WHAT BRITA

C000298659

MAX SIOLLUN

What Britain Did to Nigeria

A Short History of Conquest and Rule

HURST & COMPANY, LONDON

First published in the United Kingdom in 2021 by
C. Hurst & Co. (Publishers) Ltd.,
41 Great Russell Street, London, WC1B 3PL

This paperback edition first published in 2024 by
C. Hurst & Co. (Publishers) Ltd.,
New Wing, Somerset House, Strand, London, WC2R 1LA

Distributed in the United States, Canada and Latin America by
Oxford University Press, 198 Madison Avenue, New York, NY
10016, United States of America.

The right of Max Siollun to be identified as the author of
this publication is asserted by him in accordance with the
Copyright, Designs and Patents Act, 1988.

A Cataloguing-in-Publication data record for this book
is available from the British Library.

ISBN: 9781911723264

This book is printed using paper from registered sustainable
and managed sources.

www.hurstpublishers.com

DEDICATION

In the words of a family member, 'It all started from the sacrifice of one poor man'. For the grandfathers I never met. For the grandfather who sacrificed all he had for his children but never lived to see what they became in adulthood. For my grandmother who loved and cherished me as if I were her own son (and sometimes forget I was not actually her son!). For my grandmother who died broken-hearted after the tragedy of having to watch her son buried. For the children who did not have the honour of watching their father grow old. To my father who did not live as long as I have, yet preserved and bequeathed to me the story of our family and community. For my mother who carried the burdens of an entire family, suffered injustice, yet still did good to those who wronged her. For my aunts who proved that it takes a village to raise a child.

For Benjamin, Isaiah, Jesse, John, Rhoda, many others and future generations so they may read about those who came before them.

CONTENTS

CONTENTS

PART 4

RESISTANCE

PART 5

CULTURAL, POLITICAL
AND RELIGIOUS CHANGES

LIST OF ILLUSTRATIONS

Major Alder Burdon and Hausa soldiers. Charles Henry obinson, *Nigeria: Our Latest Protectorate*, Horace Marshall and Son, London,1900.

Sir George Taubman Goldie. Charles Henry Robinson, *Nigeria: Our Latest Protectorate*, Horace Marshall and Son, London,1900.

A Hausa Village in the 1800s. Charles Henry Robinson, *Hausaland, or Fifteen Hundred Miles through the Central Soudan*, Sampson Low, Marston and Company, London, 1900.

A Nupe man in the late 1800s. Charles Henry Robinson, *Hausaland, or Fifteen Hundred Miles through the Central Soudan*, Sampson Low, Marston and Company, London, 1900.

A Fulani man in the late 1800s. Charles Henry Robinson, *Hausaland, or Fifteen Hundred Miles through the Central Soudan*, Sampson Low, Marston and Company, London, 1900.

Lord Frederick Lugard. *The King & His Army & Navy*, Vol. XVI. No. 322, Saturday, 18 April, 1903.

Flora Shaw (Lady Lugard). *The King & His Army & Navy*, Vol. XVI. No. 322, Saturday, 30 May, 1903.

LIST OF ILLUSTRATIONS

House of the British Resident at Zaria, early 1900s. *The King & His Army & Navy*, Vol. XVI. No. 322, Saturday 27 June, 1903.

Britain installing a new Emir of Zaria after deposing the previous Emir, 1903. *The King & His Army & Navy*, Vol. XVI. No. 322, Saturday 27 June, 1903.

A compound in Zaria, Northern Nigeria, early 1900s. *The King & His Army & Navy*, Vol. XVI. No. 322, Saturday 27 June, 1903.

Location in Lokoja where the Royal Niger Company's flag was lowered and replaced with the Union Jack on 1 January, 1900. Office of The Special Adviser on Culture and Tourism Kogi State.

Location in Lokoja where the Royal Niger Company's flag was lowered and replaced with the Union Jack on 1 January, 1900. Office of The Special Adviser on Culture and Tourism Kogi State.

An Igbo woman's hairstyle—early 1900s. G.T. Basden, *Among the Igbos of Nigeria: An Account of the Curious and Interesting Habits, Customs, and Beliefs of a Little Known African People by One Who Has for Many Years Lived amongst Them on Close and Intimate Terms*. J.B. Lippincott Co., Philadelphia, 1921.

Members of an Igbo masquerade. G.T. Basden, *Among the Igbos of Nigeria: An Account of the Curious and Interesting Habits, Customs, and Beliefs of a Little Known African People by One Who Has for Many Years Lived amongst Them on Close and Intimate Terms*. J.B. Lippincott Co., Philadelphia, 1921.

Soldiers of the Royal Niger Constabulary in the late 1800s. Lieutenant Vandeleur Seymour, *Campaigning on the Upper Nile and Niger*, Methuen & Co., London, 1898.

Overami, the Oba of Benin. H. Ling Roth, *Great Benin, Its Customs, Art and Horrors*, Routledge & Kegan Paul Ltd, London, 1903.

LIST OF ILLUSTRATIONS

Captain Alan Boisragon (right)—commandant of the Niger Coast Protectorate Force, and Ralph Locke (district commissioner of Warri), both of whom survived the Benin Massacre of 1897. Alan Maxwell Boisragon, *The Benin Massacre*, Methuen & Co., London, 1897.

Ologbosere with his hands and legs chained after being arrested by British troops in 1899. Source: unknown.

King Jaja of Opobo. Harry H. Johnston, *The Story of My Life*, Bobbs-Merrill Company, Indianapolis, 1923.

King Jaja's palace in Opobo. Goodnews Epelle.

Horsemen riding to meet Lugard. Martin Kisch, *Letters and Sketches from Northern Nigeria*, London: Chatto & Windus, 1910.

Mary Slessor's adopted daughter Janie, holding babies. Mary Slessor Foundation.

Mary Slessor and a young Nigerian boy she is caring for, 1910. USC Digital Archive.

Alake of Egbaland. R.E. Dennett, *Nigerian Studies: or The Religious and Political System of the Yoruba*, London: Macmillan & Co Limited, 1910.

Bishop Ajayi Crowther and members of his clergy in the 1800s. Jesse Page, *The Black Bishop: Samuel Adjai Crowther*, Hodder & Stoughton, London, 1892.

A group of Yoruba women in the late 1800s. Lt-Colonel A.F Mockler-Ferryman, *British Nigeria: A Geographical and Historical Description of the British Possessions adjacent to the Niger River, West Africa*, Cassell and Co., London, 1902.

A group of women and children from Opobo in the late 1800s. Jesse Page, *The Black Bishop: Samuel Adjai Crowther*, Hodder & Stoughton, London, 1892.

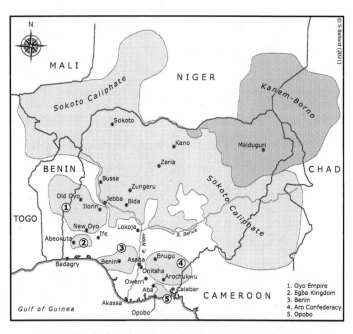

Key Pre-Colonial States in the River Niger Area, 1810

British Territories in the River Niger Area, 1887

The Colony of Lagos and the Protectorates of Northern and Southern Nigeria, 1900

Map of Nigeria, 2020

INTRODUCTION

This book's descriptive title makes a lengthy introduction to its contents unnecessary. Nigeria's colonial history matters because Nigeria matters. When the country became independent in 1960, the British Empire shrank by more than 50 per cent and Africa's independent population doubled. If India was 'the Jewel in the Crown' of the British Empire, Nigeria was the heir apparent to the throne. In the near future Nigeria will become the country with the third-largest English-speaking population in the world (with more English speakers and Christians than the country that exported the English language and Christianity to Nigeria).

Many Nigerians have a rose-tinted memory of colonialism. Although many former colonies have negative feelings towards the countries that colonised them, some Nigerians have a nostalgic reverence for British rule. Nigeria is one of the few formerly colonised nations whose people view their country's colonial era as a golden age. As recently as 2010, when a BBC journalist asked a school head teacher in the Nigerian town of Hadejia, 'Do you wish they [Britain] had stayed?' he replied, 'Yes! It would have been better,' and said he would not mind if the British 'come back again' to rule Nigeria.[1]

'The whole object of the British occupation has been the protection of the people from themselves'

Nigerians' fondness for the country that colonised them is almost bizarre given the extreme cruelty and violence that Britain used in furtherance of its colonial project. Rather than suffering from Stockholm syndrome, Nigeria is a classic case of a country suffering from a bout of winner's history syndrome. Much of Nigeria's colonial history was written by British colonial and military officers. Those narratives give the reader the impression that they are viewing Nigerians through the telescopic lens of a British rifle. They presented colonialism as a civilising mission to rid Nigerians of barbaric superstitions and corrupt leadership, and to teach and give them good governance. A Briton who wrote about early colonial Nigeria claimed that 'the whole object of the British occupation has been the protection of the people from themselves'.[2] Nigeria's colonial accounts rarely include a perspective other than from the British vantage point.

'Nigerian historians should bow their heads in shame'

To some extent Nigerians bear the blame for not presenting alternative narratives of colonialism and for allowing the British accounts to become the standard version of their history. This phenomenon of allowing the coloniser to write Nigeria's history troubled a Nigerian historian enough for him to comment, 'I feel that Nigerian historians should bow their heads in shame at the phenomenon of non-Africans doing more than ourselves have been doing on research into our past ... Historical scholarship on Nigerian peoples has been largely the handiwork of non-Africans.'[3]

I made the decision to write this book in 2017, long before the racial and social unrest of 2020. Yet the tumult of 2020 has given this book additional contemporary relevance. Colonialism is an emotive and incendiary topic. Defenders of the British Empire compare it with other empires, and point out that it was not uniquely brutal, that violence was a central feature of all colonising nations, and that modern citizens of former colonial powers have no moral obligation to feel guilt for the actions of their ancestors. This is an appropriate place to state what this book will and will not do. Those looking for a defence of colonialism or for a purely Nigerian nationalist perspective that celebrates pre-colonial Nigerian society as a utopia before Britain came and ruined everything, will not find either here. What can be found, however, is a chronological, warts-and-all account of how Britain conquered and governed Nigeria. This book's purpose is not to advocate one or the other side of value-based colonial arguments or to present a case for colonial reparations. It will not create a colonial 'league table' involving Britain, Belgium, Germany, Spain and others, to compare who had the worst colonial record. This book will discuss British colonialism in one country and demonstrate that modern Nigeria's character and problems are not organic and did not arise in a vacuum. Britain made it what it is. Accounts of Nigeria tend to jump straight to the seminal dates of 1914 (the year it was created) or 1960 (the year it gained independence), yet the core foundational ingredients of Nigeria's existence and problems were laid before and between these dates.

This book will tackle three simple questions: Why did Britain come to Nigeria? What did Britain do to Nigeria? How did the indigenes react to British presence? In answering these questions, I have tried to strike a balance between being comprehensive and being concise. Because Nigeria is so large and diverse, it is impossible to include all events of historical significance. Therefore, I have organised the chapters into five thematic sections. Although the book is chronological, the thematic nature of each chapter allows them to stand on their own as individual stories. The book will illustrate each topic by using the narrative to 'visit' as many different parts of the country as possible and use these as case studies to reveal the most important features of colonial rule. The book will also try, as far as possible, to chronicle the less well-known incidents of Nigeria's colonial history; and even when the well-known incidents are discussed, it will include their little-known or suppressed backstories.

A word on nomenclature. The first half of this book (which discusses events before Nigeria got its name) will refer to the indigenes of the land that later became Nigeria as 'natives'. This is not a clumsy use of an antiquated term, but is rather an attempt to make a simple point: that the people who lived in this land never called or regarded themselves as Nigerians before 1900. Moreover, in several places the book discusses Northern Nigeria and Southern Nigeria. This is not an attempt to drive a wedge between two different geographic regions, but is an acknowledgement that they were originally two different countries that Britain created.

Hopefully this book will interest both British people and Nigerians alike and demonstrate that, to some extent, colonialism made Nigeria a copy-and-paste version of Britain.

PART 1

THE PRE-COLONIAL ERA, 1472–1830

Britain's conquest of Nigeria was not planned from its outset. Rather, it emerged from slow mission creep. Colonialism followed different waves of British presence as various kinds of Britons pursuing their own interests came to West Africa. The first British visitors were slave traders, who were followed by explorers, then businessmen, then colonial officers and missionaries. The first three chapters will examine how trade in people was followed by trade in goods motivated European voyages to West Africa. West Africans traded and interacted with Europeans for hundreds of years outside a colonial context. A combination of European curiosity about a legendary and mysterious inland river in West Africa and the Industrial Revolution in Europe changed the nature of the relationship to one between conqueror and subject.

1

TRADING PEOPLE

A constant theme of Nigeria's history is how its trajectory has frequently been propelled and altered by unplanned events. Britain's colonisation of Nigeria was almost an afterthought. Britain was not the first European country to make contact with the land that would eventually become Nigeria. Portuguese explorers reached West Africa more than 65 years before the British did. Even the Dutch got there before Britain. One of the ironies of colonial rule is that the first people that Europeans met were not the 'big three' ethnic groups that became synonymous with Nigeria, but rather its minority ethnic groups. Depending on which account one accepts, the Portuguese first arrived in the area that later became Nigeria in either 1472 or 1485 and made contact and trade links with the Benin kingdom. Portugal brought European textiles, cowries and manilas to Benin, and in exchange exported ivory, palm oil and peppers. However, it was events on the other side of the world, rather than the Portuguese arrival in West Africa, that changed West Africa's destiny forever.

This book is not about slavery, yet it is impossible to write an accurate history of British influence on Nigeria without referring to the enormous impact that slavery and emancipated slaves had on the country's development. British interest in West Africa was also heavily influenced and shaped by the slave trade.

About one or two decades after the Portuguese arrived in West Africa, Christopher Columbus arrived in the Americas while trying to find a sea route to India. Europe's search for India inadvertently triggered the transatlantic slave trade. Had Christopher Columbus not landed on the American continent or had he taken a different route and found another place, perhaps there would have been no transatlantic slave trade. But since explorers from two European countries got lost in their attempt to find Asia and instead reached the Americas and Africa, they set in motion a series of events that would lead to the decimation of the indigenous population of both continents and to the largest forced population transfer in history. This would also sow the seeds for Britain's eventual conquest of Nigeria.

In 1470 the Portuguese found a small uninhabited island in the Atlantic Ocean off the West African coast and called it São Tomé (St Thomas). They decided to establish plantations on the island. However, since the island had no indigenous population, the Portuguese exported slaves from Benin and sent them to work on São Tomé's plantations. That was the beginning of a vast trade in people, and for the next 350 years West Africa's primary export to the rest of the world was human beings. Columbus's arrival in the Americas caused a massive decline in the native population there, who died from infections brought by the Europeans. The need for slaves to work on lands that Europeans found in other parts of the world, combined with established trade relations between Benin and Portugal, created a demand for slaves from West Africa. These slaves offset the loss of the indigenous population in the Americas.

TRADING PEOPLE

British Arrival in West Africa

The first British ships to reach the land that later became Nigeria were led by Captain Windham and arrived in the Bight of Benin in 1553. Upon arrival Windham was astonished to discover that interaction between the Portuguese and the people of Benin was so advanced that the oba (king) of Benin spoke Portuguese. Windham never returned to Britain. He and many other members of the expedition died from illness and from other issues caused by excessive drinking. Only 40 of the original 140 members of the expedition survived to make the return journey to Britain.

Portugal and Spain were the leading slave-trading nations, but Britain eventually surpassed both of them. Britain entered the slave trade in 1663 when King Charles II granted the Company of the Royal Adventurers of England Trading into Africa a royal charter and monopoly on trade in Africa. The company was contracted to supply African slaves to British colonies in the West Indies.[1] Britain became the leading figure in a triangular three-continent trade in which Europeans would travel to Africa, buy slaves there, then export them to the Americas. Badagry, Lagos, Elem Kalabari (Old Calabar), Bonny and Calabar (New Calabar) became major slave-trading ports. The number of slaves exported was staggering. In the twenty years between 1680 and 1700, according to a conservative British estimate, Englishmen alone shipped at least 300,000 African slaves.[2] In the 54 years between 1676 and 1730, Benin shipped 730,000 slaves (42 per cent of all slaves taken from the entire African continent during that time period).[3] Slavery became so routinised and associated with this part of West Africa that the area became known as the Slave Coast. In the 17th century the cost of a male slave was 13 iron bars and a female slave 9 iron bars. To give some idea of the 'price' of a human being, one iron bar could buy half a gallon of brandy, a bunch of beads, or a piece of textile.[4] A Briton said that 'neither in those days did anyone see any inhumanity in the trade, the African being looked on as an animal, only superior to a monkey in that he could be taught to work'.[5]

'The very dregs of the community'

In 1713 the Treaty of Utrecht granted Britain a 30-year monopoly on the slave trade. Although European businesses that traded in Africa were often owned by wealthy men, the traders and crews who worked for them were not from the upper echelons of society. A British slave ship captain named Hugh Crow said that 'many of the individuals composing [slave ship crews] were the very dregs of the community: some of them had escaped from jails; others were undiscovered offenders, who sought to withdraw themselves from their country lest they should fall into the hands of the officers of justice'.[6] According to Crow, 'these wretched beings used to flock to Liverpool' and attach themselves to sailing crews as a convenient method of absconding abroad to escape justice. Placing vulnerable slaves under the supervision of such criminals led to an astonishing level of casual cruelty.

In 1781 a British slave ship, the *Zong*, was on a voyage across the Atlantic Ocean with a full cargo of slaves when the crew discovered that the ship's water supply was insufficient for the number of slaves they had on board. If the slaves died of thirst, the loss would fall on the slave owners. However, if the slaves were thrown overboard, their loss would be covered by insurance. The crew came up with the ingenious idea of throwing 132 of the slaves into the ocean and claiming £30 for each slave drowned from their insurers.[7] Male slaves were usually chained to each other and kept away from female slaves. As the women were not always chained, the absence of male slaves to protect them made them vulnerable to sexual abuse by the slave crews.

Slavery remains an emotionally charged and difficult topic to address. The descendants of its perpetrators respond to it today with guilt, indifference or defiant denial. On the other hand, the descendants of its victims tend to hold Europeans solely responsible and omit or minimise African complicity in the trade. A common defence of slavery is that it existed in Africa before Europeans started the transatlantic slave trade. The British army officer Mockler-Ferryman said: 'From time immemorial the native of Africa has been a slave; the institution of domestic social slavery is part and parcel of the black man's life; he himself sees nothing outrageous nor even extraordinary in the mere fact of being held in bondage.'[8]

Slavery did indeed exist before European arrival in West Africa. However its status was fluid. A slave's position was not always permanent. Slaves could emerge out of slavery and attain high status and leadership in society. For example, one of the most influential chiefs in southern Nigeria, Jaja of Opobo, was a slave who rose to become one of the most powerful figures in his region. Additionally, many emirs who ruled northern Nigeria were the sons of slave women.

The transatlantic slave trade intensified the demand for African slaves. As the trade became more lucrative and the demand for slaves increased, African slave dealers terrorised their neighbouring communities, engaged in slave-raiding expeditions, and triggered artificial wars to capture slaves for sale to Europeans. Although transatlantic slavery was a one-way ticket, and slaves could not return from the Americas to warn their kinsmen of its horrors, in their quest for quick profit African slave dealers blinded themselves to the devastation they brought to their neighbouring communities and ethnic groups. Although it was not intentional, the slave trade disrupted West Africa in a manner that made it vulnerable to conquest by Britain. The fear of being captured and sold into slavery made some Africans voluntary prisoners of their own villages and cities. Venturing too far away from home carried a risk of being captured by slave hunters. This inhibited inter-community and inter-ethnic alliances and cooperation. This lack of African inter-ethnic patriotism later came back to haunt Africans and contributed to their inability to form a united coalition to oppose British invasion and rule. Slavery also drained the population of its able-bodied adult population, leaving behind the elderly and young children.

After centuries of slave trading between European countries and West Africans, the method of transacting became systematised. European ships anchored off the coastline and would secure a right to trade by giving gifts, called 'dash' or 'comey', to the local chief. They would then wait (sometimes for several months) for African intermediaries known as 'middlemen' to bring slaves to them from the hinterland. Once they had fully loaded the ship with a slave cargo, they would then depart, and repeat the exercise on their next journey with an empty ship.

As a result of this frequent trading, an expressive staccato language evolved in the southern coastal areas of West Africa where Europeans traded. This new language became the language of commerce between European and African slave dealers. At first it was descended from Portuguese and incorporated terms such as *sabi* (to know), which was derived from the Portuguese word *saber*, and *pikin*, from the Portuguese word for small, *pequenho*, which was used to refer to little children. As the British displaced the Portuguese as West Africa's pre-eminent trading partner, this language further evolved in an anglicised direction. Today this language is one of the most widely spoken in Nigeria. The BBC has a version of its website in this language and words from it are found in the lyrics of popular modern music. In contemporary times it is called pidgin or 'Broken English'.

Britain's increasing industrialisation, combined with a growing abolitionist movement by Christians, eventually led to Britain's decision in 1807 to make it illegal for its citizens to engage in the slave trade with effect from 1 January 1808. Britain's abolition of the slave trade seems ironic given that it was its foremost practitioner just a few years earlier. Nonetheless, the abolition was a seminal event for West Africa. European Christians who had been active in the anti-abolition movement justified Britain's entry into and involvement with West Africa on humanitarian grounds. Africa was of particular interest to Christian missionaries because in their view it was populated by heathens, and was a den of crime, immorality and misery. The early accounts of explorers and traders containing exaggerated accounts of African barbarity and savagery contributed to their determination to Christianise the area, improve the moral standards of the natives, and abolish practices such as human sacrifice and slavery.

After abolishing the slave trade, Britain stationed a naval squadron off the West African coastline to intercept slave ships heading for the Americas. The slaves recovered from these ships were sent to Sierra Leone (Mountain Lion in Italian) and resettled in a colony for freed slaves on land bought from locals. This land was later christened 'Freetown' and remains the capital of Sierra Leone to this day. Britain's abolition of the slave trade produced a generation of emancipated slaves who received a British education in Sierra Leone, converted to Christianity, and became Britain's representatives for the spread of Christianity in West Africa.

However, the end of British slave trading did not mean Britain no longer had economic interests in West Africa. It instead generated incentives for Britain to discover and explore West Africa's interior. Trade in people was about to be replaced by trade in goods.

2

CURIOSITY AND EXPLORATION

Although European ships had called at Africa's coast many times, they knew little about its inland areas. For many of them, 'Africa is the mystery of the world ... for the maps of a century ago had nothing to disclose of its vast interior but blank spaces, as undiscovered as the North Pole'.[1] This led Europeans to refer to Africa as 'the Dark Continent'.

The Great River

A river can take at least some of the blame or the credit for Britain's conquest of Nigeria. Since the days of ancient Greece and Rome, Europeans had been fascinated by legendary tales of a mighty river that flowed through Africa and drained into an inland sea. They wanted to find out whether it flowed east or west, and where its waters emptied. Some thought it flowed across the African continent into the River Nile, others that it flowed south to join the River Congo, or north from Lake Chad into the Mediterranean Sea. They speculated about the River Niger with the same sense of wonder and mystery as later generations would have about putting a human on the moon. Some legends claimed that it flowed past an African desert El-Dorado in Timbuktu, and that its banks were lined by houses with roofs made of solid gold. The river was known by many names. Some called it the 'great river' or 'Kwora', Arabs called it 'Bahr Sudan' (Black Sea), and the ancient Greek geographer Ptolemy called it 'Nigir'. In modern times it is known by its Latin name of Niger.

'I saw with infinite pleasure the great object of my mission'

Were it not for the River Niger, the interior of Africa would probably have remained unknown to Europeans for several more decades. In the 18th century, however, European fascination led to one expedition after another being dispatched to search for the river and its source. In 1795 the Royal Geographical Society sent a 24-year-old Scottish doctor named Mungo Park to locate it. After arriving in West Africa, Park started his journey in Gambia and travelled eastward. On 21 July 1796 Park made a discovery at Segu (in modern-day Mali), which he described in ecstatic terms:

> I saw with infinite pleasure the great object of my mission—the long-sought-for majestic Niger, glittering in the morning sun, as broad as the Thames at Westminster, and flowing slowly to the eastward. I hastened to the brink, and having drunk of the water, lifted up my fervent thanks in prayer to the Great Ruler of all things for having thus far crowned my endeavours with success.[2]

Nigerian schoolchildren are often taught that 'Mungo Park discovered the River Niger'. Yet, it had been known to millions of Africans who lived close to the river, fished in it, or sailed on it for centuries before Park's arrival. Park travelled through modern-day Gambia, Senegal and Mali. After navigating 300 miles of the river, he returned to Britain in 1797 as a hero. News of Park's discovery set the scientific world abuzz and it was regarded as a major breakthrough in exploration. His book about his journey was a bestseller and accounts of what he saw increased European curiosity.

'Discover the termination of the Niger, or perish in the attempt'

Having found the river, Park was determined to find its source. In March 1805 he set out again at the head of a much larger and well-funded expeditionary group with 44 Europeans, 39 of whom died by the time they reached the river in August 1805 (including his wife's brother). Undeterred, Park built an unsteady canoe, determined to continue his journey. On 17 November 1805 he wrote letters to his wife and the secretary of state for war and the colonies, Lord Camden, and handed them to his servant Isaaco[3] for delivery to the British authorities. In his letter to Camden, Park said: 'I this day hoisted the British flag, and shall set sail to the east, with the fixed resolution to discover the termination of the Niger, or perish in the attempt.'[4] It was the last letter he ever wrote. He drowned at Bussa (in modern-day Niger State in Nigeria). The faithful Isaaco kept his journals and letters and handed them over to other Britons on the coast, who eventually brought them to London. In 1827, Park's son Thomas set off from Accra (in modern-day Ghana) to search for his father whom he believed to be still alive. Thomas was never seen or heard from again.

'The white man's grave'

Park's death and those of other European explorers dampened European interest in finding out more about West Africa. The high mortality rate among Europeans who visited the area earned it the name of 'the white man's grave'. The British government had spent half a million pounds on the expeditions and had nothing to show for them. Britons wilted under the blazing hot sun and humidity and died from a mysterious fever-like illness they called 'ague', for which they had no cure. All they knew was that it was deadly and that it 'laid low all and sundry without distinction of rank'.[5] Yet despite the great hazards of travelling to West Africa and Britons' pessimistic assessments of it, Britain did not divorce itself from the area. Britons had heard tales about empires known as 'Houssa', 'Yariba' and 'Timbuctoo', of people called 'Foulahs', and of a great city called 'Soccatoo'. Other explorers set out to find and make contact with these empires and search for the River Niger's source.

Many of the pioneers of West African exploration were Scots. In 1820 the British government sent another expedition under Lt Hugh Clapperton (a Scotsman from Dumfriesshire who had been press-ganged into joining the Royal Navy), a young Scottish doctor from Edinburgh named Walter Oudney, and Major Dixon Denham (who later served as superintendent of liberated slaves in Sierra Leone). Clapperton heard about Oudney's expedition to West Africa and volunteered to join it. This time the explorers abandoned the route followed by previous explorers which had taken so many lives. Instead they arrived in Tripoli (in modern-day Libya) in north Africa and travelled south across the Sahara. The expedition had an entourage of 200 Arab horsemen and included Columbus, a multilingual biracial man from the Caribbean island of St Vincent. His real name was Adolphus Simpkins but he was known as Columbus as he had travelled halfway across the world on a merchant ship and spoke three European languages and Arabic.

The explorers arrived in Kukawa, the capital of Borno, in February 1823 and met the shehu of Borno, a brilliant scholar named Mohammed el-Kanemi. Although they had planned to stay in Borno for only a short while, they remained there for nearly a year after their camels and horses died, Clapperton and Denham quarrelled, and they became so seriously ill with fevers and hallucinations that they could barely leave their huts. Explorers like Park, Clapperton and Denham survived for as long as they did due to the hospitality of the Africans they encountered. Everywhere they went, the natives happily supplied them with food, water, housing, guides, escorts, horses to ride on, camels and mules to carry their loads, and even provided their wives, sisters and daughters to nurse them when they fell sick. The death of an Englishman, Mr Tyrwhit, in Borno in October 1824 is worth recounting for its demonstration of the lengths to which native hosts went on behalf of their British guests. After Tyrwhit's death, el-Kanemi sent a letter to the British consul in Tripoli informing him of his compatriot's death. He also produced an extraordinarily detailed inventory signed by seven Borno elders and imams itemising every single piece of Tyrwhit's property which they found (even down to mundane items such as his clothing, tin cans, towels, unused soap, glasses, an umbrella and a toothbrush). They gave all of Tyrwhit's belongings to his servants for onward transmission to the British, and also listed everyone that owed money to him, as well as those he was indebted to.

British explorers were very curious to learn about the fighting prowess of their hosts in different areas. As a soldier, the restless Denham had been given instructions to accompany any military expedition and he was anxious to conduct a reconnaissance of the natives' military capability. He observed with great interest a Fulani army defeat Borno in battle by employing a mounted cavalry charge against their opponents. Denham appears to have been an adrenaline junkie. When he heard that a Borno raiding party was going to Mandara on an expedition to plunder and capture slaves there, he decided to accompany them. El-Kanemi refused to consent to Denham's presence on the raid, arguing with some conviction that although Denham was a soldier, he (el-Kanemi) could not guarantee his safety and did not want him to come to any harm while he was under el-Kanemi's jurisdiction. Denham was insistent and accompanied the raid anyway. However, the raid did not go according to plan. The intended victims resisted with poisoned arrows and wounded or killed several of their attackers. Denham was wounded in the face and had his clothes stripped from his body, his horse was killed, and he narrowly escaped. Denham's decision to accompany the slave-raiding party proved an unwise decision as Mandara was under the jurisdiction of el-Kanemi's rival sovereign, the sarkin Musulmi (the king of the Muslims) at Sokoto, to the west of Borno.

'True Muslims have always avoided shedding the blood
of Christians, and assisted and protected them with their
own honour'

After their long stay in Borno, Clapperton and Oudney decided to visit the states of the Sokoto Caliphate to the west of Borno. Even though he was at war with them, in January 1824 el-Kanemi wrote two similar letters to the emir of Kano, Mohammed Dabo, and to the sarkin Musulmi, Mohammed Bello, asking them to grant the British safe passage, to attend to their needs, and to provide guards to escort them. In his letter to Bello, el-Kanemi advised him that, although the British were Christians, their people had 'maintained with the Muslims uninterrupted treaties of religious amity and friendship, established since ancient periods'. He cited Koranic principles of honour and reminded Bello 'that the true Muslims have always avoided shedding the blood of Christians, and assisted and protected them with their own honour'. He therefore charged Bello to be 'attentive to these travellers, and cast them not into the corners of neglect; let no one hurt them, either by words or deeds, nor interrupt them with any injurious behaviour: but let them return to us, safe, content, and satisfied, as they went from us to you'.[6]

El-Kanemi gave Islamic travelling names to the Britons. He called Clapperton 'Rayes Abdallah' and Denham 'Rayes Khaleel'. After they set off, Oudney died on 12 January 1824 from a disease known at the time as 'consumption' (tuberculosis) on the journey. After burying Oudney, Clapperton continued even though he himself was severely ill. He went first to Kano where he was gravely disappointed that the locals took absolutely no notice of him and that 'not an individual turned his head round to gaze at me, but all, intent on their own business, allowed me to pass by without notice or remark'.[7] He then travelled further west to Sokoto, which was 250 miles west of Kano (a 20-day journey). When Bello heard that Clapperton (a man he had never met) wished to travel to Sokoto, he sent emissaries and 50 armed guards on horseback to meet Clapperton and his entourage and escort them all the way to the city. Clapperton's arrival in Sokoto and meeting with Sarkin Musulmi Bello on 17 March 1824 proved to be an eye-opener for both men. Clapperton admitted that in those days most British people 'erroneously regarded the [Africans] as naked savages, devoid of religion, and not far removed from the condition of wild beasts'.[8]

During the meeting between the Scotsman and the ruler of an African Muslim state, the two men at first reacted to each other with a sense of amazement and curiosity. Clapperton was stunned when he met Bello and discovered that, rather than a 'naked savage', the man sitting on a carpet in front of him was a scholarly, portly, middle-aged man wearing a regal blue robe and a white turban. The two communicated by means of an Arabic translator. Bello condoled with Clapperton on the death of his friend Oudney, and also expressed regret that he did not get to meet him, as he would have liked Oudney to instruct his people in medical practice. Bello was no longer the young warrior who helped his father wage jihad and conquer Hausaland, yet he still retained his scholarly religious rigour. As he had never met a Christian in his life, Bello was curious about Clapperton, and peppered him with a series of theological questions about Christian denominations. The questions became so complicated for Clapperton that he admitted he 'was obliged to confess myself not sufficiently versed in religious subtleties to resolve these knotty points'.[9]

Clapperton also had to deal with a political complication created by his friend Major Denham. Bello asked Clapperton bluntly why Denham had accompanied a slave-raiding party launched into Fulani land by his rival, the shehu of Borno, el-Kanemi. Bello nonetheless returned Denham's belongings, which had been seized from him during the unsuccessful raid, and also gave Clapperton an account of Mungo Park's death and where his belongings were kept.

'We were a people that never interfered with the rights of others'

From the next day (18 March) onwards Clapperton was inundated from sunrise to sundown with a non-stop stream of curious visitors asking him questions. The most frequent query was 'What did you come for?' They were not satisfied with his reply, 'I came to see the country, its rivers, mountains, and inhabitants, its flowers, fruits, minerals, and animals, and to ascertain wherein they differed from those in other parts of the world.'[10] Bello was no fool. He had heard about, and asked Clapperton for, newspapers, which he referred to as 'news of the world'. He also asked Clapperton about the Greeks, and reminded him that Britain had fought with the Algerians and had also conquered India. Clapperton tried to reassure Bello by telling him that 'we merely afforded it [India] our protection, and gave it good laws', and that 'we were a people that never interfered with the rights of others'.[11]

Although Denham and Clapperton managed to return to England, they never reached the River Niger nor could they find its source. However, both Bello and el-Kanemi innocently provided intelligence about their lands and the river to their future invaders. Bello drew a map of the river's course for Clapperton. In late October 1824, el-Kanemi wrote a letter to the British consul at Tripoli, in which he informed him that the river was 'great and extensive', and that several other rivers emptied into it. He added that the river bisects the land and splits east and west, and that it also flows into 'the land of the Pagans, to whom no one goes' and further south. 'And God only knows what is to be found on the other side of these places.'[12]

After his time in Africa, Clapperton wrote bout his interaction with Africans: 'I found them, from my personal observation, to be civilized, learned, humane, and pious.'[13] The friendly reception accorded to Clapperton and his colleagues encouraged the British government to send another expedition. This time, instead of crossing the desert, Clapperton travelled from the south through the land of a people he called the 'Yariba' (Yoruba). After several of his companions died, Clapperton and his servant Richard Lander continued the journey alone. When Clapperton returned to Sokoto and met Bello again two years later (in 1826), he found Bello distracted by increased tensions and conflict with Borno. Although Bello hosted and granted protection to his British guests, he had been unsettled by written petitions warning him that Clapperton was an enemy spy. Bello was also concerned that Clapperton had in his possession guns which he was going to deliver as gifts to Bello's enemy el-Kanemi. Bello refused permission for Clapperton to travel through his territory to deliver gifts to el-Kanemi. Clapperton again tried to reach the River Niger but succumbed to illness and died on 13 April 1827 in a small village five miles outside Sokoto.

After Clapperton's death, his servant Richard Lander returned to England with his journals and personal papers, from which he wrote a book about their epic journeys, and reported his death. In 1830 the secretary of state, Lord Bathurst, sent Lander back to explore the River Niger. His brother John Lander joined the mission as an unpaid volunteer. Although 80 per cent of the Europeans on the mission died, the Lander brothers navigated the Niger further than any other Europeans before them. They landed at Badagry and made their way north to Bussa (in modern-day Niger State), travelled 100 miles further upstream, and then in August 1830 used a canoe to follow the river south, arriving at the Atlantic coast in December 1830. They returned to England in June 1831 having solved the mystery of the River Niger's route. They learned that European maps (which were in reality only educated guesses of what Africa's interior lands looked like) had been inaccurate for hundreds of years. They also brought back news that the Niger converged with another great river, the Benue. Lander's discovery of fertile land on the river's banks changed the emphasis of British voyaging from exploration to economic opportunity. British realisation that the River Niger provided a navigable route into the heart of West Africa caused great excitement. Explorers' accounts consistently mentioned that West Africa was teeming with produce that the natives could not exploit without British expertise and supervision. Not only could the river be used as a highway, but it could also serve as a commercial artery and outlet for British commerce.

When he heard of this, the Scotsman Macgregor Laird, who was from a famous Birkenhead ship-building family, retired from his father's shipbuilding company to focus his energy on developing business along the River Niger. Laird formed a company in Liverpool, which Richard Lander joined. They built ships specially adapted for trade in West Africa, and in October 1832 sent two steamships stocked with commodities for the first organised trading voyage from Britain to the River Niger. Of the 49 Europeans that started the journey, 40 died. Nonetheless, the two steamships travelled over a hundred miles along the Niger and Benue rivers. Laird became convinced that the best course would be to build permanent factories on the river banks, with stocks that could be replenished with goods brought from England by steamship.

For centuries British interaction with West Africans had largely been limited to the coastal areas. However, as one British expedition after another penetrated deeper and deeper into the West African hinterland, the natives became suspicious about the motives of their incessant British guests. The early British explorers who visited West Africa in the 19th century were like an advance party of spies who carefully observed the local situation and collected intelligence on the areas and natives they visited. The explorers excelled in quickly learning the language, climate, roads, topography, military strength and attributes of the places they visited. For example, Major Denham insisted on accompanying a slave-raiding expedition in Borno in 1823 because he was determined to witness the Borno forces' battle tactics. Whenever they arrived in a new village or town, they surveyed it and drew a detailed map of it. They also tried to learn indigenous languages so they were not left vulnerable to dishonest or inaccurate translators. They documented everything they did and saw in encyclopedic detail. They wrote in their journals daily: where they went, whom they met and saw, the routes they took, and the distances between different towns. They gave details of measurements, distances, numbers and even the architecture of houses and kings' residences. They were obsessive. These records were transcribed verbatim and printed when they returned to Britain. Their diaries and notes were invaluable resources at a time before cameras, photos, videos and smartphones could be used to capture images and memories.

WHAT BRITAIN DID TO NIGERIA

The British explorers' inquisitiveness (some may say nosiness) and insistence on studying and documenting everything and everyone they encountered led the natives to become watchful. There were clues that the British explorers were not just friendly tourists and might be a prelude to a forceful invasion. When Bello hosted Clapperton, he received letters warning him that the British had similarly come to India in ones and twos until they were powerful enough to take over the country. When a British expedition was shipwrecked near Jebba in 1859, the local monarch, the etsu Nupe, provided gifts and bodyguards to the survivors. However, their determination to survey and draw maps of the etsu's land, and their insistence on walking around his territory to collect botanical specimens, made the natives suspicious. When the mission's botanist, Mr Barter, refused to obey the etsu's edict that he refrain from stripping and collecting tree barks, the etsu sent an escort to accompany and monitor him during his excursions. Another member of the mission, Captain Glover, became aware of the suspicions and wrote in his journal: 'Nothing could shake their conviction that if I put all their country down upon paper, and Mr. Barter took pieces of all their trees and shrubs home, we should make charms of these things to use against them, and then return and take their country from them.'[14]

Whether or not their inquisitiveness was innocent, the records that explorers compiled were often presented to audiences at the Royal Geographical Society or the Royal African Society, and served as aides-memoires for future colonial administrators. Thus by the time Britain started its colonial enterprise, its military and political officers already had access to a huge repository of knowledge about the lands and people they were about to conquer. Crucially they knew more about West Africans than West Africans knew about them.

3

THE KINGS IN THE NORTH AND SOUTH

This chapter will examine the state of pre-colonial societies in the River Niger area prior to British rule. It will focus on five key civilisations in the area that later became Nigeria. These were not the only civilisations or kingdoms in the area (there were in fact hundreds) but their cultural and political history is important for contextualising their role as precursors of Nigeria's current primary ethnic groups. The shifting balance of pre-colonial power within and between these kingdoms is also important for examining the seismic changes brought about by Britain's arrival.

States in the area immediately to the north and south of the River Niger had existed for over a thousand years before the British arrived. As Map 1 shows, there were two large states on each side of the River Niger. To its north-east and north-west respectively were the ancient Muslim states of Kanem-Borno around Lake Chad and the Hausa states. To the south-west of the River Niger were the two interrelated kingdoms of Oyo and Benin. In addition to these, there were several decentralised societies without a paramount ruler to the south-east and north of the River Niger.

WHAT BRITAIN DID TO NIGERIA

The Kings in the North

The Kanem-Borno Empire

The thousand-year-old Kanem-Borno Empire is the longest-ruling kingdom in African history. The kingdom of Kanem arose around AD 700 in the area north-east of Lake Chad (in modern-day Chad). It was led by the Zaghawa, a nomadic people, but in the 11th century immigrants who, according to Borno oral tradition, came from Yemen supplanted the Zaghawa and established a new royal lineage called the Saifawa dynasty. The ruler had the title of *mai* and ruled through a council of twelve consisting of free-born and slave members. Owing to a series of internal conflicts and attacks from neighbouring groups, Kanem moved its capital south from a place called Njimi (whose modern-day location is unknown) to the area now known as Borno State in north-eastern Nigeria. As Kanem's early residents were nomadic it is also possible that Njimi was not a fixed location but, as they moved, they referred to each new place they camped as 'Njimi'. Borno's population was multi-ethnic and its location close to Lake Chad generated a diverse economy. Its population included farmers and fishermen from ethnic groups such as the Kanembu and Kanuri and cattle-rearing Fulani and Shuwa Arab nomads. By the 13th century, it had extended to the areas east, west, and south of Lake Chad (modern-day north-eastern Nigeria, south-west Chad, and south-east Niger Republic). The geographic move was also accompanied by a change in lifestyle from nomadic to settled agriculture. The kingdom had diplomatic and trade links with places as far away as Libya, Morocco and Tunisia, and traded in ivory and ostrich feathers.

A third transition within the ruling dynasty occurred in the 19th century. In 1808 Fulani jihadists to Borno's west invaded and captured its capital. Mohammed el-Kanemi, who we have already met, the son of a Kanembu father and an Arab mother, born in what is now modern-day Libya, came to Borno's aid, repelled the invasion and moved the capital to Kukawa in 1814. In 1846, el-Kanemi's son succeeded the mais, adopting the new title of shehu (the name by which Borno's rulers have been known ever since).

The Seven Hausa States

Many modern-day Northern Nigerian cities such as Daura, Katsina, Kano and Zaria are, to some extent, descendants of ancient Hausa city-states of the same names. The exact date of the Hausa states' formation is not known but they likely arose sometime between the 7th and 9th centuries. Each state was named after its walled capital city (known as *birnin*) and was said to have a specific duty entrusted to it. For example, Gobir, on the fringes of the Sahara desert, was the northern outpost of Hausaland, guarding it against Tuareg invaders; Zaria was the slave-raiding state; Kano and Katsina were trading states; Rano was an industrial centre; while Daura was the spiritual home of the Hausa. These walled cities were built with defence in mind. They were surrounded by ditches and made provision for withstanding sieges by leaving space inside the city walls for farming. Cities such as Kano and Sokoto also served as pre-colonial trans-Saharan trade hubs. In the mid-19th century, 30,000 camel loads of salt arrived annually in Kano for distribution as far away as Ashanti land in modern-day Ghana. The Ashanti exchanged their gold and kola nuts for livestock, cloth and salt from Hausa traders. In the 15th century Zaria had a legendary queen called Amina. She was reputed to be a fierce warrior who, according to oral legend, after conquering enemy armies in battle, would choose a lover from one of their warriors and then execute him the next morning after making love to him.

Although they were culturally related and similar to each other, the Hausa states were not governed by a single ruler and were politically independent. Each was ruled by a sarki (king), who was assisted by a titled class of aristocratic officials known as *masu sarauta*. Underneath the ruling sarkins and aristocratic *masu sarauta* were the commoners, known as the *talakawa*. Although they spoke the same language, Hausa, it was common for the people of the Hausa states to refer to themselves by the name of the state in which they resided: for example, Katsinawa (those from Katsina) and Kanawa (those from Kano).

A group of light-complexioned, tall, slim immigrants to Hausaland caused perhaps the most seismic change ever to occur in northern Nigeria. These immigrants were a cattle-rearing nomadic people who had dispersed over thousands of miles across west Africa. They looked so physically different from their neighbouring ethnic groups, and their language was so different as well, that it is certain that their origins lay far away. Many of them migrated to Hausaland from the area that is now modern-day Mauritania and Senegal. The immigrants were known by many different names. The French called them 'Peul', the Kanuri called them 'Fulata', while the Hausas called them 'Fulani'. They referred to themselves as 'Fulbe'.

The catalytic figure behind the 19th-century transformation of Hausaland was an Islamic cleric of the Torobe Fulani clan whom a British army officer described as 'the African Napoleon'.[1] Usman dan Fodio's[2] ancestors migrated to the Hausa state of Gobir from Futa Toro in modern-day Senegal. His father, Muhammad Fodio, was an Islamic cleric, hence Usman was known as 'dan Fodio' (son of the learned).

Oral tradition states that Bawa, the sarki of the Hausa state of Gobir, hired dan Fodio to be a religious mallam (teacher) for the royal house, and that one of his pupils was a prince of the royal house named Yunfa. Dan Fodio accused the Hausa states of idolatry and of contaminating Islam with animist rituals. In 1804 he declared a jihad to purify Islam and called on his followers to establish true Islam throughout Hausaland. Dan Fodio issued the jihad's commanders with flags as symbols of authority from him to wage holy war. There was a mentor-and-student element to the war, as it pitted dan Fodio against his former student, now king, Yunfa.

The Sokoto Caliphate

Dan Fodio and his followers conquered the pre-existing Hausa states and absorbed them into a massive confederation of Islamic emirates now known as the Sokoto Caliphate. It was then Africa's largest pre-colonial state and stretched as far as Mali at its western end, traversed Nigeria, and extended into Cameroon at its eastern end. Dan Fodio took the title of amir-ul Mu'minin (Commander of the Believers) and appointed his flag-bearers as amirs (commanders or rulers) of the territories they conquered (this title later became transliterated as emir). By the 1830s the Caliphate had a population of approximately 10 million and had conquered and incorporated lands that were not part of the Hausa states (including the Ilorin provinces of the Oyo Empire, areas formerly ruled by the Kanem-Borno Empire, and Jukun and Nupe people). The southward advance of dan Fodio's jihad was halted not by a superior military force, but rather by two ecological forces that even his army could not overcome. The dense forests of the south proved impenetrable for the horses of dan Fodio's cavalrymen, and the tsetse fly lurking in those forests menaced the horses with sickness. Hence, the jihad stopped in northern Yorubaland and was unable to penetrate further south.

The success of dan Fodio's jihad inspired jihads elsewhere in Africa, in what later became Guinea and Mali. The era was also a time of revolutions around the world. The American Revolution had occurred about twenty years earlier, the French Revolution five years earlier, and the Haitian Revolution which culminated in Haiti's independence in the same year the jihad started, 1804.

The Kings in the South

The two most prominent kingdoms south of the River Niger area were Oyo and Benin, both of which claimed descent from Ife in what is now south-west Nigeria.

The Oyo Empire

Before 1800 much of what is now the Yoruba-speaking area of western Nigeria was part of the Oyo Empire, ruled by the alaafin (lord of the palace) of Oyo. The empire's capital was the city of Oyo, which some outsiders also referred to as Katunga. At its peak the Oyo Empire stretched across large areas of modern south-west Nigeria and into the neighbouring country of Benin to the west. Oyo was surrounded by other powerful states, notably Ife to its south-west, the Hausa states to its north, the kingdom of Benin to its east and Dahomey to its west.

Although the people of Oyo may be considered the ancestors of today's Yoruba people, it was not a Yoruba empire, as is popularly believed. The people of Oyo shared cultural affinities and a similar language (albeit with multiple dialects), yet they did not regard themselves as one ethnic group. Much of what is now the Yoruba area of south-west Nigeria was fragmented into several kingdoms which bordered Oyo and claimed common descent with it. The people of these kingdoms did not identify themselves as Yoruba and instead used local identities denoted by the name of their clans (such as Egba, Ekiti, Ijebu, Ijesha and Ondo) or by the name of their towns. In the 18th century the word 'Yoruba' was rarely, if ever, applied to any of these people except the Oyo. Despite some early accounts describing the Oyo people as the 'Yoruba Proper',[3] they spoke several different dialects (some say languages) and did not identify themselves with a common name. Even then, the name 'Yoruba' was an external appellation and was originally a Hausa term used to describe Oyo. Although some travellers to the region in and around Oyo referred to it as the 'Yariba' country, others referred merely to the people as 'Eyo' (Oyo) or 'Jebu' (Ijebu). Additionally, many residents of the Oyo Empire were from other ethnic groups, such as the Ebira and Nupe.

Although overall political leadership of the Oyo Empire resided with the alaafin, the kingdom also had multiple provinces ruled by subsidiary chiefs known as obas. The alaafin spent most of his time in his palace and rarely appeared in public or allowed himself to be seen by his subjects. He doubled as a political and spiritual leader, yet he did not have absolute dictatorial powers. Oyo's government had a separation of powers with checks and balances, and the alaafin was expected to take advice from a seven-member non-royal council known as the Oyomesi. If they lost confidence in the alaafin, the Oyomesi could force his resignation by passing a resolution calling for him to abdicate honourably by committing suicide. The Oyomesi were constrained from abusing this power as one of them had to die with the alaafin. The alaafin did not exercise command of Oyo's military force either. The leader of the Oyomesi (the basorun) acted as a prime minister.

Abiodun, who reigned from 1774 to 1789, was perhaps the most notable alaafin. Although Oyo had become powerful and prevailed over its neighbours because of its mighty cavalry, it declined in prominence substantially after Abiodun's reign. Oyo weakened under pressure from external invasion and internal conflicts. Its distance from the southern forest belt enabled it to build a cavalry to supplement its archers, and its horses were far enough away from the forest belt to survive the deadly tsetse fly lurking there. Yet that distance from the southern forest belt also placed it within striking range of the expansionist Sokoto Caliphate to its north. In 1823 Fulani armies invaded and captured Ilorin in the northern part of the Oyo Empire, established an Islamic emirate and incorporated it into the Sokoto Caliphate. In 1836 the Fulani armies also invaded, sacked and destroyed Oyo's capital. After the capital fell, the city was evacuated and the alaafin fled south and founded a new Oyo capital about 100 miles further south. The invading Fulani armies also sacked many of the northern Oyo towns, and refugees fled south to found new cities at Ibadan and Abeokuta. Although the Oyo dynasty continued, its territory dwindled and it never regained its former glory.

By the time British colonial ambitions increased in the late 19th century, Yorubaland was in chaos. After a series of internal rebellions and secessions whereby various towns declared independence either from Oyo or from its neighbouring kingdoms, the area was destabilised by several wars. Apart from throwing the region into ferment, the flow of refugees caused long-standing societal changes. The refugees who fled south later embarked on a reverse migration several decades later that facilitated both the growth of Christianity in the area and British invasion of it. Many of those who fled the wars became educated by British missionaries, returned to evangelise in the region, invited further British involvement, and created the orthography of Yoruba that led to the merging of the different dialects and identities in the region into a Yoruba national identity and language that stretched beyond the Oyo region.

The Benin Empire

The most numerous ethnic group in the Benin kingdom were the Edo people (sometimes also called Bini). Benin is the

Nigerian kingdom with the longest history of pre-colonial contact with Europeans. By the time Nigeria came into existence, the kingdom already had over five hundred years of trade and other relations with Europeans, including the Portuguese, Dutch and British. Contact with Portugal was so routinised that Portuguese was spoken in the king of Benin's court, and Benin and Portugal exchanged emissaries to visit each other's lands. In the 16th century Benin sent some of its citizens to Portugal to receive religious instruction in Christianity and report back.

The Benin kingdom was located in what are now the modern-day Edo and Delta States in Nigeria. Although the precise date of its formation is uncertain, oral tradition places it around the 12th or 13th centuries. This tradition also acknowledges the ancestral links between Benin, Oyo and Ife. Benin had many cultural and historical similarities with the Ife and Oyo kingdoms, such as the concept of a divine royal lineage. Like his counterparts in Ife and Oyo, the Benin king (oba) was a political and spiritual leader and derived his authority from a god. The similarities in royal administration and terminology between Benin and Oyo suggest that oral traditions regarding ancestral links between the two were more than allegorical. For example, the oba had an advisory council of six chiefs known as the Ozama, who played a similar role to the Oyomesi in Oyo. Other officials in the oba's court held titles that were phonetically identical or similar to their Oyo counterparts.

Although Benin was not as geographically large as the Sokoto Caliphate to its north, from around 1440, under the expansionist Oba Ewuare, the kingdom expanded from a small area only 15 km in radius and overran neighbouring communities among the Yoruba to Benin's west and some Igbo communities to its east. Benin's influence extended so far to its west that Lagos was its vassal state.

'The largest single archaeological phenomenon on the planet'

Ewuare also reconstructed the capital city according to a new symmetrical pattern. Benin city was distinguished by great feats of engineering and technology, some of which were unprecedented at the time. It was surrounded by massive external and internal walls, which both marked the capital city's boundaries and also separated some 500 villages within it. The walls extended for over 16,000 km. According to the 1974 edition of the *Guinness Book of Records*, Benin city's walls were the largest earthworks ever constructed in the world prior to the industrial era. Another source claimed that the walls took an estimated 150 million hours to construct and described them as 'perhaps the largest single archaeological phenomenon on the planet'.[4] Benin city was also one of the first places in the world to have street lighting. The 120-feet-wide roads to the oba's palace were illuminated at night by metal street lamps fuelled by palm oil that stood several feet high. A Portuguese explorer who visited Benin in 1691 wrote:

> Great Benin, where the king resides, is larger than Lisbon; all the streets run straight and as far as the eye can see. The houses are large, especially that of the king, which is richly decorated and has fine columns. The city is wealthy and industrious. It is so well governed that theft is unknown and the people live in such security that they have no doors to their houses.[5]

'The masterpieces of world sculpture'

Evidence of Benin's and Oyo's artistry and technical sophistication is provided by the stunning array of bronzes, terracotta objects and other artwork which they produced. According to a British historian, these artworks 'rank among the masterpieces of world sculpture'.[6] Thousands of such works of art decorated the streets and homes of both kingdoms, and the details inscribed on them acted as a record of significant ceremonies, people and events in their histories. In Benin's case, British anthropologists who first saw them refused to believe that 'primitive' Africans were capable of creating such artwork and instead concluded that they were either made by a superior visiting foreign race or that the Portuguese taught them the crafts involved.

A British visitor to Benin claimed that 'no one who went there in the old days came away without being impressed'.[7] Yet by the late 19th century, British visitors described Benin 'as possessing only the ruins of its former greatness' and as being 'in a terrible state of bloodshed and disorder',[8] which led them to call it the 'city of blood'. Why did the city decay between the 16th and 19th centuries? Benin's decline corresponded with its contact with Europeans and primarily with its centuries-long engagement in the slave trade. Benin's involvement with slavery also coincided with the adoption of other practices that caused unnecessary loss of life. For example, the death of a prominent chief would be commemorated by sacrificing and burying his servants with him so that they could continue serving him in the afterlife. The oba also charged tolls for those wishing to pass through the kingdom and use its waterways in order to trade. This practice put Benin on a collision course with Britain.

The Decentralised Societies

A striking characteristic of several ethnic groups (such as the Igbo, Annang, Ibibio and Ekoi) that inhabited the area which would become south-east Nigeria was that their communities lacked paramount rulers or large states under one political administration. Some had no government at all. Other examples of such politically decentralised ethnic groups located elsewhere include the Idoma and Tiv, who lived in the middle area of Nigeria, sandwiched between the northern Muslim areas and the south. Early literature referred to such people as living in 'stateless societies', which implied a disorganised society. This has been superseded by the more modern and accepted term of 'decentralised states'. Even though such societies consisted of people with similar cultures and languages, they existed and conducted their affairs without the need for an overarching authority or government. Leadership rarely extended beyond a family or a village of a few hundred or thousand people.

Pre-colonial Igbo Society

Decentralised social organisation was prevalent among Igbos. Unlike the Yorubas, Hausas and Kanuris, there is no evidence that Igbos ever recognised one person or political authority as their ruler. Pre-colonial Igbo society operated as an idiosyncratic gerontocratic democracy. Social authority usually resided with the oldest male member of each family or clan that claimed descent from a common ancestor. The oldest male of each lineage group usually exercised authority over his lineage and, upon his death, his authority was transmitted to the next oldest male. The lineage elder was usually called upon to arbitrate in disputes between different households in the same lineage. The different lineage leaders usually belonged to a village council called *ndi ama ala*, which presided over matters affecting the entire village. In this way power was decentralised and each lineage clan was represented and had the assurance that decisions affecting them could not be taken without their consent. Additionally, any adult male in the village could attend and speak at the council's meetings.

'The Igbo knows no king'

Each village was largely autonomous, and villages often had emotional or lineal affiliation to each other through descent from a common ancestor. Even though Igbo society had age-grade fellowships, secret societies and title societies, these usually operated at village level, and rarely came under a single directing authority. The absence of paramount kings ruling over large areas was encapsulated by the maxim '*Igbo amaghi eze*' (the Igbo knows no king). In a culture without a paramount king, admission to a title society was a status symbol and evidence of achievement. Admission was remarkably democratic. Every male adult was eligible so long as they could demonstrate high achievements in their lifetime. Such titles were rarely hereditary and there were few or no qualifications for them other than achievement or money. A man could gain a title simply by raising funds and paying for it. These titles incentivised achievement and provided upward social mobility. Hence, having an honorific title in Igboland did not necessarily make the title-holder a political ruler.

There were some exceptions to the general absence of paramount kings in Igboland. Kings were present in some areas that bordered regions with monarchies (such as Igbo towns close to Benin). A good example is the Igbo town of Onitsha (on the eastern side of the River Niger, across the river from the Benin kingdom), which had a chief called the obi of Onitsha. The titular and monarchical similarities between chiefs in such Igbo towns and those in Benin suggest that they were influenced by, or sought to emulate, the ancient Benin kingdom. These phonetic similarities in royalty are supported by oral tradition. For example, monarchies in the Igbo towns of Onitsha, Aboh and other large towns on the western side of the River Niger claim descent from a man named Chima. Depending on the version one accepts, Chima was either a slave, a hostage of the oba's court during the reign of oba Esigie in the 16th century, or the son of a previous oba of Benin. According to oral tradition, Chima and other migrants left Benin and separated, with some crossing the River Niger to found Onitsha on the east side of the river, and others founding Agbor and other Igbo towns on the west side. Additionally, village-level monarchies also existed in coastal areas that dominated the transatlantic trade, such as Bonny, Brass, Calabar, Kalabari and Opobo (home to the Efik and Ijaw people).

At least six interesting themes emerge from this summary of pre-colonial states. First is the accuracy of multiple oral traditions. Much of what is now known about pre-colonial Nigeria was passed down through centuries of folklore. Although the validity of oral tradition is often dismissed and considered mythology, certain cultural and linguistic affinities and patterns corroborate its accuracy. This demonstrates its value as a historical record for Nigeria and shows that written records are not the exclusive repository of history.

A second theme is the multi-ethnic character of pre-colonial Nigerian societies. A common criticism of colonialism is that it herded hundreds of ethnic groups with no prior history of common government into one giant state. Yet, as we have seen, the Kanem-Borno, Sokoto Caliphate, Oyo and Benin kingdoms were multi-ethnic. Kanem-Borno included Kanembus, Kanuris and Shuwa Arabs; the Sokoto Caliphate was a mostly Hausa state ruled by Fulani immigrants but also included Tuaregs and other ethnic groups; the Oyo Empire included Yorubas, Ebiras and Nupes; the kingdom of Benin included Edos, Igbos, Yorubas, Esan and Afenmai; and the decentralised Aro confederacy of Igboland included common commercial and religious links among the Igbo, Annang, Ibibio and Ijaw.

Thirdly, not only was pre-colonial Nigeria multi-ethnic, but the ethnic groups that later comprised Nigeria were not unknown to each other before British colonialism. Many of them were not only aware of each other's existence, but even traded with one another. For example, Igbos, Hausas and Nupes traded in pre-colonial markets at Onitsha. The frequency of migration in pre-colonial origin stories suggests that at least some of the people of the different kingdoms were related to or descended from each other. This is certainly the case with Oyo and Benin, and the origin stories of the Hausa states suggest a link with Kanem-Borno, while those of the western Igbo societies suggest influence from Benin. British colonialism did not introduce Nigeria's ethnic groups to each other, but rather, without their consent, amalgamated them within a single political system for the first time (whereas much of their pre-colonial interaction had been limited to trading).

Fourthly, each of Nigeria's current three largest ethnic groups of Hausa, Yoruba and Igbo did not self-identify as one ethnic group in the pre-colonial era. The centralising and integrative effects of colonialism amalgamated people who had never considered themselves part of the same ethnic groups into large 'super tribes'. Fifthly, Nigeria's contemporary debate about whether the country is secular or multi-religious should be examined in a historical context, as the rulers of three of the four largest kingdoms in pre-colonial Nigeria exercised dual authority as political and religious leaders. For example, the alaafin was considered *ekeji orisa* (next to the gods) and the oba of Benin was similarly the leader of a divine monarchy. The position of the leader of the Sokoto Caliphate as amir-ul Mu'minin (Commander of the Believers) and sarkin Musulmi (king of the Muslims) made him the spiritual leader of the Muslims in his domain, and disobedience of his edicts was almost tantamount to apostasy. Sixthly, the pre-colonial states had democratic characteristics, albeit ones that did not resemble European multi-party forms. As shown above, few pre-colonial rulers exercised absolute power. Some of them were subject to the decisions of non-royal councils, while others could be deposed without their consent or even sentenced to death for misrule.

Britain commenced its colonial project when most of these states were no longer at their zenith. Their internal problems and disputes meant they had to keep one eye on each other and another eye on the British invader. By the late 1800s Kanem-

Borno had declined as a result of leadership disputes and external invasion, Benin had shrunk in size, Oyo had fractured due to civil war and the Sokoto Caliphate's invasion of its northern frontier, and the Caliphate's initial reformist impetus had subsided after the deaths of Usman dan Fodio and his son Mohammed Bello. Britain's arrival after formerly powerful pre-colonial states had weakened probably assisted its conquest of Nigeria. Had Britain commenced its invasion ninety years earlier, it would have met with very different leaders and more cohesive societies. How, for example, could it have ruled Northern Nigeria if it had encountered the charismatic and infectious zeal of Usman dan Fodio? Would any emir have dared to surrender and swear loyalty to the British Crown while dan Fodio was alive? How would a more cohesive Oyo Empire have responded to alien rule in an era before the Yoruba civil wars and when the imbalance in military technology between it and Britain was not as great as it became by the late 19th century? The answers to these questions can now be consigned to 'what if?', but the history of colonialism is enriched by contextualising the timing of Nigeria's emergence and by exploring alternative scenarios that might have changed the course of Nigeria's history.

PART 2

EXTRACTION AND TRADE, 1832–1886

Richard Lander's discovery of fertile land on the banks of the River Niger changed the emphasis of British contact with West Africa from exploration to economic extraction. In general, European economic interest in Africa was evident from the way European countries named territories after the commodities they expected to extract: the Ivory Coast, Gold Coast (later Ghana) and Slave Coast (Nigeria). By the mid-to-late 1880s European countries were almost coming to war in their haste to grab pieces of Africa for themselves.

Britain wanted territory in the River Niger area if only to stop France from getting it. Prior to the Berlin Conference of 1884–5 British influence in Nigeria consisted of a nebulous and irregular form of involvement whereby Britain appointed consuls as emissaries to West Africa and to arbitrate in disputes between British businesses and West Africans. Although the consuls lacked political authority over the natives, the Royal Navy backed them with occasional naval bombardments of native towns and villages that were not amenable to the consul's persuasion. Britain's claims to influence rested on the controversial and sometimes mysterious treaties that the consuls and British businesses entered into with native chiefs. These treaties ignited the first conflicts between British and West African authorities and planted the seeds for colonial rule.

4

PALM OIL RUFFIANS

Given how unpopular West Africa was for Europeans, and how rapidly it consumed British visitors, why did the British keep coming back? After Britain made it illegal for its citizens to engage in slave trading from 1808, British businesses engaged in the trade had to turn to other ventures to make money. The abolition of the slave trade also coincided with a time of economic, social and technological changes in Europe.

As Europe industrialised and became less dependent on human and slave labour, and more reliant on machinery for production, West Africa offered a natural supply of goods that Britain and other European countries needed. Fortunately for Britain and unfortunately for West Africans, the raw commodities that Britain required to power its industrial revolution were in the River Niger area. There was an increase in demand for oil to lubricate industrial machinery and, as hygiene standards in Europe during the first half of the 19th century were appalling, soap became essential to health and survival. The abundant palm oil extracted from palm trees which grew wild in the forests along the River Niger could supply Britain's demand for both machine lubricant and soap. The invention of the pneumatic rubber tyre in the 19th century also created a demand for rubber. Fortunately for Britain, rubber, gum and shea trees grew in the lower River Niger area.

The plentiful supply of palm oil from along the lower River Niger led the British to refer to the area as the Oil Rivers area (now in the modern-day South-South zone of Nigeria). Little did they know that beneath their feet lay another type of oil whose value far exceeded that of palm oil, and that would bring an unimaginable level of wealth a century later. They also referred to the area as the Niger Delta.

'West Africa is a proverbially unpopular part of the world'

Identifying the economic potential of the Niger Delta was far less problematic than actually exploiting it. Africa was not an empty continent, and Britain could not extract natural resources from the Niger Delta without interacting with its inhabitants. Additionally, in the 1800s the area had a hostile climate and topography for the British. It was hot, humid and criss-crossed by mosquito-infested creeks, rivers and swamps. Most Britons considered the area a death trap. It was also populated by scores of ethnic groups who spoke a myriad of languages which the British found incomprehensible. A British army officer wrote: 'West Africa is a proverbially unpopular part of the world; its climate long ago gained for it an evil reputation, which it has maintained even up to the present time. The travellers who would visit the West Coast of Africa merely for pleasure are few and far between.'[1] A British person sent there would probably have regarded the posting as a punishment. However, West Africa's economic potential made continued European interest inevitable. British industrialisation and the discovery of abundant natural resources in West Africa also coincided with medical advancements that made the tropical West African climate less daunting and deadly to British lives. They finally discovered the secret of the mysterious 'ague' that killed so many of them. The realisation that 'ague' was carried and transmitted by mosquitoes prompted them to devise defensive measures to protect themselves. They started sleeping under mosquito nets and taking a medicine called quinine pre-emptively to immunise against the disease, which is now known as malaria.

The invention of the steamship reduced the travel time from Britain to West Africa from 35 to approximately 21 days.[2] Steamships reduced not only the shipping time between Europe and West Africa, but also the cost of British shipping, allowing more goods to be exported from Africa to Britain, and with greater frequency.

Excitement about the economic opportunities that lay in the River Niger area led many European companies, British, French and German, to set up trading stations on the banks of the river, from where they traded with local chiefs and shipped produce to Europe. Between 1800 and 1830, the Niger Delta exported more palm oil than the rest of West Africa combined.[3] Since there was no monetary currency in use in the Niger Delta, natives sold palm oil to Europeans in exchange for European wares or cowries.

British business was facilitated by pre-existing networks of African contacts. The abolition of the slave trade did not alter the basis on which the British and native traders transacted with each other. Instead of buying slaves, British companies started buying other goods such as palm oil, using the same network of middlemen as before. Many of the British businesses along the River Niger were based in Liverpool and the amount of palm oil shipped from West Africa to Liverpool increased from 150 tons in 1806 to 3,000 tons in 1819 and 13,000 tons in 1839.[4] This palm oil was used to make soap, candles and margarine, and as a lubricant. By 1850 Liverpool businesses were producing nearly 30,000 tons of soap every year, a third of Britain's total soap production.[5]

'Ruffians of the worst kind'

As with those involved in the slave trade, many of the 19th-century traders and crew who worked for them came from the lower reaches of European and British society or consisted of murderers and other convicted criminals. For example, in 1841 a murderer who had just been released from prison immediately found employment as the captain of a British trading ship that sailed to the Bight of Benin. The ship crews who worked in the slave trade often repurposed themselves to become palm oil traders. Yet they behaved more like pirates, and retained their habits of dishonesty, violence and utter disregard for the safety and lives of Africans. They were known as 'palm oil ruffians'. They wore unsophisticated clothing (usually pyjamas), lived rough lives, which were usually short because of the harshness of their work and the climate and topography in which they laboured. A senior British colonial officer admitted: 'The masters of the vessels trading to the coast were, as a rule, ruffians of the worst kind, guilty of the most brutal treatment to the Africans with whom they dealt and to the crews of their own vessels.'[6] Incidents of British trading crews mistreating the natives were legion. In 1854, to amuse himself, a British trader in the Brass River area ordered a native boy who boarded one of his ships to be detained and flogged. When the boy's father, who was a prominent man in the community, discovered what had been done to his son, he ordered a raid on the British ship. Using two large canoes, his men attacked and boarded the ship and arrested the captain, took him ashore, and tied him to a tree for 12 hours.[7] Only the fear of British military reprisal restrained the natives from killing the captain in retribution.

As we have seen, British businesses paid local chiefs for permission to trade in their domains by giving them gifts or payments known as 'comey' or 'dash'. Some of the payments were intended for the chief alone, while others were shared among his community and followers. There was even a distinction between 'boy's dash' and 'gentleman's dash'. This method of trading created a systematised form of exchange and payment. Not only did chiefs or 'Big Men' become accustomed to it, but they regarded it as their legitimate entitlement. Commissions, tipping and other payments for services rendered became deeply embedded in West Africa's business and trading systems and were pervasive in the 19th century throughout the territory that eventually became Nigeria. Both the emirs of the Sokoto Caliphate north of the River Niger and the middlemen to its south-east received such gratuities from British trading companies, as did the Yoruba obas to its south-west. Although they had different cultures, religions and systems of government, these different societies came to accept these 'top-up' payments when transacting business.

In the late 20th century, these *ex gratia* payments acquired new names: bribery and corruption. When English law was transplanted to West African society, legitimate trade payments that had existed for centuries were suddenly transformed into illegal financial transactions. Nigeria's modern-day bribery is at least partially a descendant of this elaborate system of payments. Contemporary Nigeria is still trying to divest itself of the problem.

In addition, British traders also gave (usually second-rate) goods and clothing to middlemen in exchange for the palm oil they brought from the hinterland on canoes. The British traders would often trade old discarded sailor's hats and uniforms by telling the gullible natives that they were traditional attire worn by the aristocracy in England. The unsuspecting natives sometimes wore such items when they met other

Britons, who would then refer to their ill-fitting attire as evidence of African buffoonery.

A big challenge to British commercial interests along the River Niger was the competition between rival British businesses trading in the area, between British businesses and their European business rivals, and between British businesses and the native 'middlemen' traders. British companies regarded these middlemen as business rivals to be eliminated. They wanted to obtain palm oil and other goods directly from their producers without going through intermediaries. As a result, British businesses petitioned the British government to eliminate the middlemen, often complaining that they were monopolistic. Yet, as we shall see, Britain pushed the middlemen aside in order to replace them with a state-sponsored British monopoly. British commercial desire to obtain produce without the involvement of intermediaries prepared the way for eventual colonial rule.

5

JAJA OF OPOBO

In the late 1880s West African middlemen and British business-men became competitors as the latter became determined to access the inland areas of West Africa without the use of intermediaries. The treatment Britain meted out to perhaps the most famous and influential pre-colonial chief in south-eastern Nigeria demonstrated the lengths to which the British authorities would go to deal with natives who obstructed their commercial ambitions.

Mbanaso Okwara-Ozurumba was born around 1821 at Umuduruoha village in Amaigbo (which later became part of Imo State in the Igbo-speaking south-east of modern Nigeria). Kidnappers captured Mbanaso when he was about 12 years old and sold him as a slave to Chief Allison of Bonny. The chief became so exasperated with the young boy's insubordination and headstrong nature that he gave him away to Chief Madu, who was himself a former slave who had risen to become a member of a prominent family. When Madu died in 1833, his son Alali succeeded him. A leadership vacuum arose after Alali died in 1861, heavily in debt. Potential successors were reluctant to suc-ceed Alali and inherit his debts to British businesses. Hence, in

1863 they chose the young and ambitious Mbanaso, who was also a businessman, to succeed Alali.

The charismatic Mbanaso had risen in the society through sheer force of character, and had a reputation for honesty and for keeping his word. He paid off the debts he inherited from his predecessor, built good business relationships with the British, and sometimes hosted feasts and galas for British naval officers. He was articulate, intelligent, and conducted himself with a quiet dignified comportment.

Mbanaso bore the honorific name Jubo Jubogha, which his kinsmen shortened to Jojo and Europeans to Jaja. He established himself as a wealthy trader and middleman who acted as an intermediary between European traders in the coastal areas of the Niger Delta and native palm oil producers inland.

After a civil war with rivals in Bonny in 1869, he secured his independence, seceded from Bonny and moved to Opobo (taking 14 of Bonny's 18 native chiefs with him). In 1873 he signed a treaty with the British consul for the Bights of Biafra and Benin, Charles Livingstone (brother of the legendary Scottish missionary David Livingstone), that recognised Jaja as the king of a new kingdom at Opobo independent of Bonny. Jaja's dual roles as an extremely wealthy businessman and a leader who wielded political authority made him a Michael Bloomberg or Moshood Abiola of his time.

Even though he was Igbo, he had a cosmopolitan outlook. Opobo was a multi-ethnic town with Andoni-, Igbo- and Ijaw-speaking people. Jaja also married wives from different ethnic groups and understood the value of Western education. He enrolled several children from his community in schools abroad, and sent two of his sons, Mark and Sunday, to study in Scotland. Concerned that prolonged absence abroad would separate his children from their culture, he brought Sunday home and enrolled him in a secular school that Jaja opened at Opobo. In

1881, he sent his 13-year-old son Warabo to England and enrolled him in Manor House School in Cheshire. Warabo never returned to Opobo. He died from a lung inflammation after a cricket game.

Jaja was astute enough to recognise the importance of establishing and maintaining friendly relations with Britain. The British exploited the rivalry between Jaja and the king of Bonny by giving both sides the impression that they could gain Britain's favour and a military advantage over the other by having their men drilled in warfare by British officers. Using these pretexts, the adjutant of the Hampshire infantry militia, Captain Nicol, travelled to Bonny to procure men for the war against the Ashanti (in modern-day Ghana) in 1873, and convinced both Jaja and the king of Bonny to send 53 and 105 men respectively for the mission. In 1875 Queen Victoria awarded Jaja a sword of honour in recognition of his services during the war. He became so influential that the British relied on him to mediate their disputes with different ethnic groups.

'The greatest African living in the east of modern Nigeria'

As an employer of several thousand people, presiding over lands that had economic resources, its own schools, a navy with a fleet of 50 canoes, a cannon, several men armed with rifles, and treaties with foreign powers, Jaja operated as the astute and enlightened president of an embryonic state. In 1863, the British consul Richard Burton prophetically described Mbanaso as 'young, healthy and powerful and not less ambitious, energetic and decided. He is the most influential man and the greatest trader in the River and £50,000, it is said, may annually pass through his hands. He lives much with Europeans and he rides roughshod over young hands coming into Bonny. In a short time he will either be shot or he will beat down all his rivals.'[1] A historian described him as 'the greatest African living in the east of modern Nigeria'.[2] However, Jaja's commercial acumen and wealth gained him the jealousy of both local people and British businesses. His position as a 'middleman' meant that British traders who wanted to buy palm oil or trade with traders in inland areas had to go through him. Jaja bought palm oil from its producers, then resold it to British businesses for export to Britain. However, Jaja did not allow the British buyers and the palm oil producers to trade directly with each other. This put him on a collision course with British businessmen, who also had to pay him 'dash' and 'comey' in exchange for the right to trade in his areas.

Six British businesses responded to rising palm oil prices in 1883–4 by forming a cartel and refusing to pay for palm oil at any price other than that jointly fixed by them. This led to a stand-off during which Jaja and the cartel boycotted each other. Jaja's decision-making and commercial enterprise bordered on the ingenious. Always one step ahead, Jaja circumvented the British businessmen by shipping oil directly to Britain himself.

Although he self-deprecatingly told his British business partners that 'I don't know book', would plead to the British prime minister that 'I have no idea about English laws', and described himself as 'a poor ignorant man',[3] he was none of the above, and was in fact unsuccessful in his attempts to conceal his sharp intellect from others. The Foreign Office wrote that 'Jaja is the ablest of the coast middlemen. He is a man of energy and considerable ability ... he is sharp enough to hold his own with the Europeans and powerful enough to overcome the natives in the interior.'[4]

Jaja demonstrated these qualities in 1884 when he negotiated a treaty with the British consul Edward Hyde Hewett. Unlike many of the other chiefs, Jaja carefully studied the content of his treaties and hired a third party to examine them. As was standard, the proposed treaty that Hewett presented to Jaja would grant British merchants the exclusive right to trade in areas under Jaja's jurisdiction, and allow missionaries to proselytise, in exchange for those areas being placed under British protection. Even though he spoke English well, the shrewd Jaja asked Hewett to elaborate on the meaning of various clauses in the treaty. In particular he asked Hewett to explain the meaning of the word 'protection' and asked Hewett for a written assurance that it would not affect his rule over his domain nor would the British queen rule over his lands. In response, Hewett wrote to Jaja on 1 July 1884 and provided the written assurances Jaja asked for:

> I write, as you request, with reference to the word 'protection' as used in the proposed Treaty, that the Queen does not want to take your country or your markets, but at the same time is anxious no other natives should take them. She undertakes to extend her gracious favour and protection, which will leave your country still under your government. She has no wish to disturb your rule ...[5]

Jaja also negotiated a special amendment to his treaty that deleted the standard article 6, which guaranteed freedom of trade to all in his territory. This deletion preserved his monopoly in his territories. Jaja and Hewett signed the treaty on 19 December 1884.

Jaja employed a freed African American woman named Emma (born to black American slave parents in Kentucky) as his secretary, and she ran the school he opened in Opobo. She also drafted his correspondence. Events in the international arena would keep Emma busy with letter-writing duties for several years.

On 5 June 1885, in accordance with the General Act of the Berlin Conference, the Foreign Office declared a protectorate over the area in which Jaja resided. The Act also provided for freedom of navigation on the River Niger and its connected rivers, and declared that no exclusive privileges of navigation should be granted to companies or private persons. Jaja and other African leaders were not party to the treaty nor were they consulted about its provisions, which were inconsistent with Jaja's treaty rights. But Britain took the position that the Berlin Conference and its protectorate declaration overruled Jaja's monopoly rights under his treaty.

These measures gave British businesses that wanted to be rid of Jaja an opportunity to strike. They sought to trade and buy palm oil directly from the inland producers without going through Jaja, and lobbied the British government to remove Jaja. In response, Jaja petitioned the prime minister, Lord Salisbury, and two years of recriminatory correspondence between Jaja, the prime minister, Hewett and the Foreign Office ensued between 1885 and 1887.

In January 1887 Hewett ordered British traders to stop paying 'comey' to Jaja. Jaja sent letters of protest to the prime minister in which he pointed out that Hewett continued to allow all other chiefs in the area to receive their comey, and that Hewett had threatened to exile him. In the same letter Jaja identified many Britons whom he had met and who could attest to his good conduct and 'have never yet know me to rob any white men in this my river their rights'.[6] Jaja also complained: 'Should there be any meeting wherein my presence is required by him [Hewett], upon my arrival in such a meeting there is only continual abuse from him and nothing else.'[7]

'A headstrong imperialistically minded young careerist'

Hewett went home to Britain in 1887 on sick leave, and the young, impatient and brash Harry Johnston deputised for him as acting consul. Johnston did not like Jaja. A British expatriate who lived in Nigeria for several years described Johnston as 'a headstrong imperialistically minded young careerist who had no time for Jaja'.[8] The day Johnston arrived in the Niger Delta, he sent a letter to the prime minister to complain about Jaja. In official dispatches to the prime minister he described Jaja as 'the most grasping, unscrupulous and overbearing of mushroom Kings who ever attempted to throttle the growing commerce of white men with the rich interior',[9] and complained that 'here is the country where white men may hope to settle and enjoy good health, and it is from lands like these that runaway slaves and upstart Kings like Ja Ja are trying to keep us from penetrating'.[10] Johnston's and Jaja's personal differences amplified the conflicting strategic and commercial differences between British businesses and Jaja.

Johnston was unable to travel to Opobo by British gunboat or ship as they were too large to navigate the narrow and shallow creeks. Instead he contacted Jaja's enemy, the king of Bonny, George Pepple, who supplied Johnston with a canoe and armed escorts to travel to Opobo. In contrast to his invective-laden descriptions of Jaja, Johnston described King Pepple, who had converted to Christianity, as 'very civilized' and noted that he 'spoke and wrote English like an Englishman and dressed as we do'.[11] Jaja had refused to convert to Christianity and was unlikely to have perceived Johnston as a neutral arbiter after his arrival in a canoe and with an escort provided by his enemy. At first Jaja did not want to deal with the 29-year-old Johnston, who was almost forty years his junior. He informed Johnston that he would resume discussions when Johnston's 'father', Hewett, returned.

'He is an old man now'

However, Johnston summoned Jaja to a meeting on 5 August 1887 and ordered him to sign an amendment to his treaty to allow free trade in all of his markets or face a naval expedition if he refused. Jaja protested to the British secretary of state about being compelled to sign away his rights under duress. Johnston was not done with him, however, and was determined to remove Jaja. He wrote to the prime minister to express his

> conviction that this country will never be really opened to the full tide of commerce and civilization till Ja Ja has been removed from his position as King. He is an old man now, past 60, and I feel sure that his declining years would be more happily spent if he surrendered his affairs to the administration of the British Government, and retired with his family to some tranquil retreat.[12]

Johnston sent a cable to the Foreign Office on 19 August 1887 alleging that Jaja had violated his treaty obligations by obstructing free trade and by trying to trade in an area not recognised by his treaty. Johnston also forbade all British businesses to trade with Jaja and applied to the Foreign Office for authorisation to execute a plan that Hewett had devised to 'deport' Jaja by inviting him to a meeting on board a British ship, then sailing away with him.

'It would be called kidnapping'

On 29 August 1887 the prime minister considered the matter and then wrote to Johnston:

> I am unable, from the papers before me, to see what cause of complaint we have against Jaja ... It is said he is contravening the stipulations of a treaty made in 1873. I can find no provision of that treaty which is contravened by the action that he has taken ... To invite a chief on board your ship, carefully concealing the fact that you have any designs against his person, and then, when he has put himself in your power, to carry him away, is hardly legitimate warfare, even if we had a right to go to war. It is called 'deporting' in the papers, but I think this is a euphemism. In other places it would be called kidnapping ... I see no ground for hostile action so far as my present information goes.[13]

The prime minister then travelled to France on holiday but had already developed the impression that acting consul Johnston was under the influence of Jaja's British business rivals. He again wrote on the matter on 9 September 1887 to express his view that 'I am not satisfied with the entire impartiality of Consul Johnston's judgment',[14] and ordered that a British naval officer be sent to investigate the matter.

'Your action with regard to Jaja approved'

The Foreign Office transmitted the prime minister's memorandum to Johnston by cable at 3.45 pm on 12 September 1889. They also appended an annotation to the cable stating: 'Your action with regard to Jaja approved. Further instructions will be sent after communication with admiralty.'[15] The purpose of this cable was to tell Johnston to await further instructions without taking any action regarding Jaja. On the same day Johnston sent a cable to the Foreign Office stating: 'Ask immediate permission remove Jaja temporarily Gold Coast. Organises armed attacks, obstructs waterways, markets. Intrigues render this course imperative. Despatch following explains. Ask admiralty telegraph assistance.'[16] The official account by Johnston and the Foreign Office is that, by some incredible coincidence, Johnston's cable arrived at the Foreign Office at 3.55 pm the same day (only 10 minutes after the Foreign Office sent a cable telling him to stand by for further instructions). According to this traditional explanation, because the two cables allegedly crossed in transmission, Johnston misinterpreted the words 'Your action with regard to Jaja approved' in the Foreign Office cable as approval of his request to deport Jaja.[17] However, the Foreign Office was replying to his earlier, unrelated 19 August cable, not to his request to deport Jaja.

It is not possible to verify or disprove Johnston's and the Foreign Office's accounts since, in those days, telegrams were not sequentially numbered to clarify the order in which they were sent and received. However, even if the official account is accepted, there are still some puzzling features. The next day (September 13) the prime minister sent another memorandum to the Foreign Office telling them to 'Adhere to my instructions already given and execute them. Consul's language and proposals do not inspire me with confidence. Naval officer will be less under the influence of merchants.'[18] That same day a delegation from Opobo,[19] including two of Jaja's sons, who had been sent to Britain, met with the undersecretary of state for foreign affairs, Sir James Fergusson, to present a petition on Jaja's behalf.

Yet for some strange reason the officials at the Foreign Office, several of whom had been fed on a diet of Hewett's and Johnston's incendiary reports about Jaja, did not execute the prime minister's twice-cabled instructions. Also, they oddly did not send another clarifying cable to Johnston in order to clear up the potential misunderstanding caused by two unrelated cables arriving almost simultaneously. Johnston immediately acted upon the part of the cable that stated 'Your action with regard to Jaja approved', but strangely he ignored the other parts of the cable that told him to await further instructions, as well as the prime minister's memorandum, which very clearly deferred any action on Jaja until after a naval investigation had been completed. It was also odd that he presumed that a cable that referred to his 'action' (i.e. something he had already done) as approval of something he was asking for permission to do in the future.

'I am afraid to come'

Back at Opobo, the impetuous Johnston was still at work. Armed with what he thought was authorisation to deal with the situation, he again invited Jaja to a meeting on 19 September

1887 at the Opobo premises of the British trading firm Thomas Harrison & Company, a competitor of Jaja's that had been campaigning for his removal. Jaja was unaware of events in England but nonetheless the meeting request aroused his suspicions. He replied to Johnston: 'I am quite sensible of your position and your capability of doing me any harm. Therefore I am afraid to come.'[20] Jaja asked Johnston to prove that 'you mean no harm against me' by sending a British hostage to be placed in his house as a surety for his safe return. Johnston refused to agree to this condition but, in his words, 'advised Ja Ja strongly, and in his own interest, to attend the meeting'.[21]

Jaja then said he would attend only if Johnston gave him an assurance that he would not be arrested and that he would be free to leave when the meeting concluded. Johnson wrote a letter to Jaja on 18 September 1887 to reassure him:

> I have summoned you to attend in a friendly spirit. I hereby assure you that whether you accept or reject my proposal tomorrow no restraint whatever will be put upon you, you will be free to go as soon as you have heard the message of the government. If you do not attend the meeting no further consideration will be shown you, and you will be simply treated as an enemy of the British government. I shall proclaim your deposition, and hand your markets over to the Bonny men. If you attend tomorrow I pledge you my word that you will be free to come and go ...[22]

'You will be declared an outlaw'

Based upon Johnston's assurance of safe passage and that he would not be detained, Jaja agreed to attend the meeting. When he arrived on the morning of Monday 19 September, he was confronted by Johnston, British naval officers and the British gunboat HMS *Goshawk*, which had pointed its guns at Opobo. Johnston had also conscripted armed men from Bonny to block-

ade the creeks around Opobo to prevent Jaja from escaping.
Johnston read out aloud an ultimatum to Jaja:

> should you be so misguided as to refuse to submit to the orders of
> the British Government it will be taken as an admission that you are
> guilty of the charges brought against you. I shall then proceed to use
> an armed force, which will mercilessly crush any resistance you may
> offer. You will be deposed, and tried for your misdeeds, as a common
> malefactor; your property will be confiscated, and your country
> brought to ruin by the stoppage of trade. Should you attempt to
> evade me by escaping into the interior you will be declared an outlaw,
> a reward will be offered for your capture, which will be sufficiently
> large to tempt the greed of your treacherous followers, and your
> bitter enemies among the surrounding tribes ... will be free to avenge
> on you old grievances. No man ever stood in a more critical position
> than you are in at the present moment, King Ja Ja ... But refuse to
> do so, and you leave this Court a ruined man for ever, cut off from
> your people and your children.[23]

Johnston gave two choices to Jaja: surrender immediately and
go to Accra in the Gold Coast to face trial, or decline to surrender and be declared an outlaw, with a bounty placed on his
head for his capture. Johnston gave him one hour to decide.

Jaja surrendered, and Johnston took him on board HMS
Goshawk and sailed with him to Accra for the trial. Further evidence that Johnston arrested Jaja without authorisation is provided by the fact that, when the Foreign Office discovered what
Johnston had done, they cabled him: 'Report by telegraph precise circumstances under which you thought arrest necessary.' It
seems that the Foreign Office knew Johnston acted illegally by
luring Jaja into custody with a false promise of safe passage, and
then arresting and deporting him. However, they retrospectively
ratified the illegal acts by hurriedly enacting the Opobo Political
Prisoners Detention Ordinance in October 1887 to enable Jaja to
be investigated.

What started out as an investigation turned into a trial or military-style court martial presided over by Rear Admiral Sir Walter James Hunt-Grubbe, the commander-in-chief of the Royal Navy's Cape of Good Hope and West Africa Stations. Jaja's trial commenced on 29 November 1887 at Fort Christiansborg in Accra. Hunt-Grubbe presented three charges against Jaja:

1. Have you at any time barred the trade to the inland districts beyond your own jurisdiction ...?
2. Have you at any time blocked the highway?
3. Have you, since the Protectorate treaty of 19 December 1884, loyally endeavoured to carry out the provisions of that treaty?

An African lawyer, Edmund Bannerman defended Jaja, who was 'allowed to call witnesses'. Calling witnesses was of course virtually impossible because every conceivable person that could testify on his behalf was in Opobo, hundreds of miles and an ocean journey away. The charges against Jaja were strange. The questions that Hunt-Grubbe presented to Jaja were akin to asking him whether he had done things his treaty allowed him to do. The proceedings were made more bizarre by the reversal of the British legal doctrine of innocence until proven guilty. Rather than having to present evidence to prove the charges, Hunt-Grubbe asked Jaja to provide evidence that he was innocent of them.

Hunt-Grubbe found Jaja guilty on the second and third counts. The second was proved by the fact that during a trip to Opobo, Johnston's path along a river had been obstructed by beams placed by people he suspected to be Jaja's employees. Hunt-Grubbe somewhat absurdly claimed that the third was partially proven because Jaja sent a delegation to see the British secretary of state without Johnston's permission. He exiled Jaja and his son Sunday[24] to the West Indian island of St Vincent, with an annual stipend of £800 a year to be paid to Jaja from his own savings. Jaja was dethroned and exiled for operating a monopoly. Yet, strangely, the government allowed a British company to do exactly the same thing, with legal authorisation under a royal charter, and even compensated the company when its charter was revoked.

The treatment meted out to Jaja was a serious matter that left the British government with a lot of explaining to do. Johnston had deported a foreign chief against the express wishes of the prime minister. In Parliament, opposition MPs peppered the government with questions about Jaja's fate and demanded details about his medical condition and date of return to his homeland. In May 1888, MP Arthur Pease complained in Parliament that he was sure that Jaja's exile 'would not have been sanctioned in the case of the Ambassadors of any other Power, and was only sanctioned in this case because Ja Ja happened to be a black King'.[25] Jaja's powerful British and African friends lobbied the British government on his behalf for him to be sent home.

While in exile, Jaja succumbed to depression, illness and homesickness. The terms of his detention forbade him from leaving his residence for more than four hours, required a police officer to escort him wherever he went, and ordered that his correspondence be censored. As his health deteriorated he repeatedly submitted appeals, requesting to be returned home so he could die in his homeland rather than in a foreign land. However, British businesses trading in and near Opobo submitted counter-petitions objecting to his return.

The government allowed one of Jaja's wives, Patience, to join him in exile, and subsequently moved him to Barbados. When his petitions for repatriation continued, they approved his request to return home in 1891, after he signed an undertaking that his return would be conditional on his becoming a private individual, abstaining from fomenting disturbance, and conducting himself with loyalty to the Crown and its representatives. As Opobo made preparations to give him a heroic welcome home, sometime in July 1891[26] he died mysteriously on the way back on the Spanish island of Tenerife. His body was returned and buried in the courtyard of his compound at Opobo in a ceremony featuring music and cannon fire that could have been a state funeral. A statue of him was also erected in Opobo.

The Jaja controversy had wider ramifications, and generated native mistrust of Britain. In 1896 an Itsekiri chief Nana Olomu (from a different region from that of Jaja) rejected an invitation to attend a meeting with the British high commissioner for the Niger Coast Protectorate, Sir Ralph Moor, and replied, 'I fear you go catch me all same JaJa' (I fear you will kidnap me the same way you kidnapped JaJa).'[27]

As we shall see, Jaja's deposition exacerbated the vacuum of political authority in an area where paramount rulers were already scarce. Jaja's constant resort to dialogue and negotiation throughout his conflicts with British businesses and consuls arguably demonstrates that his exile was also to Britain's detriment. By exiling him, Britain lost the influence and economic and political dexterity of an interlocutor who could have helped them negotiate economic access and political accommodation in this area of West Africa. By deposing a leader with whom they could bargain, to some extent Britain ensured that its encounters with natives of the area would become violent.

The Reverend M.J. Elliott, who once met Jaja, subsequently described his fate as 'a tragic mistake, which those who knew Ja Ja best, and felt for him the esteem of which he was worthy, have never ceased to regret'.[28]

6

GOLDIE

Although this book is a record of the colonial relationship between two nations, and not a biography of an individual, it would not be possible to document that relationship without an account of the individuals who made pivotal contributions to it. A nation's development is essentially the accumulation of actions by multiple individuals. When books and articles discuss the leading British figures behind colonial Nigeria, the usual suspects, such as Sir Frederick Lugard, Sir Hugh Clifford and Sir John Macpherson, are named. However, there is another captivating yet little-known person who arguably played a greater role in forming Nigeria than these men, who are frequently touted as Nigeria's British founding fathers. He does not have airports or city centres named after him, yet history did not forget him. His lack of fame is of his own doing. Perhaps no other man in Nigeria's history has put so much effort into his life's work, only to invest even greater effort to ensure that what he did would not be remembered. He told a friend, 'I never want to be spoken of—the less you say about me the happier I shall be.'[1]

Son of the Nunnery

George Dashwood Taubman Goldie was born into an aristocratic Scottish–Manx family on 20 May 1846. He was born and raised in a mansion called 'the Nunnery'[2] near Douglas on the Isle of Man. His paternal family was the product of a combination of two wealthy families, the Goldies and the Taubmans. The Goldies were a Scottish family from Goldie Leigh, in Dumfriesshire, who owned substantial properties in Dumfriesshire and Kirkcud-brightshire (modern-day Galloway). The Goldies had impeccable military credentials–George's father, older brother, paternal grandfather, great-grandfather and great-uncle were all army officers (the last three were generals). His father, Lt-Colonel John Goldie-Taubman, was a lawyer and magistrate and served as a member of the Scots Fusilier Guards. Incredibly, his father, grandfather, great-grandfather, and brother all served as Speaker of the House of Keys, the Isle of Man parliament.

In 1803 George's paternal grandfather Alexander Goldie married Isabelle Taubman, the daughter and heiress of Major John Taubman of the Nunnery. Major Taubman was also a member of the House of Keys and had numerous business interests, including his investment in a slave ship, the *Prince Vada*, that set sail from Liverpool in December 1760, purchased 203 slaves in Angola and deposited the 180 who survived the journey in Barbados. The Taubmans were landed gentry who made a fortune from smuggling spirits, tea and wine. When Isabelle Taubman died in 1824, the couple's eldest son, John (Goldie's father), appended his mother's maiden name to his surname by royal licence, and thus became John Goldie-Taubman.

Goldie's mother Caroline was his father's second wife and was the daughter of a wealthy barrister, John Eykyn Hovenden. Both of Goldie's parents died before he was five years old, and the family employed staff to help look after the young children. He trained at the Royal Military Academy in Woolwich and qualified as an army engineer in 1865, although he admitted, 'I was blind drunk when I passed my final examination for the engineers.'[3] However, two immutable traits in his character ensured he would not stay long in the engineers: his restless spirit and his voracious appetite for seducing women.

After two years in the engineers, a relative died and left him a fortune. He was so excited by the freedom that the new wealth gave him that he immediately departed from England and moved to Egypt where, by his own admission, 'I fell in love with an Arab girl'.[4] He spent three years living with her in a Bedouin camp during which time she taught him to speak Arabic. After she died from tuberculosis, Goldie said, 'I came home to lead a life of idleness and dissipation.'[5] His excitability ensured that his idleness was not likely to last.

Family business reignited Goldie's interest in Africa. Goldie's older half-brother, John Senhouse, married the daughter of Captain Joseph Grove-Ross. Grove-Ross was the secretary of the English trading company Holland Jacques & Company, which began trading on the River Niger in 1869. By 1875 the company was in serious financial trouble and Captain Grove-Ross appealed to his son-in-law John for help. John in turn got his younger brother, George, involved in the project of reviving the company's fortunes. On 13 May 1876 the family registered the Central African Trading Company Limited, in which George and Grove-Ross were the only directors, which in turn bought Holland Jacques & Company.

In 1877 the 31-year-old George and his brother Alexander planned an expedition to the River Niger to assess its commercial potential for themselves. For this purpose Goldie ordered the construction of a 90-ft-long steamboat called the *Benue* and had it sent out to Africa in pieces. However, Alexander became so ill with fever when they arrived in Nupe-land that they prematurely aborted the mission and returned to England. Nonetheless, the trip made George realise the huge potential in trading along the River Niger. George said: 'On the journey back I conceived the ambition of adding the region of the Niger to the British Empire.'[6] That is the official story that Goldie told his friends and that British accounts have repeatedly given. However, there were other reasons for Goldie's venture to West Africa. A British colonial administrator later claimed: 'West Africa was deemed the provided dumping ground for the unfit, a home for lost husbands, or at best a market for *pêches à quinze sous*.'[7] Goldie was not lacking in ambition or intellect. However, Dame Margery Perham's comment that Goldie was 'no plaster saint'[8] was a great understatement. West Africa offered him the chance to make a fresh start and escape his scandal-ridden personal life in England. At the age of 24, he caused a scandal among his friends and family by becoming infatuated with Matilda Catherine Elliott, who worked as a nanny at his family home. He eloped with Matilda to Paris. They returned to England in 1871 and, to avoid further scandal, were married at St Marylebone parish church in London in a quiet ceremony.

Goldie was not the only one who realised the abundant economic opportunities along the River Niger. His task of reinvigorating the family business was made even more formidable by the fierce competition he faced from French and German companies and from the Liverpool businessmen whose long-standing business interests along the River Niger preceded his. In modern times, some countries have pursued their economic interests overseas by first invading foreign countries, then sending their companies to trade in the occupied countries. Britain's practice in the 19th century was the inverse. British businesses usually entered foreign countries before their government did. A century before the United States and the USSR used Africa as a proxy battleground for their Cold War, European countries were using

Africa as a proxy battleground for economic competition between themselves. Trading companies from different European countries competed fiercely with each other to secure trade on the River Niger. French trading ships had reached the upper banks of the river and were trying to establish trade links there. British trading companies feared that the French-Italian explorer Pietro Paolo Savorgnan di Brazzà (after whom Congo-Brazzaville was later named) was planning to enter into an exclusive trading agreement with the ruler of Bussa near the River Niger which would bar them from trading there. British traders also complained that, although they had opened up trade there, France threatened to reap what they had sown. The Anglo-French economic rivalry in the area threatened not only to halt or repel the advance of British economic interests in West Africa, but also endanger existing British territories.

Britain's West African territories were not geographically contiguous. They were encircled in a noose of territories controlled by, or under the influence of, its European rivals. To the west of the Oil Rivers area France had Senegal, and to the east Germany had Cameroon. The British colony of Gambia was also surrounded by French colonies. French prospecting for business in the River Niger area meant that the British colony of Lagos was at risk of becoming a small British island in a sea of French-controlled territory. If that happened, Britain might be forced to cede its West African territories to France, whose plan to build a railway line from Senegal to Algeria provided further evidence of its extensive ambitions in Africa. Britain also feared that France planned to annex West African territories and establish one giant, continuous West African French colony.

Goldie's interest in Africa was reinvigorated at a time when Britain was losing interest in colonial acquisition. The abolition of the slave trade curtailed the economic benefit of African colonies to Britain, and there was no reason to keep possession of territories that were no longer generating economic gain. In 1865 a House of Commons Select Committee advised that Britain should avoid 'all further acquisitions of territory or assumption of government, or new treaties offering any protection to native tribes', and should consider withdrawing from all of its African colonies except Sierra Leone, because of its value as a naval base and as a refuge for repatriated slaves. Britain wanted to do business and make money, but sending its citizens and armies abroad to conquer and colonise foreign territories involved trouble and expense it could do without unless there was a commercial incentive. It had to find a method of protecting its economic interests that was cheaper and less laborious than colonialism.

Britain considered three options. The first was to share trade areas on the upper and lower parts of the River Niger with France. The second was to establish a British protectorate in the Oil Rivers area, and the third was to enter into trading agreements with native chiefs. In November 1883 the British cabinet chose the third option. However, they still faced the hurdle of how to capture trade in an area that did not have one paramount government or ruler with whom Britain could enter into business treaties. The areas along the Niger instead had hundreds of chiefs, each of whom governed lands no bigger than small villages or towns. The cabinet therefore approved the conclusion of treaties with native chiefs who were willing to place themselves 'under British protection' subject to certain conditions.[9] Still, the question remained as to how the government's decision could be implemented, and who would be willing and able to do it.

While the British government was filled with concern and ambivalence, Goldie was laying the foundations for a business empire. Goldie wanted not only to overcome competition from foreign companies, but also to eliminate competition from British business rivals. Of the British companies trading on the

River Niger, four were particularly prominent. These were Alex Miller, Brother & Company of Glasgow, the West African Company Limited[10] of Manchester, James Pinnock of Liverpool, and the Central African Trading Company Limited of London (99.72% of shares in this company were owned by the Taubman family). In 1879, Goldie set up a new company, the United African Company (UAC), which bought out these four companies. The acquisition was all the more remarkable because at the time Goldie had no experience of trading in West Africa, no experience of shipping, and was still a young man in his early thirties. Goldie paid for these acquisitions by granting to the owners of the acquired companies shares in the newly incorporated UAC. The granting of shares provided simultaneously an asset and a trap. In an early demonstration of Goldie's monopolistic intent, the UAC's articles of association forbade its shareholders to trade on the Niger or Benue rivers or within 25 miles of them. Any shareholder who violated this rule would forfeit his shares in UAC. By spearheading this merger Goldie simultaneously eliminated his British competitors and created a more unified British rival to foreign businesses.

Yet despite the elimination of his British competitors, Goldie was still not satisfied. He sought not only economic opportunity, but economic exclusivity. His aim was to secure for his company the exclusive right to trade with the natives living adjacent to the River Niger. He entered into many treaties with native chiefs. Estimates regarding the number of treaties vary considerably from 250 to 500, depending on the source consulted.[11] His determination to secure trading rights for his company became almost obsessive. On one occasion he told friends the story of a chief who was holding out and refusing to agree to a treaty with his company. When he met the leprosy-afflicted chief for dinner, the latter took a piece of meat from his own plate and with 'his leprous fingers'[12] raised it to Goldie's lips. Not wanting to risk losing the benefit of years of hard work by declining the chief's kind gesture, Goldie ate the meat.

These treaties were interesting (see an example in the Appendix). Although modern-day European businesses ostensibly operate in a free market capitalist environment, their trade practices in Africa during the 1800s were quite different. They were fond of trying to secure trading monopolies for themselves by using exclusive treaties to bar their competitors from trading. The treaties that UAC entered into with native chiefs granted the company the exclusive right to trade with and extract produce from the territory under the chief's jurisdiction. The treaties also forbade the chiefs to trade with other companies. The treaties were perpetual, could not be terminated, and did not state whether English or native law applied to them. In return for granting these rights, the chiefs were placed under British 'protection', which usually meant that the British would side with them should an outside party attack their community. Many of the treaties were incredibly one-sided. In exchange for being granted extensive trading rights, European businesses 'paid' the chiefs with guns, pieces of cloth, hats and alcohol. Only the most important chiefs were paid an annual stipend, which varied in amount according to the importance of the chief and his kingdom. For example, the company's 1894 treaty with the amir-ul Mu'minin in Sokoto obliged the company to pay the amir 3,000 bags of cowries (approximately £1,500) per year.[13]

Goldie also exploited Britain's nervousness about France's aggressive economic entry into West Africa to nudge the British government into actions that would further his own business ambitions. He not only envisaged trading as a businessman, but also wanted direct governing responsibility over the natives in the areas where he wanted to trade. Goldie claimed that most publicists and geographers 'know, in short, that all that is needed to convert the Niger Sudan into an African India is the strong hand of a European protector'.[14] He pursued a three-pronged strategy of eliminating competition from British rival companies, doing the same to foreign and indigene competitors, and lobbying the British government to set up direct jurisdiction over the River Niger area. When the government did not respond to his letters and petitions with the haste he expected, he resorted to scare-mongering and constantly exploited the British government's insecurity about losing the River Niger area to France.

The British government had in the past used royal charters to authorise British companies to trade, negotiate treaties with foreign chiefs, levy taxes, establish their own armed forces to guard their premises, and fight against hostile elements in the areas where they operated. The granting of governing responsibilities to a private commercial company benefited both the British government and the company itself. It allowed the British government to simultaneously protect its economic interests in foreign territories and avoid the expense, resources and risk of involvement in direct governance. It could delegate the burdens and risks of governing responsibility to the company. The British government could also absolve itself of blame for the acts and mistakes of a company that it did not own. Conversely, if the company governed successfully, the government could claim the credit for having the foresight to select such a company for the granting of a royal charter. Goldie applied for a royal charter on behalf of UAC in 1881, but his application was rejected mainly because UAC was not large enough to be entrusted with such responsibilities. As British interest in colonial acquisition waned, the practice of granting royal charters became rare. Things were not looking good for UAC. Nonetheless, rejection did not deter Goldie from his ambition. A former UAC employee later said that Goldie was 'a very intelligent but most difficult person either to control or to divert from his intentions'.[15]

Events on the other side of the world unexpectedly came to Goldie's aid. In November 1881 the Crown granted a royal charter to the British North Borneo Company to administer North Borneo (in present-day Malaysia). Goldie carefully studied the parliamentary papers regarding the North Borneo Company's royal charter and obtained legal advice about it from eminent lawyers. He was determined to use the Borneo charter as a template to press his own demands. In June 1882, for the third time in only six years, Goldie set up a new company called the National African Company (NAC).[16] NAC bought out UAC, increased its issued share capital almost ten-fold from £125,000 to £1,000,000, and invited share purchases from the public. In a covering letter dated 6 June 1882, which accompanied NAC's prospectus, the new company's agent-general, David McIntosh, revealed his concern that unless NAC stepped in, other companies 'will have the honour and profit of opening trade in countries, the resources and requirements of which are unlimited, and which are teeming with produce for which they have now no market'.[17]

However, NAC still faced competition from French companies. French businesses had over 30 trading stations along the River Niger area and claimed to export at least 50,000 kg of ivory a year from the River Benue area.[18] Commandant Mattei, a French officer who was France's consul at Brass and was later the agent-general of the *Compagnie Française de l'Afrique Equatoriale* (French African Equatorial Company), returned to the West African coast in June 1882 with authorisation to establish factories wherever Goldie's company was operating. Goldie sent several letters to the British foreign secretary, Lord Granville, with complaints about the French presence. Competition between the French and British trading companies became so intense that Mattei challenged the NAC's agent-general, David McIntosh, to a duel.[19]

In 1884 NAC sought to expel the French companies from the River Niger area by offering to buy them. As an incentive, NAC offered the French firms not only money, but also shares in NAC itself. Had they known what would occur over the next twenty years, the French companies would have refused the offer. However, they accepted, and NAC finally prevailed in its war with its French competitors when it bought the French African Equatorial Company and the *Compagnie du Sénégal et de la Côte Occidentale d'Afrique*. With excellent timing, NAC completed the final purchase deeds for the French companies on 14 November 1884, just one day before the Berlin Conference (sometimes called the Berlin West Africa Conference) began. Although Goldie attended, no African chiefs were invited to a conference whose purpose was to partition and share African lands among European countries. Although European nations rarely questioned their right to divide African lands between themselves as they saw fit, a British expatriate did later ask himself 'as a matter of abstract morality, what justification is there for European Powers to divide and apportion for themselves Africa without the assent of the Native inhabitants? But this is a barren question of casuistry.'[20]

Largely on the basis of the treaties that NAC had concluded with West African chiefs, the Berlin Conference recognised British claims to sovereignty from its coastal colony of Lagos in West Africa all the way to the Cameroons in the east, and from the Niger Delta's coastline northwards to the River Niger's confluence with the River Benue. The British Foreign Office declared a protectorate over this area on 5 June 1885 and called it the Oil Rivers Protectorate,[21] an area that corresponds to modern-day Southern Nigeria. However, the protectorate was largely a paper document and lacked effective application on the ground. There was no direct British governance or uniform system of laws over the territories supposedly under British jurisdiction.

Nonetheless, the treaties that Goldie entered into with native chiefs gave him leverage to present himself as the most significant representative of British commercial interests in West

Africa, and he kept trying to convince the British government that it had to act quickly to grant his company a royal charter. To aid his cause, Goldie made astute appointments when he incorporated NAC. He invited the rich Welsh industrialist and former home secretary, Lord Aberdare,[22] to be the company's chairman, and Goldie became its vice-chairman. Aberdare was a prominent politician and also a close friend of prime minister Ewart Gladstone and Lord Granville. Goldie was the company's heart and soul, while Aberdare's presence ensured that the company had access to the highest levels of government. Aberdare applied to the British government for a royal charter in February 1885. The government finally relented under Goldie's incessant pressure and granted a royal charter to the NAC on 10 July 1886. Incredibly, the charter did not contain a map or a description of the territories over which the company would have jurisdiction. Thus we are guided by the areas to which the company presumed that its charter applied (shown in Map 2). Although the borders of the charter territories were imprecise, most of them originally corresponded to what later became the Middle Belt of Nigeria (along with some areas of what later became Southern Nigeria that were on the southern side of the River Niger's confluence with the River Benue). By means of its dubious treaties (discussed in the next chapter), the company later claimed to have extended its jurisdiction to northern Nigeria through treaties with the emir of Gwandu and the amir-ul Mu'minin at Sokoto.

Three days after it received the royal charter, the company changed its name to the Royal Niger Company, Chartered and Limited (RNC). Aberdare became the RNC's governor and Goldie its deputy governor. Goldie succeeded Aberdare as governor on his death in 1895. Although the RNC was already a well-established business with a board of directors and a registered office in London, the royal charter meant that it also had to start conducting itself as a government. Four days after receiving the royal charter, RNC issued its first regulations, containing 13 different edicts. As a sign of how it was to operate, the company did not bother to consult with or inform the Foreign Office before enacting these new laws.

The RNC established a constabulary force of soldiers in August 1886 to protect its trade, employees and facilities, and also established a high court. Apart from Goldie and Aberdare, the RNC made three other significant senior appointments to run its administration: David McIntosh as its agent-general, the Scotsman Sir James Marshall (a former chief justice of the Gold Coast) as its senior judicial officer, and Major Vetch from the British army as commandant of the Royal Niger Constabulary. The agent-general was RNC's de facto chief of staff, the senior judicial officer its chief justice, and the Constabulary commandant its chief of army staff. The RNC even operated its own post office and used its rubber stamp instead of postage stamps. Both the Constabulary and the court had their base in Asaba, which was also the location of the RNC's administrative headquarters.[23] The Constabulary originally consisted of 400–500 men commanded by officers loaned by the British army. The Constabulary's African soldiers were mainly Hausas, Yorubas and Fantis recruited from the Gold Coast. Its soldiers were armed with Snider rifles and bayonets. They were required to enlist for three years and were paid a bonus if they renewed their enlistment for an additional three years.

The royal charter was a game changer. It marked the moment when Britain declared its intent not just to anchor ships off the coast and trade from there, but to enter the inland areas and directly interfere in the lives of the native peoples. Britain now had interests in three different West African territories close to the River Niger: the Colony of Lagos under the Colonial Office, the Oil Rivers Protectorate under the Foreign Office, and the RNC's charter territories. However, this increased contact would give rise to a series of new conflicts and controversies. Perhaps no other company had as much influence on Nigeria's creation as the RNC.

7

THE ROYAL NIGER COMPANY

Since the Royal Niger Company (RNC) exercised vast powers and played a pivotal role in the events that led to the formation of Nigeria, its history is to some extent also the history of early Nigeria. Yet there are massive gaps in historical accounts regarding the time it was most influential (between 1885 and 1900). The gaps exist because the company's founder made a concerted effort to obscure the history of that era and to prevent its story from ever being told. A former RNC employee hit a brick wall when he tried to write about the company's history and was astonished to find that 'virtually no official documents of any historical value have been handed down'. He further noted that 'it seemed incredible that nothing further could be traced, but it has now been regretfully assumed that whatever other documents there may have been in the past must since have been destroyed'.[1] This lacuna in Nigeria's history is due to the actions of one man, Sir George Goldie. What can explain Goldie's pathological commitment to secrecy and ensuring that history would not remember him? What did the swashbuckling son of an aristocratic family with political ties and a long and proud history of military service have to hide?

WHAT BRITAIN DID TO NIGERIA

Corporate Terrorism

Like many other large corporations, the RNC has a dark history. Its actions at times resembled corporate terrorism. It had the remarkable knack of managing to antagonise the natives and its British rival companies simultaneously. This chapter will focus on three elements of the RNC's conduct: the actions of its leader, the brutality of its employees towards natives, and evidence of serious fraud by the company's personnel.

'His wish to remain unrecognised amounted almost to mania'

It is also a mark of Goldie's obsessively secretive personality that, although he set in motion the chain of events that eventually led to Nigeria's creation, many people today have not heard of him and are unaware of what he did. A friend of his said that 'his wish to remain unrecognised amounted almost to mania'.[2] On two separate occasions Goldie burned his personal papers. One of his former employees claimed that he destroyed his documents just after the outbreak of World War I, then he repeated the exercise after collating documents and writing notes for a planned autobiography. He changed his mind about the book and, according to his daughter Alice, again burned his documents and forbade his family to assist in the writing of his biography. Never a man to take chances with secrecy, he also ordered his private diaries and documents to be destroyed on his death and made his children Alice and Valentine promise that they would never write anything about him, nor assist anyone else to do so.

Goldie also took measures to ensure that people outside his family would not disclose details about him or his company's dealings. The RNC adopted its leader's desire for secrecy. All RNC employees (even temporary staff) were required to enter into a £1,000 bond and sign contracts that forbade them to disclose any information about the the company's dealings to newspapers or any other outside party without the RNC's prior written consent (a consent that was rarely granted). What was the source of this secrecy and what did Goldie want to prevent the public from discovering?

'A violent and uncompromising man'

One of Goldie's friends described him as 'a violent and uncompromising man. He had a good deal of uncontrolled temper.'[3] His company also conducted itself with similar uncompromising brutality and violence. Despite Goldie's impressive attempts to impose total discipline on the RNC and run it like a secret society, some of the company's acts of cruelty were so outrageous that they could not and should not be erased from history. Even before being granted a royal charter, the company had engaged in shocking behaviour. In October 1885 the company kidnapped three young boys from the village of Mblama in the Niger Delta, held them as hostages, and refused to release them for seven months despite the British consul ordering them to do so. This was not the company's only outrage. The Royal Niger Constabulary was another instrument of the company's corporate terror. The Constabulary undertook at least 56 military raids between 1886 and 1899.[4] The targets of these raids were usually villages or ethnic groups that clashed with the company or that damaged or seized its property. The Constabulary often inflicted staggering collective punishments. Its standard modus operandi was to punish an entire village for the actions of one or a few of its residents by burning the village down, destroying farms, and seizing or killing livestock. For example, in 1890 the Constabulary destroyed the Igbo town of Aguleri after one of its residents punctured one of its palm oil barrels with his knife.[5]

To achieve his objectives, Goldie maintained an obsessive devotion to his job, and expected the same from his employees. As a boss he was a hard taskmaster and acquired a reputation for being a difficult man to serve. He was a workaholic, an early riser and late sleeper, who worked 16 hours a day. The first employee that Goldie hired said that 'those who were associated with him had to work early and late, in season and out of season ... To be in his service was to realise you were with a masterful man, whose instructions had to be obeyed ... Those who did not carry out his instructions, or showed slackness, were severely dealt with.'[6]

Goldie admitted that he exercised 'almost uncontrolled powers'.[7] The RNC in turn granted massive powers to its employees. For example, its district agents (the lowest rank for its European staff) had the power to sentence Africans to death. Armed with such arbitrary powers, RNC employees often treated natives with arrogance and appalling brutality. A British colonial administrator later admitted that 'generally speaking, the British trader in Nigeria in the early days appears to have been an unpleasant person'.[8] Several incidents corroborate this view. An RNC employee raped the wife of a prominent Ijaw chief on board a ship. Instead of the employee being punished, the chief's wife was further humiliated by having 'presents' forced upon her as if she was a prostitute being paid for her services.[9] In another incident, an RNC employee named Captain Christian seized a native woman, stripped her naked and covered her body in tar.[10] There seemed to be little appreciation of the effect such appalling treatment had on the natives.

'A case of hot-blooded butchery'

Natives mistreated by the RNC could not expect justice even when they complained. An incident from 1887 illuminates this.

In December of that year an RNC employee named Josue Zweifel,[11] who was 'acting as a sort of traveller and explorer for the Royal Niger Company',[12] hired about 160 Sierra Leonean labourers for a rubber-gathering expedition along the River Niger. Zweifel had extensive knowledge of the River Niger area, and had been an employee of the RNC's former French business competitor *Compagnie du Sénégal et de la Côte Occidentale d'Afrique* until the RNC acquired it. Many of the labourers hired for the project had worked for Zweifel before. After a gruelling three-month march over several hundred miles, the party's food supplies were running low. When they arrived at Lokoja on 15 March 1888, Zweifel informed them that the expedition would continue down to Asaba, a town over 110 miles to the south. The labourers, who had been limited to food rations of two bananas a day, complained of hunger and thirst, and protested that their mission to gather rubber had been completed and that they did not want to travel any further on a dangerous and endless journey of undetermined duration through bushes and rivers. Zweifel interpreted the labourers' complaints as a 'dangerous mutiny' and called the RNC's acting agent-general, William Wallace, for help. Wallace arrived with troops from the Royal Niger Constabulary. Zweifel confined the labourers in a factory in Lokoja and forbade them to leave. A historian described what happened next as a 'case of hot-blooded butchery'.[13] Zweifel took out his gun, shot one of the labourers in the head and killed him. Wallace ordered the Constabulary troops to open fire on the remaining labourers; and between 6 and 17[14] of them were killed in the process and 21 others wounded.

'Blew his brains out with a revolver'

Some of the surviving labourers fled. After a gruelling 300-mile journey south, they reached Lagos on the southern coast, where they narrated their ordeal to the governor of the Lagos Colony, Cornelius Alfred Moloney. Both Moloney and the governor of Sierra Leone, supported by the Colonial Office, urged the prosecution of Wallace and Zweifel for murder. Even though 'the whole affair is believed by the Royal Niger Company to have been owing to lamentable mismanagement on the part of Mr Zweifel',[15] the RNC continued to employ both Zweifel and Wallace after the killings. The matter came to the attention of the prime minister, Lord Salisbury,[16] who wrote a memorandum in July 1889 stating his view that there was 'strong ground for viewing this act as one of wilful murder, or at least manslaughter' and deploring the RNCs continued employment of two men being investigated for murder. The prime minister added:

> it could not be said that Wallace's life was in any danger. There is no evidence that the porters uttered any threat or announced any design except that of going home. Sanadu's offence was that he tried to leave the ranks to fetch a blanket. On his doing so, Zweifel shouted that he was the man who had advised the porters to go home, and blew his brains out with a revolver. A general mêlée followed in which six men were killed and a great number wounded.[17]

The RNC's chief justice, Sir James Marshall, was a 'I will order him to be hanged on Monday morning'[18] type of judge, who in the past had ordered the execution of native chiefs and diviners. Marshall, who also happened to be one of the company's directors, investigated the matter but exonerated both Zweifel and Wallace, whom he found not guilty of any wrongdoing. Marshall did, however, imprison two of the Sierra Leonean 'mutineers'.

'An indifference for African life'

The Foreign Office sent an official dispatch to Goldie to complain that his continued employment of Zweifel and Wallace demonstrated 'an indifference for African life which is the worst possible recommendation for an extension of their power over new and more populous regions'.[19] Rather than dismissing the two men, Goldie asked for a meeting with the prime minister and the secretary of state for the colonies, Lord Knutsford.[20] After the meeting, Goldie somehow convinced the government to end its inquiry into the murders and stop its censure of his company. After these meetings the murder of the Sierra Leonean labourers mysteriously vanished from the official records, and the government kept silent about them. Marshall's biography did not mention the murders either. However, shortly after giving his judgment, Marshall resigned from his position as the RNC's chief justice and, on his way home to Britain, stopped in Lagos and gave an account of the murders that corroborated that of the surviving labourers.

The RNC's misconduct, judicial miscarriages of justice and brutal treatment of natives were not limited to the Wallace and Zweifel controversy. One commentator believed that 'the Niger company's courts had been characterised by irregularities of the gravest kind'.[21] One of the company's employees was found guilty of murdering a young girl in 'circumstances of the most dreadful brutality'.[22] A senior executive officer sentenced the employee to death for the murder. However, the RNC's council commuted the death sentence and released him after only two years' imprisonment. Two other RNC employees who were convicted of murder were imprisoned for only one year, while another employee found guilty of manslaughter served only three months in prison.[23]

X Treaties

The RNC's treaties with native chiefs were another source of friction. Disputes frequently arose about the meaning of the treaties or the interpretation of specific clauses within them. The treaty controversies that led Britain to exile King Jaja of Opobo and Nana Olomu were discussed in chapter 5. In the RNC's case there was doubt as to whether its purported treaties existed at all, and allegations were made that some treaties were fraudulently obtained or even altered.

The treaties were written in English even though many of the chiefs who assented to them were illiterate and could not read, speak or understand English, allowing them no way of verifying that the written treaty was identical to what they had been told. Sometimes native chiefs with whom the RNC claimed it had signed treaties would contradict the RNC's account and deny ever having entered into an agreement. Some treaties were blatant forgeries. For example, the RNC asserted that it entered into treaties in the Forcados region with illiterate chiefs. Since the supposedly illiterate chiefs were unable to sign their names, the RNC claimed that such chiefs used an X to 'sign' the treaties instead. However, the X marks on the treaties were identical and symmetrical, clearly giving away the handiwork of a literate writer.[24]

A treaty-making expedition in 1894 to Borgu (in the Baribaspeaking area of modern-day north-western Nigeria and northeastern Benin Republic) is worth revisiting for its revelation of the skulduggery that accompanied the RNC's treaties. The RNC often engaged agents to negotiate treaties on its behalf. Perhaps its most famous agent was the British army captain Frederick John Dealtry Lugard, who would later become the Briton most synonymous with Nigeria. After spending time in Uganda in East Africa, Lugard arrived in the River Niger area. His job was to negotiate treaties with indigenous chiefs on behalf of Goldie's RNC. The mission was delicate, as the RNC needed Lugard to reach the Borgu area and secure treaties with its chiefs before France, which had sent emissaries there for the same purpose.

In October 1894 Lugard secured a treaty between the RNC and the 'king' of Nikki. However, the king did not sign the treaty himself. Lugard's official explanation for the absence of the king's signature was that the king deputed three of his subordinates to sign the treaty on his behalf, as the king was blind and had a superstitious fear of white people. According to Lugard, he had no choice but to conclude a treaty with the king's intermediaries since he was unable to meet the king personally. The tale became more bizarre when the same king signed a treaty with France shortly after Lugard's departure, revealing that he was not blind after all, or morbidly afraid of white people. What is even more damning of Lugard's account is that closer inspection of the treaty revealed that the signatures of the three deputies who allegedly signed for the king were all written in identical handwriting. Additionally, the name of the king (Lafia) on whose behalf they signed was that of a king who had died six years earlier. Lugard made the situation worse by trying to clean up the mess. He subsequently tried to 'fix' the treaty after it was signed by annotating its margin with a note stating that the king was 'also called Absalamu'. Sadly, Absalamu was not the king's name either. The king's real name was Sire Toru and he denied ever having agreed to a treaty with Lugard, claimed that he did not delegate anyone to negotiate on his behalf, and said he had never met Lugard or any of the RNC's agents.[25]

In the same month Lugard also claimed to have signed a treaty with another king of a town (Kiama) in the same area. This king and his advisers signed with a cross. Although Lugard maintained that this treaty was genuine, the name of the king (Musa Pobida) written on the treaty was actually that of one of the king's clerks. Lugard tried to explain this away by averring that the king had a superstition that made him afraid to append his name to any written record. Yet, curiously, when France signed a treaty with the same king after Lugard's expedition, the real king (Kemura) signed his name in Arabic.[26]

A charitable explanation for these controversies is that Lugard was duped by intermediaries. This interpretation requires one to accept that Lugard, who had worked extensively in three different African countries, could be easily conned. Another interpretation is that Lugard, who was under pressure to deliver results for his superior, George Goldie, and beat the French, did whatever he had to in order to secure the treaties. The subterfuge that Lugard and the RNC employed calls into question the authenticity of many treaties that the RNC claimed to have entered into. Were these treaty forgeries an anomaly or were they a widespread practice? If the latter, it means that much of colonial Nigeria was acquired by fraud.

The thuggish behaviour of the company's employees and the ruthless manner in which they preserved the company's monopoly won them few friends among other British businesses, especially the Liverpool companies that resented the RNC's monopoly. As far back as June 1885 the RNC's predecessor, the National African Company (NAC), forbade all trade except its own on the Niger and Benue rivers. When the chief of Onitsha gave John Lander and Company of Liverpool permission to trade at Onitsha, the NAC responded by blockading the town with armed ships. When Lander's agents moved north-west into Nupe-land to trade there, the NAC captured them and beat them up.

'There was a great deal open to censure in the early conduct of the Company'

On many occasions, MPs raised in the British Parliament their concerns about the RNC's appalling treatment of natives. For example, an MP from Liverpool, William Lawrence, repeatedly complained that 'some very questionable things had been done by agents of the Company', that 'there was a great deal open to censure in the early conduct of the Company', and that 'many things were done by people who bore our name and sailed from our shores which could not be defended'.[27] On 7 April 1887, Lawrence asked the undersecretary of state for foreign affairs, Sir James Fergusson, about 'the policy of the Royal Niger Company in seizing certain children as hostages'. He also asked Fergusson to provide copies of the 237 treaties which the RNC had alleg-edly entered into with native chiefs and written evidence of the RNC's dealings with the natives. Yet there was a strange deter-mination by the British government to either shield the RNC from censure or deliberately turn a blind eye to its outrages. Fergusson curtly replied that the treaties 'were in the possession of the Foreign Office'. Fergusson also mentioned that the RNC's troops had cause to 'chastise some slave-hunting tribes' who allegedly attacked one of its factories, but that 'there are no papers on the subject'.[28] When Lawrence pressed Fergusson fur-ther and asked him whether it was true that the RNC had detained native children as hostages for seven months, Fergusson again tersely replied that he did not know how long the children had been held hostage.

On 13 April 1896 an MP from Newcastle-under-Lyme, William Allen, asked the undersecretary of state for foreign affairs, Sir Charles Dilke, whether it was true that RNC staff on board a ship had chased a native in a small canoe and shot him, as a consequence of which he drowned. Allen also alleged that some native staff of the RNC had resigned in protest at the cruel treatment that the company meted out to the natives. Dilke replied that the RNC had launched 'a full inquiry' into the incident and that the RNC's chief justice, Sir James Marshall, reached a verdict of 'death by misadventure'. Dilke also claimed that the dead man had not been shot but instead 'jumped overboard' for unexplained reasons and that his corpse 'could not be found'.[29]

The RNC seemed to have friends in high places watching its back. Its governor, Lord Aberdare, was a former politician with many close friends in Parliament and, in a strange conflict of interest, the secretary of state for the colonies Joseph Chamberlain was an RNC shareholder.

The Anglo-Ijaw Rivalry

Since neither the RNC's courts nor Parliament would come to their aid and protect them from the RNC's outrages, the natives had to engage in self-help. The brutal and contemptuous treatment that the RNC meted out to natives elicited great bitterness. Ethnic groups close to the company's operations bore the brunt. The Ijaws were one of the most numerous of such ethnic groups. For centuries they had been traders and fishermen and navigated the Niger Delta's rivers and creeks long before the British arrived. Their maritime lifestyle led one British administrator to describe them as 'almost amphibious people'.[30] The RNC's elaborate licensing and taxation system set it on a collision course with the Nembe, a sub-group of the Ijaw. The British referred to the Nembe people and the area they inhabited as 'Brass'. Some less kind British descriptions portrayed them as 'devil-worshippers and cannibals'.[31]

Although it was a company, the RNC operated in part like a government. It imposed an elaborate system of licensing and taxation on the territories to which its charter applied, in the same way a sovereign nation would impose customs duties and excise on trade across its borders. Although section 14 of the RNC's royal charter forbade it from operating a monopoly, it blatantly violated its charter by imposing trading terms that were monopolistic and at times resembled a Mafia protection racket. It arbitrarily imposed extortionate taxes on natives and other companies for engaging in regular trading activities in which they had participated for years before the RNC arrived. Since it had a virtual monopoly, the RNC could charge whatever price it deemed fit and others had to pay because there was no alternative. Additionally, the company made a handsome profit by buying produce at below-market prices from West African natives and then reselling it in Europe at a marked-up price.

Despite Goldie's insistence that he did not want to interfere with or change the lives of natives, and that his preoccupation was to regulate the activities of foreigners, he had a very liberal interpretation of the term 'foreigner'. Foreigners were not just non-Africans. From Goldie's perspective, the term applied to anyone not born in the company's territories, including those from Lagos, Sierra Leone and, most problematically, from the Niger Delta. The Nembe lived outside the areas under the RNC's jurisdiction and so they were 'foreigners' to the RNC. Classification as 'foreigners' was a huge and incendiary problem for the Nembe. Any foreigner that wanted to trade in the RNC's territories had to procure a bewildering range of licences, including a general trading licence costing £50; a spirit licence costing £100; and a licence costing £10 for each separate port at which he wished to trade.[32] This minimum annual trading charge of £160 was a very large sum of money in the 1800s. The penalty for trading without a licence was a minimum fine of £500. Even if he could afford to acquire these prohibitive licences, any Nembe who wanted to transport goods across the river had to declare them to the RNC and pay a tax on each item. If he purchased goods and wished to take them out of RNC territories, he also had to pay an export fee equivalent to 20 per cent of the value of the goods. If, by some good fortune, a Nembe was wealthy and motivated enough to acquire and pay for all these licences, he still faced another hurdle. Most of the Nembe were either illiterate or not literate enough to complete customs forms, nor could they read or draw up invoices in English. These requirements were deliberate measures to block trade by competitors and natives, but cloaked as a licensing and taxation system. The ruthless efficiency of the regime was demonstrated by the fact that in the five years between 1895 and 1900, no one was granted a licence to export from the RNC's territories, and no one except the RNC exported from those areas.

Faced with these outrageous fees and licences, smuggling goods in and out of RNC territories became a risky alternative for the Nembe. However, the RNC strictly enforced the licensing regime and dealt harshly with smugglers. Its ships blockaded the river and fired on and killed people in canoes suspected of smuggling or who failed to stop at its ports. The licensing regime not only prevented the Nembe from trading but also prevented them from crossing the river to collect payments from their debtors. The RNC seemed determined to make life miserable for the Nembe. It even issued a regulation forbidding the collection of debts in its territories (another blatant attempt to punish the Nembe), and seized Nembe canoes which were transporting yams and cassava, the staple foods of the area. Food became so scarce that some Nembe began to starve.

'If we cannot trade we must starve'

The Nembe aired their grievance to British authorities. In a letter to the Foreign Office in 1876 King Okiya of Nembe lamented that the RNC's practices were driving them into penury and that 'We have no land where we can grow plantains or yams, if we cannot trade we must starve'.[33] A group of Nembe chiefs later complained to a British commission of inquiry:

> We do not call ourselves Brassmen; but Nimbe [sic] ... There are many Christians in our country; but many have gone back to the old faith, owing to the oppression of the Niger Company ... Many chiefs who were brought up as Christians have now gone back to fetishism, among these King Koko (of Brass), the reason for this being that they had lost faith in the white man's God, who allowed them to be

oppressed, and their trade, their only means of livelihood to be taken from them without just cause or reason.[34]

Goldie did not care. He claimed that the licensing regime would 'exclude from the territories—a class of men ... who were formerly the worst enemies of civilisation in central Africa. These were disreputable coloured men who ... lived by surreptitious dealings and slaves ... stirring up the natives to discontent and bloodshed.'[35]

From the perspective of the Nembe, they had done exactly what the British had told them to. The British told them to abolish the slave trade, and they did. The British told them to trade instead in agricultural products, and they did. Then the British stopped buying palm oil from them and obtained the palm oil directly themselves, and they also blocked the Nembe from fishing and trading on the rivers, as they had done for centuries. It was so unconscionable that a British army officer admitted:

> I was in a position at the time fully to understand why they were driven to desperation by what they reasonably considered was unjust treatment at the hands of the white man ... You only needed a superficial acquaintance with the people of Brass to see at once that the licences demanded were prohibitive ... It is not surprising that the poor Brassmen were at their wits end to know how they were to gain their livelihood.[36]

The Nembe were faced with a stark choice. They could either submit to the RNC's regime and die slowly of starvation, or they could resist and die quickly from RNC gunfire. In January 1895, the Nembe made their choice.

Vengeance in Akassa

On 27 January 1895 the RNCs vice-consul in the Nembe area, Harper Harrison, received an anonymous letter with the following warning: 'Brass people leaving tomorrow to destroy Royal

Niger Company's factories and lives at Akassa on Tuesday morning. Be sure you send at once to stop them. An Observer.'[37] The vice-consul passed on the letter to the company's agent-general, Joseph Flint, but neither of them took any further action in response to it.

29 January 1895

At 4.30 on a misty morning, dozens of canoes approached the RNC's factory at Akassa (in modern-day Bayelsa State). On board were several Nembe warriors armed with machetes and Dane guns. The early morning mist and poor visibility allowed their canoes to reach the headquarters undetected. The Nembe king, Frederick William Koko, shrouded the journey in mystery and did not tell his warriors its objective until just a few days before they departed. Koko had converted to Christianity but then abandoned it and returned to his traditional religion in disgust at what the country that brought Christianity was doing to his people. He also withdrew his son from the Roman Catholic Church at Onitsha.

As they arrived at dawn, most of the RNC's staff were still asleep. Captain Morgan of the Constabulary came downstairs from the staff residence (a wooden house on stilts with a zinc roof), to be greeted by a bullet that grazed his head. As the Nembe rushed from their canoes and swarmed into the RNC's premises, Morgan quickly ran back upstairs while two other staff members named Russell and Hughes barricaded themselves in a room. Morgan and a French naval lieutenant called Grigg barricaded themselves into another room and took turns to open the door at intervals and fire gunshots to keep the attackers at bay. Some of the attackers tried to get at them by climbing over a dividing wall, but Morgan pointed his revolver over the top of the wall and fired at random without looking.

THE ROYAL NIGER COMPANY

In the melee, the agent-general, Joseph Flint,[38] and some other employees fled in a dinghy.

The Nembe attackers wreaked havoc and destroyed or removed most of the company's equipment and property including files, weapons, spirits, tobacco and furniture. They also sank two of its ships, damaged a third, and killed 24 of the RNC's labourers—so-called 'Kruboys' (West African sailors and labourers hired from Liberia). Before departing, the Nembe took 60 Liberian and native hostages, whom they divided among King Koko's chiefs. Splitting the hostages also split opinion about what to do with them. Some wanted them killed while others wanted to use them as bargaining chips with the British. Unable to reach consensus, some chiefs executed 43 of the hostages.[39] Some British accounts claim that the Nembe ate the hostages they killed. One of the witnesses to this alleged cannibalism was a priest who, strangely, was allowed to leave Nembe country unharmed by the alleged cannibals.

The Foreign Office ordered a retaliatory raid against the Nembe. Vice-Admiral Sir Frederick Bedford arrived on 20 February 1895 with a force of four ships and 150 sailors and marines. The RNC's Constabulary reinforced them with another 150 soldiers. The land forces captured a Nembe island known as Sacrifice Island,[40] where they discovered the remains of some of the executed hostages, while in late February and March the naval ships destroyed Nembe towns and villages such as Nembe and Kaiama with shellfire. The troops also killed hundreds of people, drove the survivors into the bush and seized and destroyed Nembe war canoes, cannons and gunpowder. They also released the surviving hostages. King Koko fled into exile and died in a village called Etiema on 25 February 1898; his remains were brought back to Nembe country for burial.

The most puzzling aspect of the bloodshed and destruction is how avoidable it was. It could easily have been prevented by the simple measure of adjusting the boundaries of territories under RNC jurisdiction to include the Nembe. The RNC's failure to ask the Foreign Office to do this was symptomatic of its utter disregard for the effect its activities had on the native population. The RNC staff's contempt for the locals and refusal to learn their language facilitated the attack's secrecy and blinded them from seeing what was coming. They also failed to take note when the Nembe suddenly and mysteriously stopped trying to trade in areas near the RNC's districts just before the attack.

Nonetheless, the Nembe incident had serious repercussions. The focus of the attack solely on the RNC's facilities gave credence to the Nembe position that their quarrel was solely against the RNC and not against Britain. In June 1895 the Foreign Office sent Sir John Kirk to the Niger Delta to conduct an inquiry. His report noted that the attack was provoked by RNC regulations which made the Nembe foreigners in an area in which they had traded for years. He also suggested that the RNC territories should be eventually taken under direct British government control. To some extent the Akassa raid was a watershed. It put the RNC in danger of losing its charter. The RNC could no longer conceal its mistreatment of natives from British officialdom, and the British government became less inclined to turn a blind eye when the RNC's activities damaged Britain's reputation.

Feeling the pressure from domestic and international rivals, Goldie considered maintaining his company's influence by divesting itself of its commercial activities but retaining its administrative powers. In July 1897 he wrote to the Colonial Office to inform them:

> I think it is desirable, in Imperial interests, that the administration of Nigeria should no longer be conducted by a company which is also engaged in trade ... This duality of the Niger Company's functions has produced a bitter hostility amongst a handful of persons in

Liverpool, which has had serious international effect ... Now, political interests of the Niger Company are those of Great Britain.[41]

'He must be with us or against us'

In the same memorandum Goldie also recommended merging his company's territories with the Niger Coast Protectorate and the Colony of Lagos, and that all three territories 'should be thrown into one West African territory'.[42] This was essentially a proposal for the formation of the country now called Nigeria. However, Goldie's position had weakened. Lugard's treaty shenanigans in Borgu had created an international controversy, with France both protesting and refusing to recognise the validity of the treaties and sending its soldiers into territories under the RNC's charter. A private company could not match the French government in economic or military resources. Britain's creation of the West African Frontier Force (WAFF) in 1897 provided a British military counterforce to France but it also undermined Goldie. Since the WAFF was controlled by the government, its officers could not be commanded by a private company. This was an additional complication and gave Colonial Office officials the impression that Goldie was content to reap profits while the government spent money and undertook military operations on his behalf to secure territories that were supposed to be controlled by his company. Once Goldie realised that the revocation of his company's charter was likely, he became intransigent (even by his standards), withheld cooperation from Colonial and Foreign Office officials, and prioritised securing as much compensation as possible from the government. Relations between Goldie and the government soured. On 19 September 1897, the British secretary of state for the colonies, Joseph Chamberlain, wrote a memorandum to the parliamentary undersecretary to the Colonial Office, Lord Selborne, threatening 'to expropriate him [Goldie], lock, stock, and barrel ... In fact I should take a very high line with him and tell him that in this crisis he must be with us or against us, and that we cannot allow him to dictate terms.'[43]

It is a damning indictment of the RNC's tenure that despite enjoying and exercising the powers of a government, it did none of the things a government is supposed to do. It did not build schools or hospitals or provide amenities for the natives living around its premises. Its legacy to the natives was destruction, fraud and oppression.

Most events discussed in this chapter are unknown to all but a specialist audience. Since Goldie did such a good job of covering his tracks, we will probably never know the full story of what Lugard did during his treaty-making expedition to Borgu, the pretext for the Royal Niger Constabulary's military operations, if they were justified, and whether appropriate or excessive force was used. Just how many treaties did the RNC forge or manipulate? To accept the treaties as valid requires us to believe that hundreds of native chiefs willingly surrendered economic and political sovereignty for a few bags of cowries, clothing and gin. How many people did the RNC defraud and kill? How many villages did it destroy? Thanks to Goldie's efficient destruction of his company's records, we may never know the answers to these questions. Goldie not only burned details of his life, but also erased significant portions of Nigeria's early history forever.

PART 3

INVASION AND WAR, 1851–1920

Britain's conquest of Nigeria was not instantaneous. It took nearly seventy years of military conflicts to accomplish and it lasted ninety-nine years overall. It followed a consistent pattern whereby Britain would send in naval gunboats and soldiers if British business interests were compromised. The invasion force would then take on a permanent character as the soldiers would remain as an occupying force, and Britain would eventually turn the invaded territory into a colony. The next six chapters will examine how Britain effected its conquest of Nigeria, and how and when the foundations of the Nigerian state were laid.

8

GLOVER'S HAUSAS

A chief once said to him, 'I know what happens to our poor country. First comes missionary—well, he very good man; he write book. Then come Consul; he write home. Then come merchant; he very good man, he buy nuts. Then come governor; he—well, he writes to Queeny, she send him back—she send man-o'-war. Our country done spoil—no more of our poor place left.'[1]

Although it was not intentional, Britain was responsible for creating the organisation that played the greatest role in reshaping Nigeria after its independence. A seemingly innocuous naval accident in the 19th century set off a chain of events that eventually led to the creation of the modern-day Nigerian army and police force. In 1858, while on an expedition on the River Niger, a British ship named the *Dayspring* struck a rock and sank near Jebba (in modern-day Kwara State in Northern Nigeria). The crew, which included Dr J. Baikie and Bishop Ajayi Crowther, escaped and reached safety before the ship sank. They camped by the riverside and remained there for a year, surviving on food provided by friendly residents of nearby villages. One of the ship-wrecked crew, a British naval officer named Lt John Hawley

Glover,[2] who was the mission's cartographer, travelled overland to Lagos in the south to bring back help and supplies to his colleagues.[3] Glover was the son of a clergyman who, after training to follow in his father's footsteps, changed tack, joined the Royal Navy, served in the Middle East and China and fought in the Burma and Crimean wars.

There are two contrasting stories about what happened after the shipwreck at Jebba. The Nigerian army's official history states that when travelling overland to Lagos, Glover met and conscripted some runaway Hausa slaves. The second story is that after arriving in Lagos, Glover travelled to Sierra Leone and there met Hausa slaves who wished to return to their homeland. Glover brought the Hausas with him on his journey back to Lagos.[4] Whichever of the two accounts is accurate, Glover's presence and planned journey back to Jebba caused much excitement in Lagos.

Glover ordered one of his Hausa servants named Sani to recruit porters for his journey back north to his shipwrecked colleagues. As news of the mission spread in Lagos and neighbouring cities such as Abeokuta and Ibadan, the knowledge that Glover was heading north enticed approximately 200 slaves to escape from their masters to join Glover's expedition. The mission offered the slaves, many of whom were Muslim northerners, including Hausas and Nupes, not just a chance to escape from their masters, but also to use Glover's expedition as a way to return north and be reunited with their families in their homelands. Glover took the runaway slaves as his escorts and porters when he set out to rejoin his party at Jebba. However, the runaway slaves included some formerly held by powerful and wealthy slave owners including Oba Dosunmu and Madam Efunroye Tinubu. When some of the slave owners tried to retrieve their slaves by force, a gunfight erupted. During the battle, Glover was impressed by how readily and precisely his Hausa escorts carried out his orders to lay down their loads and kneel beside them in a circular formation if they were attacked. From this incident Glover formed the impression that the Hausas would one day make good soldiers.

Following Britain's annexation of Lagos in August 1861, Glover was promoted to captain on 24 November 1862 and was appointed administrator of Lagos on 21 April 1863. Since British influence was strongest in the coastal areas, its extension to inland areas was dependent on the presence and demonstration of physical and military force. When Glover was appointed, the only security force in Lagos was the 100 soldiers of the West India Regiment. Of these, only 36 were on active duty as the remainder were either sick or on guard duty.

'They do not get footsore on long marches, and the simplicity of their dress renders it both convenient and economical'

On 9 October 1862 the Governor of Lagos, Sir Stanhope Freeman, wrote to the Duke of Newcastle, then the British secretary of state for the colonies, to argue for the establishment of a security force in Lagos. Freeman made it clear exactly which people should be recruited for the new force:

> The expense of this establishment is about one-fifth of what a similar number of regular troops would cost the Imperial Government, and the [Hausa] force is more efficient than the West India Regiment, one-fifth of the men are usually on the sick list in this place, while there is rarely more than one per cent of the Hausa men ill; besides this, they [Hausas] require no commissariat, little or no transport, and nourish themselves on the products of the country, which are always to be had. Wearing no shoes, they do not get footsore on long marches, and the simplicity of their dress renders it both convenient and economical.[5]

Glover's Hausas

In June 1863 the Colonial Office granted Glover permission to train and deploy 30 of his Hausa companions as a security force for Lagos. They were known as Glover's Hausas, as well as 'the Forty Thieves' (for unknown reasons) and later were renamed the Hausa Militia. Their remit was enlarged to encompass internal security and military matters, and by December 1863 they had grown to 600 members.[6] They were used to mount punitive expeditions and to protect British trade routes around Lagos. They were also deployed in military operations against the Egba Yorubas in 1870, and 100 members were sent to Kumasi in the Gold Coast (which later became Ghana) to fight against the Ashanti in 1873–4. When the Ashanti conflict ended, half of Glover's Hausas remained in the Gold Coast and the other half were sent back to Lagos and renamed the Hausa Constabulary in 1886. The unit that remained behind formed the foundation of what later became the modern-day Ghanaian army. The Hausa Constabulary was later renamed the Lagos Constabulary and operated as the police force for the Lagos Colony. An independent Hausa force was carved out of the Constabulary and given exclusively military functions.

Hausas 'form the best fighting material in Africa'

British stereotyping of Hausas as a martial race led to a deliberately racialised military recruitment policy that would have long-term consequences for Nigeria's military and political stability over the next 150 years. Glover recruited Hausas as fighting troops while other ethnic groups, many of whom were from areas near the southern coastline and whom the British regarded as less warlike, were used to perform menial duties as porters and interpreters. The diaries, memoirs and recollections of British military and colonial officers are replete with a fascination and admiration for the Hausas as a warrior or martial race. A British army officer boasted that Hausas 'form the best fighting material in Africa: they are short, sturdy-looking men, and excellent

marchers',[7] while another Briton spoke of their 'force of character, combined with a physical strength which is, I believe, unsur-
passed by any people in the world, that makes the Hausa the
efficient soldier he is'.[8] A British admiral said: 'They make admirable soldiers, being of great physical strength, and are cool and
brave in action.'[9] These impressions were reinforced by the history of success in warfare that Muslim states acquired in West
Africa. The British regarded Hausas as natural warriors whose
religion imposed discipline on them and who were members of
a culture accustomed to battle and victory.

Apart from their racialised perceptions of the Hausas and
other ethnic groups, there were practical reasons why the British
chose them as a martial race. The British habit of identifying
martial races was not unique to West Africa. In its other colonies
Britain had similarly identified races that it considered to be
imbued with martial credentials, recruited them into the colonial
armies, then used them to conquer other ethnic groups far away
from their homeland. The Sikhs were the preferred martial race
in India and the Gurkhas were their counterpart in Nepal. Hausas
were chosen in West Africa because the majority of British military campaigns at the outset in the area were against non-Hausa
and non-Islamic ethnic groups with whom the Hausas had no
allegiance. Captain Lennox said:

> The reason that the men are mostly recruited from far away north
> is because they make far and away better soldiers ... and also
> because the majority of the fighting which now takes place occurs
> against the tribes in the south, and it is of great advantage to have
> men who are in no way connected with those against whom the
> fighting is taking place.[10]

For example, many Hausa soldiers who were formerly slaves in
Yorubaland were deployed in military campaigns in that area, and
were unlikely to show restraint when given the opportunity to
wield weapons against communities in which they had been

enslaved. Owing to West Africa's massive linguistic diversity, British military authorities imposed Hausa as the army's language of command and communication. British soldiers took courses and exams in Hausa. Hausas were also itinerant traders who travelled and traded throughout West and North Africa. The geographical knowledge they acquired from trading journeys and their long habit of trekking great distances barefoot without complaining made them desirable army recruits.

On 30 September 1885 Glover died at the age of 56 in Harley Street, London. He was buried in Kensal Green. A monument to him, a life-sized marble bust, was erected in St Paul's Cathedral and was placed in the crypt next to that of Lord Nelson. The legacy of the militia he founded survived long after him.

The Army as a Colonial Force

Other colonial paramilitary armed groups later combined with the Hausa Constabulary. The Royal Niger Company created a constabulary in 1886 to provide military and police security in areas where the company traded and exercised administrative control. Sir Ralph Moor[11] created a third paramilitary group called the Oil Rivers Irregulars in 1891. They were later renamed the Niger Coast Constabulary. When the Royal Niger Company's royal charter was revoked in 1900, the Lagos Constabulary, Royal Niger Constabulary and Niger Coast Constabulary were amalgamated into the West African Frontier Force (WAFF).

The Royal Niger Constabulary became the Northern Nigeria Regiment of the WAFF and the Northern Nigeria police force, and the Niger Coast Constabulary formed the Southern Nigeria Regiment of the WAFF and Southern Nigeria police force, along with units of the Royal Niger Constabulary stationed in Southern Nigeria.[12] The Lagos Constabulary became the Lagos Battalion of the WAFF. The WAFF was renamed the Royal West African

Frontier Force (RWAFF) in 1928. The Nigeria Regiment of the RWAFF then underwent several changes in nomenclature over the next 35 years in its lineal evolution to the modern-day Nigerian army. In 1956 it was renamed the Queen's Own Nigeria Regiment following the state visit of Queen Elizabeth II to Nigeria in that year. It was renamed the Royal Nigerian Military Forces in 1959, then the Royal Nigerian Army when Nigeria became independent in 1960, and finally the Nigerian Army when Nigeria became a republic in 1963.

From Glover's Hausas to 'Pagan' Army

Although British officers marvelled at the martial qualities of their Hausa soldiers, some of their names indicate that not all were ethnic Hausas. In the 19th and early 20th century the use of a father's family name as a surname was not common among West Africans. To differentiate between soldiers with identical first names, their village or town name was usually adopted as a proxy surname. Thus, although the early members of the nominally 'Hausa' WAFF included Hausas with names such as Awudu Katsina, it also included men with names like Suberu Ilorin (from Ilorin in the northern part of Yorubaland) and Atta Igala (an Igala from the non-Hausa areas of Northern Nigeria). The army also included people described by the British as 'Hausa-speaking pagans'. Who were these men from other ethnic groups and how did they end up in an army that was supposed to be a Hausa Muslim force?

British officers believed that Islam imposed a natural civilisation and discipline on Hausa troops,[13] but were apprehensive about the religion's potential for being a rallying point for mobilising rebellion. In 1910 there was only one Christian among the 3,142 troops in the Northern Nigeria Regiment.[14] Mutiny by Hausa troops was less of a concern while they were deployed in Southern Nigeria, but might become a serious danger if they were ordered to attack fellow Muslims in Northern Nigeria. The WAFF's first commander, Brigadier General Lugard, said: 'I consider it an important matter to maintain a balance not merely of races but of Mohammedans and pagans in the corps. Indeed, though I have a great respect for the Mohammedan religion ... I do not consider it politic to enlist too great a number of Mohammedans as soldiers. Already, in my view, we have an excess of Mohammedans.'[15] (I have omitted the remainder of Lugard's quote in order not to offend modern religious sensibilities.) However, concern about the dangers of Islam led the British to devise ways to dilute the Muslim composition of the army. It pursued a two-pronged policy of maintaining Hausa as the army's official language while simultaneously trying to recruit other 'martial races' from non-Hausa areas, then teaching them to speak Hausa. This policy of ethnic manipulation unwittingly created dangerous ethnic and regional divisions within the army that would contribute to the Nigerian civil war in the 1960s.

There were three primary ways an ethnic group could become stereotyped as a 'martial race' in British eyes. Firstly, ethnic groups who fiercely resisted British army patrols would sometimes win grudging respect from the British and make themselves targets for army recruitment. However, the south-east's frequent opposition to, and revolts against, colonial authorities ironically worked against the region. Although in 1905 the army tried to recruit Ejaghams from an area in modern-day Cross River State, British army recruiters did not regard men from south-eastern Nigeria as good soldiers for several reasons. For one, British recruiters believed that 'most of the local tribes are too impatient of any form of authority to submit voluntarily to military discipline'.[16] Igbos ranked high on the list of ethnic groups that recruiters regarded as undesirable military candidates.

In British eyes, Igbos could not be trusted to obey orders. Constant armed revolts and other protest movements against British authority in Igboland gave its people a reputation for being headstrong and rebellious. Placing guns in their hands and training them in how to use them was a very dangerous proposition. The feeling of antipathy was mutual. Constant British military assaults in Igboland did not make the area a friendly place for British recruiters, and Igbos were not favourably disposed to joining an army that was in the habit of machine-gunning their families and burning their towns and villages to the ground. The language barrier between British military recruiters and south-easterners also made it difficult for any affinity to develop between them. The recruiters did not speak any south-eastern languages, and south-easterners could not speak Hausa.

It was much safer to recruit such southerners for non-combat roles as carriers, bandsmen and drummers. However, as large numbers of Igbos underwent Western education and became literate, British recruiters were almost forced to recruit them out of necessity to serve in technical roles such as clerks, mechanics and signallers. This created two conflicting stereotypes of south-erners as being educated and technically adept, but far too soft natured to be warriors, and of northerners as brave and disciplined fighters, but not educated or intellectually adroit. The natives themselves absorbed these stereotypes in ways that paved the way for future conflict between them. Northern soldiers had little respect for the martial credentials of their southern colleagues, who did not carry guns or fight but instead spent their working lives reading documents, writing and counting stock. They regarded these literate southerners (especially Igbos) as too articulate and erudite to be warriors.[17] Their attitude to the southerners was summed up by an old Hausa maxim: '*mai gudun fada ba zai yi surutu ba*' (the warrior is not talkative).

'We only want men of northern origin'

Since the south-east in particular could not provide a large pool of combatant soldiers, Britain had to recruit from elsewhere. The second marker for army recruitment was proximity to Hausaland or the ability to quickly learn to speak Hausa. Lugard claimed that 'the pagan Gwaris, Kedaras, and other tribes yield to none in bravery. They all speak Hausa and I hope to enlist many.'[18] Lugard's primary concern was to dissolve the army's mono-religious character. Yet he had little interest in making it a nationally representative army that reflected Nigeria's ethno-regional composition. He informed the Colonial Office: 'It is, in fact, my desire to make the West African Frontier Force, as far as possible, a Hausa-speaking Pagan force.'[19]

The third way for an ethnic group to earn the tag of 'martial race' was to demonstrate a history of resistance to the Sokoto Caliphate. Since the Caliphate was, in British eyes, the zenith of military and political achievement in the area, they regarded ethnic groups that successfully resisted its raids and occupation as natural warriors. These factors gave the Hausa's neighbouring ethnic groups an advantage, but made it difficult to recruit ethnic groups from faraway locations in Southern Nigeria.

The Tivs, who lived in the lower part of Northern Nigeria, had fought off frequent slave raids from the Caliphate, maintained their independence, and refused to be converted to Islam. Such attempted invasions made them resistant to strangers and they became feared for attacking intruders with their mysterious and deadly poisoned arrows. British authorities referred to them with a derogatory Hausa word, 'Munshi', and regarded Tivland as dangerous bandit country. Tivs acquired a reputation among the British for being 'truculent', 'a most intractable people', who 'have proved themselves aggressive and inimical to a degree towards any effort to establish law and order'.[20] The Tivs fulfilled these stereotypes. One month after Britain declared a protectorate over Northern Nigeria in 1900, they attacked an armed British patrol that was installing telegraph lines on their land. In the past they had also attacked the Royal Niger Company's trading stations in Tivland and murdered two of its agents, causing the company to close all but one of its trading stations in Tivland, at Abinsi. In January 1906 they sacked and burned the remaining factory at Abinsi. Although these attacks brought British military reprisals against the Tivs, it also made them, in British eyes, a potential warrior race and targets for military recruitment. In his 1906 annual report, Lugard reported to the Colonial Office: 'The Munshis are stated to be an extremely fine race, fearless and independent and very industrious.'[21]

In 1923, only 11 out of 3,000 soldiers in the army were Tivs, but By World War II, the army had 6,000 Tiv fighters. Thereafter the Tiv became synonymous with the army. They remain one of the most heavily represented ethnic groups in the army's infantry units. In 1950 the commander of the Northern Nigeria Regiment issued recruiting instructions: 'We only want men of northern origin, and Tivs from Benue.'[22] British colonial authorities also recruited large numbers of the Tiv's neighbouring ethnic groups, such as the Idoma, Igala and Jukun, and other groups, such as the Bachama, Tarok, Darkakari, Nupe and Kataf, who either lived on the periphery of Hausaland and resisted conquest by the Sokoto Caliphate, or who spoke Hausa in addition to their indigenous language. Lugard's desire to make the army a Hausa-speaking non-Muslim force succeeded, and men from these ethnic groups still dominate the Nigerian army's combat units. Sixty per cent of post-independence Nigerian chiefs of army staff came from these parts of the country. This ethnic manipulation meant that for much of its history, the army tended to be an ethnic anomaly in most of Nigeria.

WHAT BRITAIN DID TO NIGERIA

'We in England owe our negro brother-subject a great debt of gratitude'

Although it is understated in the historical literature, Nigerian soldiers served with distinction and played a key role in the two World Wars. Britain recruited over 20,000 Nigerian soldiers for World War I, and during both World Wars I and II they fought for Britain and gained a reputation as brave and loyal soldiers. A British soldier who fought alongside Nigerian soldiers during World War I paid tribute to them:

> I hope that when my readers have read this account ... they will in future respect the fighting black man of Africa, for he has at least proved himself a man. We in England owe our negro brother-subject a great debt of gratitude for all he has done for our beloved Empire. Many a native of Nigeria has trekked his last trek and fought his last fight far away from his own land for the sake of the Empire.[23]

The legacy of Nigerian army participation in British wars lives on in the name of army institutions such as Dodan Barracks in Lagos, which was the government headquarters for 25 years from 1966 to 1991, and which is named after a region of Burma in which Nigerian soldiers fought. The army's 81 and 82 divisions are named after historic West African army divisions that fought during World War II. Some early Nigerian soldiers of the WAFF acquired near-legendary status for their exploits in battle. These include Company Sergeant Major Bello Akure, 'the hero of a dozen fights',[24] Private Afolabi Ibadan and Company Sergeant-Major Sumanu, who was awarded five medals. While fighting for the British army during World War I, Afolabi carried his wounded British commander, Captain Robinson, on his back, while Sumanu followed behind to shield Robinson from rear fire with his own body. Sumanu was shot and wounded, and as Afolabi turned back to help him, he too was shot. For their actions Afolabi was decorated with the Military Medal and

Sumanu was mentioned in dispatches. Another renowned Nigerian soldier in the WAFF was Regimental Sergeant-Major Chari Maigumeri, who became a legend in the army. Maigumeri was a Kanuri from Borno. He enlisted in 1913 and fought in both World Wars I and II. During World War I, he fought for the Germans in the Cameroons, where he was awarded the Iron Cross for bravery. He was captured by the Nigeria Regiment in 1915 and remained a prisoner of war for two years until 1917, when he volunteered for the Nigeria Regiment. He served against the Germans in East Africa and was promoted to Regimental Sergeant-Major in 1928. Maigumeri also fought in World War II, in which he was awarded the Military Medal for fighting against the Italians, and the British Empire Medal for fighting against the Japanese. He retired in 1953 after 36 years of service and was promoted to honorary captain in retirement.

Despite these accounts of gallantry, Nigerian soldiers were not particularly well treated in comparison with their British contemporaries. For one thing, they were paid far less than British soldiers, even though they had to carry heavier loads and baggage than British soldiers when marching. The salary of the five British officers in the Royal Niger Constabulary was more than £3,000 greater than the combined salaries of more than 500 native soldiers in the Constabulary. Native soldiers could be punished for disciplinary infractions by flogging and were forced to march barefoot. British soldiers were not so punished and had boots. Native soldiers also had to stand to attention and salute both white soldiers (no matter their rank) and civilians. Yet British soldiers did not have to return the gesture to natives and did so only for British officers of superior rank. Britain placed a rank ceiling on the native soldiers and barred them from becoming commanding officers. They also had to perform some unpleasant missions on behalf of their British commanders. Civilians feared and resented soldiers because their presence tended to have a scorched-earth effect. While marching through the countryside, British commanders often ordered native soldiers to seize crops, yams and cattle from villagers' farms in order to feed themselves.

'We did not like the soldiers'

The army's colonial origins and the involvement of its soldiers in campaigns of destruction caused problems for it long after colonialism ended. The fact that Nigerian soldiers helped the British to conquer and subjugate their fellow Nigerians made them feared and unpopular among the civilian population. The soldiers got the blame for the colonial army's actions, but little of its benefit. They, like the civilians, were part of the same conquered African people. They obeyed orders from their British commanders without appreciating the consequences of what they were doing. They shot, invaded and burned by order. The sardauna of Sokoto and first indigenous premier of the Northern Region, Sir Ahmadu Bello, said: 'We did not like the soldiers: they were our own people and had conquered us for strangers and had defeated our people on the plain just before us. This feeling was very common all over the North.'[25]

While the tactic of using Hausa soldiers to conquer other ethnic groups was successful in the colonial era, the racialised division of labour that it introduced into the army survived into the post-independence years. When Nigeria became independent in 1960, approximately three-quarters of the fighting troops were northerners, while the majority of officers in the army's support and technical units, such as education, ordnance, finance and signals, were southerners. Less than six years after independence, southern officers staged a military coup during which they killed four northern soldiers. When northern soldiers avenged the murders of their brethren six months later, it inevitably resembled an ethno-regional fratricidal battle between northern infantrymen and southern officers and descended into a brutal blood-bath. This ethnic layering of the army contributed to several military coups in Nigeria during which different ethnic factions of the army turned their guns on each other, and to a civil war in which over a million people died. The ethnic composition of the army remains a controversial and difficult problem with which Nigeria still grapples in the 21st century. Its effect on national stability is so serious that to make military recruitment more balanced, Nigeria still applies an ethnic quota to military recruitment and promotions.

Nigeria's army and police were the country's first national institutions, and both are ironically older than the country itself. Although Nigerians are reluctant to admit it, the story of Nigeria is to some extent the story of its army. There are few countries where the country's fate and that of its army are as tightly interwoven as Nigeria. For the first 102 years of its existence, Nigeria's army was under British command. At various points in time, the army has played different roles as conqueror, destroyer, ruler and protector of the country it is supposed to defend. Without it, Nigeria would not exist. Yet it has a complex history, including its role as a tool that helped foreign invaders conquer its own people.

9

THE SOUTH-WEST INVASION

Ever since Portuguese traders and travellers arrived at the city
of Eko in what is now south-western Nigeria, the city has been
the location of pivotal events in the country's history. It was
Nigeria's first post-independence capital city, and it was also the
first Nigerian city that Britain colonised. Its location on the
Atlantic coast and its features, criss-crossed by lakes and
lagoons, led the Portuguese to refer it as Lagos ('lakes').

Lagos's importance to Britain has largely been ascribed to its
being a major slave port on the so-called Slave Coast of West
Africa. But it was also the gateway to inland areas around the
River Niger, used by both missionaries and traders. In the
1850s Lagos was a diverse city. The repatriation to Lagos of
emancipated slaves from Brazil and so-called 'Saros' from Sierra
Leone changed the city's linguistic, political and religious
dynamic. Many of the returnees from Brazil were educated,
Roman Catholic, Portuguese-speaking and had Portuguese
names. The Saros were the anglophone counterparts of the
repatriated Brazilian slaves. Saros were also educated and
Christian, but spoke English and had English names. The

returnee slaves and Christian missionaries were not on good terms with the oba (king) of Lagos, Kosoko, whom they portrayed to the British as a pro-slavery, anti-Christian tyrant. The combined effort of lobbying by the missionaries, British businessmen who wanted to trade with the hinterland, and the returnees placed Kosoko in Britain's crosshairs.

The 'usurper at Lagos'

A succession dispute gave Britain an excellent opportunity to interfere in Lagos's internal politics and remove Kosoko. The oba of Benin to the east of Lagos had the right to select the oba of Lagos. He chose Akitoye in 1841 but, owing to a leadership dispute, Akitoye was deposed and expelled by his nephew Kosoko in 1845. Akitoye went into exile firstly at Abeokuta and later at Badagry (both close to Lagos), and kept trying to return, but Kosoko put a bounty on his head. The missionaries complained to the Foreign Office about Kosoko's hostility towards them and called him the 'usurper at Lagos'. Akitoye realised that his best chance of getting his throne back was by allying himself with the British, who had their own grievances against Kosoko. The British consul for the Bights of Benin and Biafra, John Beecroft, met Akitoye and obtained his assurance that if Britain restored him to the throne, he would outlaw slavery in Lagos and admit missionaries and British businesses. On 20 November 1851, Beecroft and a British naval delegation met Kosoko, but he refused to sign a treaty abolishing slavery on the grounds that as he was a vassal of the oba of Benin, he could not agree to the treaty without the oba of Benin's consent and unless the oba signed first.

The First Battle of Eko

Five days later Beecroft returned with a flotilla of British naval ships commanded by Commander T.G. Forbes. Around 6.15

am HMS *Bloodhound* and four other ships entered the Lagos Lagoon. When they arrived within a mile of Lagos, Kosoko's forces opened fire on them from both sides of the river. The British returned fire with cannons and guns while Kosoko's warriors fired muskets from behind the city walls. About 160 marines used canoes to get ashore but never got further than 300 yards inside Lagos. When the marines landed, Kosoko's forces drove them back with flanking fire as they tried to advance down the narrow streets and alleyways. Every time the British marines tried to advance or turn down a street, they were met by defenders brandishing guns or swords. After two of their party were killed and another 16 wounded, they retreated and set houses ablaze as they left. They fled back to their ships and the attack was aborted. After discovering that four British sailors had been killed and another 29 wounded during the failed mission, Commodore Henry Bruce reprimanded Forbes for his 'extremely ill-advised' decision to confront Kosoko without prior authorisation.

The Boxing Day Rematch at Eko

On Christmas Eve 1851, British naval officers met Akitoye's forces at a pre-agreed rendezvous point in preparation for a second invasion of Lagos. The British navy gave white neckties to Akitoye's men as a distinguishing mark, and one pound of bread each (three days' rations). In the early evening, HMS *Bloodhound* and HMS *Teazer* anchored out of range of Kosoko's guns. On Christmas Day, Kosoko's warriors rained musket fire on the British ships in a futile attempt to prevent the marines from landing. It was largely a wasteful exercise, as the navy was out of range.

Around 6 am on 26 December 1851, the British navy commenced their second invasion of Lagos. As the troops tried to get ashore, they had to run a gauntlet of heavy musket fire from Kosoko's warriors, who had lined up behind sandbanks along a two-mile stretch of coastline. The marines managed to damage and prevent some of Kosoko's cannons from firing, but at a cost. Kosoko's men pounced on them with swords and killed or wounded 80 to 90 marines while they were trying to return to their lifeboats. Two men who were left behind were killed.[1] Meanwhile, Beecroft was on board HMS *Victoria* when its anchor broke loose and the ship floated within range of fire from Kosoko's men. A spent shell hit Beecroft, then bounced onto the ship's deck. To prevent the ship's guns from falling into enemy hands, Captain Lyster led several men to board it and disable its guns.

From 7.15 am to 3 pm the next day the British ships bombarded Lagos with constant cannon and rocket fire, which destroyed Kosoko's ammunition dump and the house of his deputy, Tappa. The detonation of the ammunition store sent shells flying and caused much death and devastation. Vast areas of the city were set ablaze as the fire jumped from house to house. The terrifying sight of the explosion and fire broke the resistance. Late that night Kosoko evacuated the city with his supporters. Britain had deposed Kosoko but in the process lost 15 men killed in action while another 75 were wounded.[2]

At 5 pm on Sunday, 28 December, Beecroft and Captain Jones went ashore to inspect the devastation. They found that Kosoko's men had built excellent military fortifications for a lengthy battle. Beecroft said:

> Had an engineer from Woolwich been on the spot it could not have been better planned: strong stockades, and ditches without, with trenches within, deep with their sleeping mats, fire, water, and provisions; and at every point an enfilading piece of ordnance; they must have used every energy and perseverance for an attack; the beach was fenced within 15 yards, having 5 or 6 feet for canoes at a narrow entrance near Chief Tappa's house.[3]

British marines were tempted to destroy the rest of the city but refrained from doing so as they wanted to preserve some buildings for Akitoye. The next day Beecroft and British marines escorted Akitoye to the ruins of the palace and reinstated him as oba. Akitoye sent a town crier around the city to announce his restoration. On New Year's Day 1852 the reinstalled oba boarded HMS *Penelope* and signed a treaty with Commodore Henry Bruce and Consul Beecroft that forbade slave trading in Lagos by Britons or Lagosians, as well as banning human sacrifice, allowing missionaries to freely proselytise, and granting British businesses favoured nation protection. In 1861 Britain declared Lagos a British colony, and thus began Britain's colonial acquisition of Nigeria. Lagos became corridor that Britain used to project its influence inland, initially to the north and east of the city.

The Anglo-Ijebu War

The Ijebu kingdom was situated in what is now the Yoruba area of south-west Nigeria. The Ijebu king was known as the awujale. His capital, Ijebu-Ode, is now in modern-day Ogun State, just north of Lagos. Ijebu became a British priority because the passage of trade through it was crucial for Lagos to generate revenue. Lagos earned customs dues from goods that were transported from the areas to its east, west and north. This economic dependency placed Ijebu, immediately to the north of Lagos, in the line of sight of British colonial authorities. Ijebu was an obstacle between Lagos and access to the interior. Around this time, too, France began to show an interest in the areas to Ijebu's north.

In May 1891 the acting governor of Lagos, Captain George Denton, visited Ijebu-Ode on a mission to secure for British businesses the right to enter Ijebu and trade freely. However, the Ijebu leaders rejected Denton's demand, declined the gifts

Denton brought for them, and refused to grant him permission to pass through their territory on the way to Abeokuta. Consequently, the Colonial Office demanded an apology from the Ijebu for the way they had treated Denton and insisted they enter into a treaty to grant British businesses access to their land. The acting inspector general of police in Lagos gave the awujale a 30-day deadline, with an implied threat of using force if he refused to comply with the ultimatum. An Ijebu delegation arrived for negotiations in Lagos in January 1892. After they apologised for the way they treated Denton, the new governor of Lagos, Gilbert Thomas Carter, told them that their practice of requiring goods to be sold in their markets at prices set by them was unacceptable. He also warned them that although the British queen did not wish to take over their territory, she would do so if they did not open it for trade with the British. During the meeting Carter presented them with a written agreement in English requiring free trade and British passage through their land. When the Ijebus protested that they could not read or understand English, British officials brought Ijebu residents of Lagos to sign the agreement on their behalf. It is doubtful that an agreement entered into in such circumstances was valid or legally enforceable. However, it generated acrimony only one month after it was signed.

Young Ijebus objected to the agreement and allegedly blocked a Wesleyan minister, Reverend Williams, from passing through Ijebuland. In February 1892 Britain claimed that the Ijebus had breached the agreement and had again blocked trade. In March 1892 the British secretary of state for the colonies, Lord Knutsford, authorised a military invasion of Ijebuland. The invasion force mobilised in May 1892 under the command of Colonel Francis Scott. It consisted of 450 soldiers, including 17 British officers, men from the West India Regiment, the Hausa Constabulary from Lagos, Hausas from the Gold Coast, and a contingent of Ibadan warriors who acted as scouts.

'The Ijebus are near, we have smelt them'

The decisive encounter took place on 19 May 1892. In order to invoke supernatural intervention against the invasion force, the Ijebu placed charms along the road taken by the invasion force and allegedly sacrificed a man, woman and some animals. As the British force marched towards Ijebu-Ode, the Ibadan contingent suddenly stopped, began drumming, and put on their war charms. Captain Bower ordered them to continue advancing, but the Ibadan contingent leader, Toyin, replied, 'The Ijebus are near, we have smelt them.'[4] After marching less than 20 more paces, the force came to a bend in the road where the Ijebus opened fire. The British claimed that the Ijebus deployed between 6,000 and 10,000 warriors. After three hours of fighting, the Ijebus retreated and crossed a river. The Hausa Constabulary was ordered to pursue them, but they hesitated because of rumours that the Ijebus had cursed the river. The West India Regiment was instead ordered to cross, after which the Hausas gained the confidence to follow them. The British forces pursued the Ijebu while firing Maxim guns and rockets, which set the surrounding forest ablaze and killed about a thousand Ijebu warriors.

Late in the afternoon the British troops found a white flag planted beside the path to Ijebu-Ode. Despite the signal of surrender, Scott feared that it might be a trap and remained vigilant, expecting more resistance. Instead, the awujale sent six emissaries to meet the British forces the next morning with a flag of truce. Scott sent two of them back to the awujale with a demand that the capital Ijebu-Ode surrender and kept the remainder as hostages. The British forces continued advancing and at 11.30 am they entered Ijebu-Ode. The town had been evacuated and was deserted except for the awujale and a few elderly followers. The British forces took the awujale into custody and placed him under house arrest. He was allowed out only once a day to take a stroll in the evenings and was guarded while he did so. After some looting by the soldiers, Governor Carter arrived from Lagos to meet the awujale, who claimed that his young men had fought against the British contrary to his wishes and orders.

News of the destructive speed and ease of the British victory reverberated throughout the region. Tales of the ferocity of the British assault discouraged further anti-British resistance in the area that is now Yorubaland in south-west Nigeria. Carter undertook a treaty-making tour of the area in 1893. He was accompanied by Hausa soldiers and a Maxim gun. In 1893, the area's kingdoms and rulers, including the Egbas, the alaafin of Oyo, Ibadan and Abeokuta signed treaties in which they agreed to free trade with Britain and which forbade them to conduct human sacrifices or cede any portion of their territory to a foreign country.

Most of what is now Yorubaland, except for Ilorin, became a British protectorate attached to the Colony of Lagos. In this way Britain added large tracts of territory to the Empire without firing a shot. The conquest also opened the door for missionaries to enter and proselytise in Yorubaland. The British advance, which had started in Lagos over forty years earlier, had conquered Yorubaland. Its next destination was the neighbouring kingdom of Benin to the east.

10

THE INVASION OF BENIN

For almost 125 years Britain's invasion of the ancient kingdom of Benin (see Map 1) has been presented as a British mission to avenge a native outrage committed against peaceful British officials. However, as we shall see, it was actually the execution of an already approved and pre-planned British military operation which culminated in the greatest incident of colonial looting in Nigeria's history.

Although Benin is the Nigerian kingdom with the longest history of interaction with Europeans, by the 1890s it had become a mystery to outsiders. The kingdom's isolation from Europeans increased after Britain captured and exiled a wealthy and powerful Itsekiri chief and middleman in the area named Nana in 1894. The Binis thought they would be next and were apprehensive of contact with Britain. Goods from the Benin kingdom usually reached Britain by an indirect route through Itsekiri middlemen. However, Benin's king, the oba, insisted that trade was conditional on them continuing to pay him 'dash' according to age-old traditions. British officials and trading companies refused to pay the dash and advised the Itsekiri middlemen to do the same. The oba accordingly refused to trade with them. In response British traders of the African Association Limited petitioned officials of the Niger Coast Protectorate to take action against the oba. Britain considered an invasion of Benin city in the dry season of 1895 but postponed it.

By 1897 Britons had visited Benin only twice in the previous five years. Vice-Consul Henry Galway visited Benin in 1892 and a Royal Niger Company official named Mr McTaggart visited in 1894. In August 1895 Consul-General Ralph Moor directed one of his officials, Major William Copland-Crawford (vice-consul of the Benin and Warri district), to establish trading relations with the oba. However, the oba refused to receive Copland-Crawford because he was observing some traditional ceremonies. Moor advised that in the dry season they should try again to establish trading relations with the oba and, if he refused again, his kingdom should be invaded. In 1895 and 1896 several British army officers, including Copland-Crawford and Lt Arthur Maling of the Niger Coast Protectorate Force, tried several times to visit Benin, but the Binis turned them back. These attempted visits by British officers carrying weapons alarmed the oba and his officials, who suspected that Britain planned to give them the same dose of treatment they had already administered to other native chiefs such as Jaja and Nana. Officials of the Niger Coast Protectorate also tried to gather intelligence from locals about Benin city, but very little information was forthcoming.

In November 1896, when Ralph Moor was on holiday, the acting consul-general, James Phillips, reported that the oba had again refused to open his kingdom to trade with Britain, and he requested permission from Moor to depose him. Moor, who had served as a police officer in the Royal Irish Constabulary before going to Nigeria, usually needed little persuasion to use military force, and he approved the request. The military authorities felt that at least 400 soldiers were required for an invasion, but since they could not provide so many troops at that time, Moor postponed the invasion.

Yet Phillips was undaunted. He was determined to visit the oba without an invitation. Without authorisation from the Foreign Office, he sent a letter to the oba saying that he would visit him to discuss opening trade and allowing white men to enter Benin at will. In January 1897 Phillips decided to visit Benin city along with six officers of the Niger Coast Protectorate, namely Major Copland-Crawford, Captain Alan Boisragon (commandant of the Niger Coast Protectorate Force), Lt Maling, Ralph Locke (district commissioner of Warri), Kenneth Campbell (district commissioner at Sapele), Dr Robert Elliot (the medical officer of Sapele and Benin district), Mr Lyon (assistant district commissioner at Sapele), and two European traders, Thomas Gordon of the African Association and Harry Powis of Miller Brothers. They were accompanied by servants, a clerk, interpreters and about 250 carriers, of whom 180 were 'Jakry' (as the British called the Itsekiri ethnic group) and 60 so-called Kruboys from Liberia. Each white man had three porters to carry his camp bed, food, water and other luggage. The expedition was also accompanied by the Niger Coast Protectorate Force's drum and fife band.

When the oba heard of the impending visit from uninvited guests, he sent a messenger to tell them that he was unable to receive them at this time as he was engaged in the sacred annual *ague* traditional festival during which he was not allowed to meet non-Binis and foreigners were not permitted to enter Benin. The *ague* ceremonies involve a month-long period of abstinence, spiritual rededication and cleansing. The oba added that he would be able to see Phillips a month or two later, so long as he was accompanied by only one Itsekiri chief and no other white men. Phillips replied: 'He regretted he could not wait two months, as the king [*oba*] suggested, but he had so much work to do in other parts of the protectorate that he was obliged to come up now, as there were several matters he wished to talk over with the king [oba].'¹

Phillips' stubborn determination to visit Benin after being told not to do so, unnerved the oba's court and split opinion within it. By declining the offer to visit later without a large entourage, Phillips failed the test of good faith that the oba had set for him and missed an opportunity to show the oba that he meant no harm. Instead he triggered memories of recent British visitors who came with weapons. The last British visitor to Benin, McTaggart of the Royal Niger Company, had arrived with armed soldiers, and other British military officers had also attempted uninvited visits accompanied by armed troops. The fact that these visits occurred in the same year as, or in the year following, Nana's exile probably did little to reassure the Binis. While the oba and some others counselled that the expedition should not be blocked if they insisted on coming, two senior Bini officials, the *ologbosere* (a hereditary warrior title similar to general) and *iyasere*, were convinced that Phillips was leading an invasion force and must be resisted. The oba also commented that he had heard of white men travelling around and kidnapping native chiefs, in an obvious reference to the subterfuge Britain used to capture and exile Jaja and Nana.

'We thought nothing of his advice or warning'

Chief Dore, an Itsekiri chief who was on good terms with the Protectorate, warned Phillips that continuing with the journey in defiance of the oba's instructions would result in certain death. However, one of the expedition members later recalled: 'We thought nothing of his advice or warning.'² Phillips sent Chief Dore back to the oba with a message to tell him he was coming anyway. On the night of 3–4 January 1897, another Itsekiri messenger arrived and warned Phillips not to proceed with the expedition and said the Itsekiri were frightened. Phillips dismissed the messenger's concern and told him to prepare accommodation for them at a place he called Gwato (Ughoton). Phillips also recalled that an Itsekiri chief called Dudu Jerri 'was also full of warnings and forebodings, all of which we laughed at at the time. He declared that Gwato was full of Benin soldiers, who wouldn't let us land there, and would fire on us if we attempted to do so.'[3]

When Phillips and the expedition arrived at Ughoton, three messengers (whom Captain Boisragon very unflatteringly described as 'very like monkeys in personal appearance')[4] from the oba met them and said they had been sent to lead them to the oba. The messengers asked Phillips to delay for two days to give the oba time to prepare to meet them. Phillips rejected the request and 'regretted much that he couldn't wait at Gwato [Ughoton] for 2 days as he had been told to do, but he had so much work to do elsewhere that he couldn't afford to lose a day, and so must start early the next morning'.[5] An argument ensued between Phillips and the messengers, and they again warned Phillips that it was not a good time to visit the oba. However, whether he was being superbly brave, stupendously naive, incredibly obtuse, or just full of hubris (or all the foregoing), for the fourth time Phillips ignored the warnings not to visit a king who had explicitly told him that his presence was not welcome at that time. He pressed ahead anyway.

Perhaps the most puzzling (and yet unanswered) question is why Phillips was so insistent on proceeding with the expedition despite all the warnings to postpone or turn back. The reason for the expedition is shrouded in mystery and it is not clear what Phillips was trying to achieve. He did not notify the Foreign Office before embarking on the trip, and did not have prior authorisation for it from his superior, Ralph Moor. What was Phillips up to? Since none of the others on the expedition explained why it was necessary, we may never know the true reason behind it. However, there are two plausible explanations. Protectorate officials were frustrated at the lack of cooperation from Benin and the fact they had little information about it. It is possible that Phillips wanted to use the visit as a reconnaissance and intelligence-gathering exercise for the armed invasion that had already been approved. Another possible reason is that the visit offered an opportunity to accelerate the invasion. Moor's instructions before going on holiday meant that a Bini refusal to allow the expedition to enter Benin would trigger the invasion of Benin and the overthrow of the oba.

After Phillips ignored all the warnings, Copland-Crawford, Boisragon and some natives advised Phillips that, as the uniformed drummers from the Niger Coast Protectorate Force might look like an invasion force, they should be dispensed with. Accordingly, Phillips sent the band back, but by this time they had already been seen. The British officers also decided not to openly display their guns and locked them inside their boxes. On 4 January the expedition continued its journey without the uniformed drummers. Yet they did not seem to consider that, despite their professed friendly intentions, a group of British military officers from the same country that had used force to capture and exile powerful native chiefs nearby, who had on four separate occasions ignored messages from the oba that he could not receive them, and who were accompanied by 250 others, might be perceived as an invading force rather than a friendly party. This was especially the case in the light of prior attempts to visit Benin city which caused the oba and his court to believe that a British invasion was imminent. As the expedition continued its determined march to Benin, something went very wrong.

'No revolvers, gentlemen'

At 3 pm on 4 January 1897, when the expedition was about 25 miles from Benin city, gunshots suddenly rang out from the bush. At first the British officers assumed it was a gun salute to welcome them. They were stunned when they heard some of their carriers screaming in pain after being cut down by the gun-fire. Philips shouted, 'no revolvers, gentlemen,'[6] as Boisragon and Copland-Crawford ran back to try and retrieve their revolvers, but were prevented from so doing when several snipers in the bush started picking off the expedition members one by one. The ambush chased down and killed several porters or took them hostage, and killed all British members of the expedition except Boisragon and Locke, who escaped with wounds. They wandered around in the bush for five days until they came across an Ijaw man who carried them to safety in his canoe.

'It was rather Phillips's fault that the massacre took place'

The ambush and 'Benin Massacre', as the British press reported it, reinforced pre-existing British stereotypes of Benin as a barbarous 'city of blood'. The British accounts presented the ambush as a case of the oba and the Bini people deliberately luring friendly and peaceful British emissaries into a savage, unprovoked bloodbath. There was no mention of the fact that the visit was a precursor of an already approved armed invasion. Evidence of the warnings that several intermediaries gave to Phillips (and his utterly obtuse decision to ignore them) and of the fact he was an uninvited guest were suppressed and did not come to public knowledge until two or three years after the event. A British medical officer who spoke to the survivors later admitted:

> I have had a talk with Locke and Boisragon, and from this conversa-tion I gather it seems that it was rather Phillips's fault that the mas-sacre took place. The members of the expedition all tried to persuade him to give up the idea of going, even Crawford, who was a sort of dare-devil, was against his going up, and several of the friendly chiefs

went down on their knees, begging him not to go, as they felt very certain all would be killed. Yet after all this warning, Phillips persisted in attempting to go to Benin.[7]

When news of the murders reached the Foreign Office, Britain assembled a combined naval and land force composed of a naval squadron under Rear Admiral Harry Rawson and Niger Coast Protectorate Force troops under Lt-Colonel Bruce Hamilton. An advance guard of troops arrived in the Benin countryside in the first week of February 1897. To prepare the way for the invasion force, they cleared roads, built bridges across waterways, delivered equipment, food and supplies, and scouted Benin's military positions. A combined force of naval marines and soldiers, numbering about 700 in total entered Benin City at 2 pm on 18 February 1897. Rawson admitted that the number of troops far exceeded what was needed to complete the mission, but they decided to deliver a decisive knockout blow. They also had native scouts who acted as guides. Since the scouts walked in front of their marching columns, they were usually the first ones to be hit by enemy fire. One of the scouts was shot in the neck before the force reached Benin. As they advanced, they stopped every few minutes to fire 'clearing volleys' (bursts of machine-gun fire into the bush and the road ahead) to eliminate any snipers or assailants who may have been hiding in the undergrowth. Despite several of the British officers, including Rawson, suffering from sunstroke, fever, thirst and insect bites (as well as a smallpox outbreak among the carriers), they captured Benin city with very few casualties. Only three British officers, ten seamen and marines, and four native soldiers were killed or died of sunstroke and thirst. Five British officers, twenty-two seamen and marines, and twenty-three African soldiers fighting for Britain were wounded.

One of the wounded officers in the British contingent was a multilingual African officer named Lt John Daniels. In an era when Africans were mere subalterns and were rarely, if ever, given command or commissions as officers, Daniels was a rarity. He may have been the first native to be admitted as an officer in Britain's colonial army in Nigeria. Daniels had an excellent reputation. A British Army officer described him as 'an exceptional man. Fearless himself, and having natural ability for command, he was able to inspire confidence in his men, who would follow him anywhere.'[8] The fact that he could speak Hausa and Yoruba fluently, as well as other languages, made him an invaluable part of the mission as it facilitated his communication with the mostly Hausa and Yoruba soldiers of the Niger Coast Protectorate Force. Lt-Colonel Hamilton recommended that Daniels should be given a reward for his performance and said that he 'was invaluable whenever the troops were engaged. He behaved with great dash, and is well deserving of reward.'[9]

The oba and Benin city's residents had fled in terror as the British soldiers approached. Although the city was abandoned by the time they arrived, British officers reported seeing horrendous scenes of blood and sacrifice, with mutilated corpses lying around the city. The medical officer Dr Roth wrote in his diary: 'Dead and mutilated bodies seemed to be everywhere—by God! may I never see such sights again!'[10] The stench of the decomposing bodies caused nausea among some of the British officers. Although we have only the accounts of British witnesses to rely on, their vivid descriptions and corroboration of each other make it very likely that they encountered a gruesome scene of death.

The corpses were a mystery. Who were they and why were they killed? The British accounts portrayed them as victims of human sacrifice. If this is the case, why were they sacrificed? Was it in a religious ceremony to ward off the British invasion or were they executed as prisoners of war? Since the records do not contain the Binis' explanation for the presence of the corpses, we do not have answers to these questions. If the British account is accepted, then it means that in the middle of a war and invasion by British marines and soldiers, the Binis spent time sacrificing people rather than prioritising the defence of their land. However, one curious omission from the British accounts may provide a partial answer to the mystery. The usually meticulous British officers did not calculate or estimate the Bini casualties. As the British forces advanced, they had bombarded Benin with long-range artillery fire and rockets. Rawson's biographer described devastation that the rockets inflicted on Benin and how 'war-rockets, soaring sky-high and breaking into a terrifying cascade of flame, were regarded with awe and dismay'.[11] It is possible that at least some of the corpses that British officers saw in Benin city were Bini casualties of the British assault.

On 20 February, two days after the invasion, the British forces started the systematic destruction and looting of Benin city. They burned the house of the oba's mother and about a hundred other houses. Further destruction to the city occurred when a blaze accidentally broke out the next day and jumped from house to house, even burning the surrounding woods and artworks in Benin.

Meanwhile, having fled the city, the oba and many of his supporters remained fugitives. Convinced of his guilt, British forces sent messages urging him to surrender. As Moor's troops pursued the oba, they resorted to their familiar scorched-earth tactic of laying waste to the surrounding countryside as a way of pressuring people to turn him in. They destroyed villages that refused to give information on his whereabouts or that were suspected of harbouring him. Oba Overami eventually tired of running from place to place to evade capture. On 3 August 1897, he surrendered after nearly six months as a fugitive in a procession consisting of drummers, 20 wives, 10 chiefs and 800 followers, one of whom carried a white flag of surrender.

THE INVASION OF BENIN

The Trial of Oba Overami

When Overami met acting resident Captain Roupell, the former was dressed regally, bedecked with coral beads across his arms, chest and legs, and wearing embroidered trousers and a white robe. Overami was perturbed by the presence of a large crowd and he asked whether he could submit in private. Roupell rejected his request and insisted that he submit in front of a crowd of about a thousand people. Overami knelt on the ground in front of the young Roupell and rubbed his forehead on the ground three times. His chiefs followed his example and did the same.

The trial of Oba Overami and his chiefs took place on 1 September 1897. Before the trial started, Moor informed the defendants that the trial was about the murder of Phillips and others, and not about their fighting against British forces, since they had the right to resist invasion of their land. Neither the prosecution nor the defendants were represented by lawyers. Strangely, the trial records did not address the identity of or reason for the large number of corpses that British officers found in Benin.

When witnesses claimed that men working for four Bini chiefs were responsible for murdering one of the Britons, the four chiefs were arrested. One of them, Obayiuwana, committed suicide by slitting his own throat from ear to ear after being arrested. His captors hung up and displayed his body in front of the oba's compound for a day.

It seems that there had been a split of opinion within the oba's court, with some of them wishing to do the British no harm, while others believed that they were an invading force. Several witnesses testified that after Overami heard about Phillips's impending visit, he ordered his chiefs not to harm them, cautioned that no blood should be spilled, and reminded them that no white man had ever been killed in Benin city. However, two of his senior officials, Ologbosere and Iyasere, who were convinced that the British expedition was an invasion force, rebelled against the oba's orders and insisted that the British must be killed. In his defence Overami testified that he had always been a friend of white men, had exchanged presents with them and had previously allowed them to visit Benin. He also added that his orders were that the British should not be killed.

The trial adjourned, and on 3 September 1897, found seven chiefs guilty of murdering members of the Phillips expedition. Moor insisted that, since the Binis had killed seven British chiefs, seven Bini chiefs had to die too. The seven sentenced to death included Ologbosere, who was still at large. However, since two of the condemned chiefs had already died in captivity, and a third could not be executed since he was still a boy, Moor said he would select more chiefs to make up the full number. He also proposed granting amnesty to anyone who apprehended and brought in Ologbosere, who was Overami's son-in-law. Moor executed the condemned chiefs the next day, deposed Overami, but promised to allocate a few minor villages to him if he could demonstrate his ability to govern.

Moor proposed to send Overami and a few of his chiefs to Calabar, Lagos and the Yoruba areas to see how other lands were governed. He asked Overami and the chiefs to meet him on 9 September to give him their response and their proposals for catching Ologbosere. However, Overami feared that the 'tour' was merely a British ruse to permanently exile him, as they had done to Jaja and Nana. He refused to meet Moor on the appointed day. In response, Moor sent Major Charles Carter and Lt Gabbett with 50 soldiers to bring Overami to him. When Overami became aware of the force of armed men coming for him, he fled into the bush. Moor summoned the other Bini chiefs and told them that if they did not find Overami by 4 pm that day, he would shoot every one of them and burn every remaining house in Benin. The threat scared the chiefs enough for one of them, Ojumo, to divulge where Overami was hiding. When Captain Roupell and his soldiers entered the cottage where Overami was hiding, he, ran out of the back door, straight into the arms of other members of the search party. The soldiers marched Overami to Moor, who instantly exiled him from Benin for the rest of his life. Overami's 80 wives were separated from him and returned to their families. After failing to regain his liberty by trying to bribe Moor with 200 puncheons of palm oil (worth about £1,500), and offering to disclose where his 500 ivory tusks were buried, Overami became dejected and refused to eat. He was put on suicide watch. In order to avoid his people seeing him being deported, British troops decided to take him into exile in the early hours of the morning. When troops woke him in the dark at 4 am on 15 September, the terrified Overami began screaming for help. The soldiers gagged him, restrained him with chains and bound him in a hammock before leaving for a ship in the company of 60 soldiers and a Maxim gun to thwart any rescue attempt. Overami's sense of terror must have been great since he was unaccustomed to leaving his compound, let alone his city. The ship took him to exile in Calabar.

Ologbosere on the Run

However, Ologbosere was still at large and mounted a guerrilla warfare campaign in the countryside for almost two years. Rather than fight pitched battles against the British troops searching for him, he and his supporters used ambushes to harass them and evade capture. They dug sniper trenchers and set ambushes around the village of Okemue. On 23 April 1897, Ologbosere's forces ambushed a Royal Niger Constabulary patrol, killed nine of its members and wounded another 70.[12] These casualties were more than three times greater than the total incurred during the initial invasion of Benin. The Constabulary patrol withdrew to their base after exhausting their ammunition, and their commander, Lt Fitzgerald, whose cousin Lt Gabbett was serving in the the Niger Coast Protectorate Force, later died from his wounds. A British army commander admitted: 'It is exceedingly annoying to a commander when, instead of two or three really decisive engagements, the enemy will not fight, but resorts to the tactics of sniping and cutting off stragglers.'[13] Ologbosere's rural insurgency and the casualties he inflicted on the Constabulary were sufficiently disruptive for the Royal Niger Company to attempt to negotiate with him. As a result, Ralph Moor submitted a vehement complaint to the Foreign Office about the company's interference.

As troops under Major Carter searched for Ologbosere, they conducted a campaign of destruction in the countryside around Benin city, burning villages they deemed uncooperative, destroying food stocks and seizing livestock. This scorched-earth campaign achieved its aim of wearing down the resistance, and some of Ologbosere's hungry and weary supporters deserted, surrendered to the British troops and betrayed him by giving away his position. British forces arrested him on 27 May 1899. On 27 June a trial ratified the death sentence passed on him in absentia two years earlier. He and his supporters were hanged the next day. Ologbosere's descendants continued his martial tradition. His great-grandson Brigadier Samuel Ogbemudia enrolled as one of the early members of Nigeria's post-independence army and became governor of Edo State (whose borders are within the historic Benin kingdom and whose residents are mostly Bini).[14]

Colonial Looting

The most noteworthy incident after the Benin invasion that still generates controversy forms one of the most brazen cases of colonial looting that Britain committed in Africa. After capturing Benin city, the British officers noticed that it was full of a spectacular array of carved bronze, ivory and wood artworks, insignia and sculptures, some of which were hundreds of years old. Rawson, Moor and the officers took some of them as trophies for themselves.

'Her Majesty the Queen was graciously pleased to accept some trophies'

Moor then supervised the looting of the artefacts, which he ordered to be collected at one location. He selected some as gifts for Queen Victoria and Prince of the Wales, and for officials at the Foreign Office. Moor later recalled: 'I may mention that Her Majesty the Queen was graciously pleased to accept some trophies of the operations sent through Lord Salisbury—and I believe that His Royal Highness the Prince of Wales and the First Lord of the Admiralty also accepted trophies.'[15] The British officers did not think they were doing anything wrong. As the victors in a war, they deemed it their right to collect war booty, and considered it as harmless as picking up a dropped penny from the street. While it is not known whether the looting was premeditated, several British officials had prior knowledge of the presence of large quantities of ivory in Benin. One month before the invasion, Lt-Colonel Galway wrote to the Foreign Office to advise them that 'the ivory at Benin city should fully pay the cost of the expedition'.[16] Phillips had also sent an identical message to the Foreign Office prior to the ill-fated visit.

'A race so entirely barbarous as were the Bini'

Rawson was impressed by the artefacts and suggested sending them to the British Museum, as they might have historical value.

His biographer referred to his finding 'castings of wonderful delicacy of detail, and some magnificently carved tusks'.[17] Six crates containing several hundred of these artefacts were dispatched to the British Museum. When they arrived, museum officials were stunned by their decorative artistry and the technical expertise required to make them. They could not believe that the Binis, whom they viewed as primitive savages, were capable of creating art with such attention to detail, using the same techniques as Europe's best sculptors. They instead speculated that an alien race from North Africa, China or the Mediterranean had taught the Binis how to make the artefacts. Charles Read of the British Museum was amazed that 'at the first sight of these remarkable works of art we were at once astounded at such an unexpected find, and puzzled to account for so highly developed an art among a race so entirely barbarous as were the Bini'.[18] The British experts did not know that Portuguese traders who had seen the Benin artworks hundreds of years earlier had already corroborated their authenticity.

Museum personnel were also intrigued to discover that each artefact was unique, and even when different artefacts looked similar or addressed the same theme, there were small design variations to distinguish one from another. The artefacts were not merely ornamental; they served religious purposes and also acted as a historical record of key events and personalities in Benin's history. Their looting constituted a substantial loss of Benin's cultural, intellectual and historical legacy. Rawson declared that he had found a thousand artefacts, but this excluded an unknown number that officers claimed as personal trophies and another unknown quantity that Moor admitted he had sold and whose proceeds he credited to Protectorate funds. German anthropologists also bought several hundred artefacts.

Within a year the artefacts had been scattered across the globe and ended up in British, German and American museums. The

British Museum alone currently holds about 700 or 800 of them, while the Ethological Museum in Berlin and the Metropolitan Museum of Art in New York hold approximately 580 and 160 items respectively. Probably at least 2,000 artefacts were looted from Benin, but the exact number is not known, nor is it known how many ended up in private collections.

The Benin treasures have generated a contemporary controversy, as in recent years both Binis and many Europeans have called for them to be returned. Almost 120 years after they were looted, the first case of repatriation of the Benin treasures took place in 2014. Mark Walker, a retired Welsh medical doctor, inherited two Bini sculptures from his grandfather Captain Herbert Walker, who was a member of the British force that invaded Benin. The younger Walker's conscience would not allow him to keep them, and in 2014 he travelled to Benin to return them to the reigning oba, who was the great-grandson of Overami. Oba Overami had lived out the remaining 16 years of his life in exile at Calabar until his death in January 1914, the month that Nigeria was amalgamated into one country. After his death the Benin monarchy was restored by his son, who took the title of Eweka II, naming himself after the original founder of the Benin kingdom. In November 2019 Cambridge University announced its decision to return a bronze cockerel sculpture to Benin. Whether these repatriations will be followed by many others remains to be seen.

11

FOUNDERS OF NIGERIA

How did Nigeria come into existence? By the late 1800s Britain had sustained almost fifty years of administrative presence in the River Niger area. Yet it had not created a country or a consolidated colony. Instead, there were three different territories under British jurisdiction in the same area, each of which was administered by a different authority and independent from the others. The Royal Niger Company's territories were run by a trading company that was answerable to a board of directors in London. The Colony of Lagos had been controlled by the Colonial Office since 1861 and was ruled by governors residing in Sierra Leone (until 1874) or the Gold Coast (1874–86) until Lagos was granted its own governor. The Niger Coast Protectorate was administered through consuls appointed by the Foreign Office and had its headquarters in Calabar. The Niger Coast Protectorate had been known as the Oil Rivers Protectorate from June 1885 until it was renamed on 13 May 1893. Each of the three territorial units had ill-defined borders and different rules of administration, and did not cooperate with one another. This haphazard arrangement generated a debate about what to do with these three territories. A London newspaper editorial in May 1897 complained that this 'trebling of administration is illogical and absurd'.[1] Additionally, the British government had to decide what to do about the Royal Niger Company. The mysterious treaties that the company had entered into were of dubious legal enforceability, and France had challenged some of them. The company's shady dealings, dubious treaties and abuse of locals caused uncomfortable questions to be raised in Parliament. Apart from the internal problems of administration, Britain's European rivals like France and Germany were making competing claims to the territories and were keen to take at least some of them away from Britain. These internal problems and external threats made the prevailing system untenable. Something had to change.

The Niger Committee

Analyses of Nigeria's formation usually start at 1914, yet the foundational principles of Nigeria's existence were actually laid down 16 years earlier. In June 1898 the British prime minister, Lord Salisbury, formed a Niger Committee to advise him on the future administration of the three territories. It is unfortunate that this committee is overlooked and little is known about it. Yet despite its obscurity, its eye-catching findings are extremely important, as they paved the way to Nigeria's creation and laid down the contours for its future existence. The committee had six members. They included the governor of Lagos, Sir Henry McCallum; the commissioner for the Niger Coast Protectorate, Sir Ralph Moor; and three senior officials from the Colonial and Foreign Offices: Sir Clement Hill, head of the African Department of the Foreign Office; Reginald Antrobus, permanent undersecretary for the colonies; and Lord Selborne, parliamentary undersecretary for the colonies, who was the committee's chairman. The sixth member was George Goldie.

Although Goldie's company was about to have its charter revoked, his knowledge of the area made his membership of the committee essential.

On 4 August 1898 the committee submitted its recommendations, most of which had Goldie's fingerprints all over them. It recommended reorganising the three territories into two: a southern maritime province and a northern Sudan province. Yoruba would be the lingua franca of the maritime province, which would include Yorubaland and the 'pagan' regions of the Niger Delta. The committee suggested that if the maritime province was further subdivided, there should be western and eastern provinces with their capitals at Lagos and Asaba respectively. These subdivisions corresponded to the Western and Eastern Regions of southern Nigeria which emerged at Nigeria's independence in 1960. The Sudan province's capital would be at Lokoja, and it would consist of the emirates of the Sokoto Caliphate, the Kanem-Borno Empire, and the 'pagan' lands to their immediate south. The Sudan province's lingua franca would be Hausa, and it would be governed by Muslims.

One striking aspect of these recommendations was how little the committee cared about dividing the country into territorial units consistent with ethno-linguistic zones. The committee also declined (for unspecified reasons) to subdivide the Sudan province. Owing to the failure to maintain the contiguity of ethno-cultural zones, the northern Sudan province ended up being more than two times larger than the southern province. Although the Niger Committee could not be expected to see into the future, this territorial imbalance contributed to the political crisis and structural flaws that brought Nigeria's first republic crashing down in 1966. Creating a country where one region was geographically larger, with more people, than all the other regions placed a huge albatross around Nigeria's neck and immobilised its politics until Nigeria finally found a way in 1967 to break up the uneven territorial system that Britain had created.

On the question of how to deal with the powerful emirates of the Sokoto Caliphate, the committee deferred completely to Goldie, as he had more knowledge of the Caliphate than any other committee member. Goldie's recommendations essentially provided a template for British conquest of the northern Sudan province. Goldie advised that the sarkin Musulmi at Sokoto would not accept the presence of a British representative in his territory and that posting such a representative there prior to military conquest would probably result in his death. He therefore advised postponing sending a British representative to Sokoto 'until the Fulah power is crushed'.[2] Goldie also advised against trying to conquer the Caliphate in one sudden surprise attack, and instead recommended that 'it should be done gradually, each Emir being taken in turn'.[3] That is exactly what Britain did.

The committee also made two other recommendations which have reverberated throughout Nigeria's history. Firstly, it recommended having one military force for all of the provinces. Secondly, it recommended that the three former territories should be amalgamated under one government at a future date. Goldie felt that, owing to the West African climate, only a young man could work as the head of the new combined government, and, even then, a young man would have to be away for at least a third of the year for the sake of his health. However, they deferred the amalgamation of the territories because of the absence of telegraphs and roads, which made efficient communication between them difficult.

Who would lead this new combined administration? Goldie's long involvement with, and knowledge of, the River Niger area made him an excellent candidate. He became embittered when, although the British government considered appointing him as the governor general of the northern Sudan province or of all British West African territories, he was eventually overlooked.

He took this as a slight and felt that the prime minister, Lord Salisbury, had forgotten his and his company's service to Britain. The man Britain instead chose to administer the northern Sudan province was well known to Goldie; in fact he had once worked for him: Frederick Lugard. Goldie and Lugard were not only friends, but were also very similar in temperament. Their love lives also intersected when the same woman fell in love with both of them. The writer Flora Shaw was a close friend of three men most associated with British imperialism in Africa: Cecil Rhodes, Goldie and Lugard. Her relationship with the latter two ran parallel to Nigeria's history. Lugard's biographer describes Shaw as 'Goldie's unqualified admirer'.[4] Like Goldie and Lugard, Shaw's father was a British army officer, and her mother Marie de Fontaine was a French noblewoman and daughter of the last French governor of Mauritius. Shaw fell intensely in love with Goldie, and when Goldie's wife died in 1898, Shaw expected that Goldie would propose to her. Goldie was not a man known for committed and steady relationships with women. When the proposal did not materialise, Shaw herself proposed to Goldie. She was devastated, and suffered a nervous breakdown, when he rejected her. Lugard wrote to his brother's wife Nell to tell her that Shaw 'had a blow which has left her broken down mentally and physically ... she has barely escaped brain fever'.[5]

A love affair in Asia set in motion a chain of events that led Lugard to Nigeria. In 1886, while serving at Lucknow in northern India, Lugard met and fell madly in love with a prominent married woman. Before meeting her, he had been almost indifferent to women. We do not know the name of the woman who, in the words of Lugard's biographer, was famous for her 'many conquests'.[6] We do know, however, that the two had an intense love affair and that they bonded through their shared love of horse racing. Lugard was captivated by the beautiful, intelligent woman who was a published writer and who shared his love of adventure. While on duty in Burma, Lugard heard that his lover had been badly wounded in an accident. He was so concerned for her and anxious to see her that he threatened to resign from the army if his superiors did not grant him leave. By the time he returned to India, she had departed for England. Lugard immediately set sail for England. As soon as he arrived after the long sea voyage, he went straight to her house. By this time she had recovered from her injuries and in fact was so reinvigorated that Lugard stumbled upon her in the arms of another lover. Lugard found that she had also 'established herself in a pleasure seeking circle'[7] back in London. The distraught Lugard was so heartbroken that his mental health suffered and he did not go home for two months. In an attempt to escape from his misery, he volunteered for the London Fire Brigade, and would sneak out at night to fight raging fires without telling his family (who were concerned that his mental health was so badly damaged that he no longer cared about his safety).

With his sanity in the balance and in order to escape his grief, he decided to go to Africa and start a new life. Like Goldie before him, Lugard immersed himself in hard work to try to forget his unhappy memories. Yet, despite creating physical distance from his former lover, he could not escape 'the dark moods which sometimes enveloped him'.[8] Lugard saw in Flora Shaw, not just a woman who was his intellectual equal, but someone like him whose heart had been broken in love. After a lengthy correspondence with Shaw, which drew the two heartbroken souls closer together, Lugard overcame the awkwardness of sharing his life with a woman who used to be in love with his closest friend, and he married her in 1902, four years after she had been rejected by Goldie. At the time they married, Shaw was almost 50 years old and Lugard was six years younger. Lugard's former lover died just before his wedding to Shaw, but before her death she found time to write some poisonous letters to Lugard in an attempt to wreck the impending wedding.

FOUNDERS OF NIGERIA

Nigerian Origins

One of the problems the Niger Committee discussed was what to call the new maritime and Sudan provinces. The origin of the name 'Nigeria' remains opaque. The word has a long and ancient etymology. While it is certainly a derivative of the River Niger that bisects the country, its origin as a country name is more obscure. Nigerian schoolchildren are routinely taught, and it is widely presumed, that Lugard's wife, Flora Shaw, invented the name. But this is strictly speaking not accurate. The future Lady Lugard suggested the name Nigeria in a newspaper article published anonymously in *The Times* on 8 January 1897. Yet, even before she wrote this article, the terms 'Nigeria' and 'Nigerians' had been used informally for decades to refer to the territories and people in the River Niger area. By the time Shaw wrote her article, 'Nigeria' had already crept into casual, albeit imprecise and irregular, use. However, credit cannot completely be withdrawn from Shaw. While she is definitely not the inventor of the name, she may take credit for being the first to suggest using it as an official territorial name for part of the lands that would eventually become Nigeria.

Shaw did not use the term to refer to the entirety of the lands that are now Nigeria. Rather, she suggested using the name to describe only the territories administered by the Royal Niger Company (which approximate in extent to modern-day Northern Nigeria), to differentiate them from the other British territories of Lagos and the Niger Coast Protectorate. Shaw's reasoning was that

> the title 'Royal Niger Company's Territories' is not only inconvenient to use but to some extent is also misleading, it may be permissible to coin a shorter title for the agglomeration of pagan and Mohammedan states which have been brought by the exertions of the Royal Niger Company within the confines of the British Protectorates, and thus

need for the first time in their history to be described as an entity by some general name.[9]

In other words, Shaw recommended that Nigeria should be used as a less cumbersome name to describe lands then administered by the Royal Niger Company and to distinguish them from two other neighbouring British-controlled territories. 'Nigeria' was a shorthand that rolled off the tongue far more easily than 'the territories of the Royal Niger Company Chartered and Limited'. She suggested by way of conclusion:

> The name 'Nigeria' applying to no other part of Africa, may, without offence to any neighbours, be accepted as co-extensive with the territories over which the Royal Niger Company has extended British influence, and may serve to differentiate them equally from the British colonies of Lagos and the Niger Protectorate on the coast and from the French territories of the Upper Niger.[10]

Thus, Shaw originally conceived the name as a geographical term for what are now the north-west, north-central and northeast zones of Nigeria. So, if 'Nigeria' was originally intended only to apply to the territories controlled by the Royal Niger Company, how did it enter official usage? Five months after Shaw's article, the *Saturday Review of Politics, Literature, Science and Art* published an article under the title 'The Future of Nigeria' in which it referred to 'that vast area of the African continent which, for want of a better name, we must be content to call Nigeria'.[11] Two months later, Goldie delivered a lecture at the London Chamber of Commerce also entitled 'The Future of Nigeria', in which he repeatedly used the word 'Nigeria' to describe the territories under British jurisdiction.[12] This seems to be the first written reference that, in a geographically precise way, applied the word to all three British territories in the River Niger area.

Goldie spoke of Nigeria as consisting of two sections, southern and northern, with the southern section 'for the most part occupied only by pagans, occupying as yet only a low rank of civilisation' and who were 'divided into hundreds of tribes'.[13] He described the northern section as the 'larger, more important, and more interesting part of Nigeria', which consisted 'of the inland two thirds of Nigeria lying between the Great Sahara on the north and the two great branches of the rivers Niger and Binue[14] [sic] on the south'.[15] He referred to this northern section as 'Hausaland'. However, Goldie seemed to change his mind about exactly which geographical areas he considered to be Nigeria. In July 1897, he sent a memorandum to the Colonial Office in which he referred to 'the administration of Nigeria' and to 'Nigeria, the Niger Coast Protectorate and the Colony of Lagos'.[16] By differentiating Nigeria from the Niger Coast Protectorate and Lagos, this memorandum seemed to suggest that, like Flora Shaw, Goldie regarded the term 'Nigeria' as applying only to what is now Northern Nigeria. Despite the geographically inconsistent nature of its use, from mid-1897 onwards 'Nigeria' seems to have caught on and stuck.

Yet despite its adoption by the media and the public, the term did not immediately move from colloquial to official use. British officialdom did not adopt 'Nigeria' until two years after Shaw's famous article. The Niger Committee also discussed names for the new maritime and Sudan provinces. Goldie rejected the suggestion of calling them 'Goldesia' after himself (following the example of Cecil Rhodes and Rhodesia) and instead recommended 'Niger Soudan' and 'Niger Coast' for the northern and southern provinces respectively. Reginald Antrobus of the Colonial Office did not like 'Soudan', as France wanted to use that name for its territory to the north-east of British territories. He instead suggested 'Lower Nigeria' and 'Upper Nigeria' or 'Southern Nigeria' and 'Northern Nigeria'.

WHAT BRITAIN DID TO NIGERIA

'It must be Nigeria'

In official minutes and correspondence in 1898 and 1899, officials at the Colonial Office considered many other names including Nigritia and British Soudan. When the bewildering alphabet soup of suggested names reached the British secretary of state for the colonies, Joseph Chamberlain, he wrote a note in the file: 'Northern and Southern are really more descriptive—but Upper and Lower are more euphonious to my ear. But I do not care of those which it is. It must be Nigeria—and not Soudan.'[17] He preferred Nigeria, not because it had a deep historical or symbolic meaning, but simply because it sounded better to him. Although he did not realise it at the time, Chamberlain's hand-written note gave birth to the name of a new nation. So to whom should credit be given for giving Nigeria its name? The originator of the name 'Nigeria' will probably never be known. But by being the first person to suggest it as an official name for part of the territory that later became Nigeria, Flora Shaw provided the stepladder which others would climb to apply the name in a more geographically precise way. Colonial officials sealed the deal, by following, firstly, Antrobus's recommendation and, secondly, Chamberlain's almost casual 'It must be Nigeria' annotation, which became official policy and which gave the country the name by which it has been known for over 120 years.

In late 1899, the British government revoked the Royal Niger Company's charter and purchased several of its assets, including ships, buildings, machinery, and its Constabulary, for £865,000. The company was also granted a 99-year licence to receive half of the proceeds from the sale of all minerals from its former territories.[18]

At 7.20 am on 1 January 1900 in Lokoja, Northern Nigeria, the Royal Niger Company's flag was removed and the Union Jack was hoisted to replace it. Britain declared two new protectorates in the River Niger area: the Protectorates of Northern Nigeria and Southern Nigeria. There was a difference between colonies and protectorates: the African indigenes living in colonies were British subjects, while those in the protectorates were protected persons with no right of entry to Britain.

After the government revoked its charter, the Royal Niger Company was reorganised and some of its old directors stayed on in the new company. Since the company knew the area well, the British government needed the expertise of its employees. Some of them left the RNC to join the colonial government. Examples of this continuity of personnel include the company's agent-general, William Wallace, who left to place his considerable local knowledge at Lugard's disposal in a new appointment as Lugard's deputy high commissioner in Northern Nigeria. The Royal Niger Constabulary's commander, Major Alder Burdon, left to take up a new political post in Northern Nigeria. Burdon was a Cambridge University alumnus and an army instructor in Arabic and was also fluent in Hausa. His linguistic skills were key commodities for the new colonial government. The Royal Niger Constabulary was absorbed into the West African Frontier Force.

To Goldie, the British government's revocation of his company's royal charter was a massive personal blow from which he never recovered. He resigned from the company after the charter was revoked, and it continued as a private company without him. On 1 January 1900 it dropped the 'Royal' from its name and renamed itself the Niger Company Limited. Goldie said: 'Probably my name will soon be forgotten in connection with Nigeria, and to this I am indifferent.'[19] The loss of the charter was one of a series of personal misfortunes that Goldie suffered. His wife Matilda ('Maude') died in March 1898 of heart failure. In August that year he travelled to South America to try to forget Africa. After returning to England, his health deteriorated; after World

War I he suffered from emphysema. Illness caused him so much discomfort that he was unable to lie down and slept in a sitting position. As his condition worsened, he was forced to spend winters in Italy to avoid the cold. When he came back to England in 1925, he became so ill that he had to be carried from the boat at Dover. He died on 20 August 1925 in a hotel room near Piccadilly in London at the age of 79.

'Founder of Nigeria'

Three important traces of Goldie remained in Africa after his death. Firstly, he had fathered at least three children with a woman from the Niger Delta, and there were possibly others. The grandchildren and great-grandchildren descended from his unions with local women live in Nigeria and other countries. Secondly, there was the company he founded. What became of it in his absence? It is to Goldie's credit that the company eventually merged into a massive multinational conglomerate business that today has over 150,000 employees, and generates over $50 billion in revenue every year. That company makes hundreds of brands as well known and varied as Vaseline, Ben & Jerry's ice cream, PG Tips and Lipton tea, Dove soap, Marmite and Domestos bleach. Its name is Unilever. Thirdly, he paved the way for the eventual creation of Nigeria. Before his death he said: 'The foundations of Nigeria have been fully laid, and it may be left to natural causes to raise that great structure of Nigerian prosperity which I shall not see, but in which, under reasonable conditions, I have the most absolute faith.'[20] He is buried in Brompton cemetery in London, where his wife is also buried. His gravestone reads: 'Sir George Taubman Goldie: Founder of Nigeria'.

12

THE NORTHERN INVASION

Britain's declaration of a protectorate in Northern Nigeria in 1900 was essentially a legal fiction. What Britain had was a mere paper protectorate over lands most of which British eyes had never even seen, and which were inhabited by people most of whom had never seen a white person in their lives, and knew nothing about Britain's claims to rule over them. Having declared a protectorate, Britain now had the task of demonstrating to its European neighbours and the protectorate's residents alike that it also exercised de facto control of it. The man that Britain chose for this task was a child of the British Empire, born in Madras, India, to British missionary parents. His name was Sir Frederick Dealtry Lugard. More than any other Briton, his name is synonymous with Nigeria, and he is considered, rightly or wrongly, to be Nigeria's 'founding father'.

Lugard's father was a chaplain in the East India Company and his mother, Mary Howard, was her husband's third wife. She died when Lugard was only seven. Lugard enrolled in the British army and graduated from Sandhurst in sixth place out of a thousand candidates. While serving in the British army, he was posted to India where experiences would change his life and send him into a tailspin that would eventually land him in Nigeria. After an emotionally tempestuous affair with a married woman (which was discussed earlier in chapter 11), he travelled to Africa to escape from unhappy memories. He worked for the British East Africa Company from 1889 to 1892 and helped capture Uganda for the British Crown, albeit not without controversy. He defended himself against accusations that he had conducted a massacre of natives and used excessive force. He came to Nigeria for the first time in 1894 to negotiate and execute treaties with indigenous chiefs in the Borgu area on behalf of the Royal Niger Company. On his way back from the expedition, Lugard and his entourage were attacked, and he was nearly killed after being hit on the head by a poisoned arrow. He survived after native doctors gave him herbal potions which acted as an antidote to the poison. He was appointed commandant of the newly formed West African Frontier Force in 1897 and then high commissioner for Northern Nigeria in 1900, when he was only 42. As high commissioner, it was his job to show the natives that they had a new master.

Britain's desire to conquer Northern Nigeria seems puzzling given that it had no overriding commercial interest in the region, and that the region's rulers clearly did not invite or desire British presence. Unlike the Niger Delta area of Southern Nigeria, it did not have the economic resources that Britain needed. The conquest of Northern Nigeria seems to have been either a land grab, just because Britain could, or a pre-emptive British move to block their European rivals from seizing territory to the north of its protectorates. Both France and Germany showed interest in the area and would almost certainly have seized Northern Nigeria if Britain had not.

British accounts[1] repeatedly justified their invasion on the grounds that the Sokoto Caliphate's initial reformist zeal had subsided and had been replaced by corrupt, oppressive rule, an addiction to luxury, and incessant slave raiding. Lugard claimed that the rule of the emirs 'grew sensual, avaricious, and cruel'.[2] British accounts also claimed that the Hausa were on the verge of rebelling and overthrowing the Fulani on the eve of Britain's arrival.

It is difficult to obtain an objective account of the British invasion of Northern Nigeria because most of the evidence and written accounts of it originated from one man, Lugard. Although he was certainly qualified to comment by way of being a direct participant, he was not an independent witness. He also had to convince a sceptical Colonial Office, which was against the use of force, that the violence he deployed was justified.

'I will read no more letters from these white men'

The correspondence between Lugard and the sarkin Musulmi, Abdurrahman, soon after the former's arrival is worth revisiting given the controversy and war that followed. Abdurrahman, a great-grandson of Usman dan Fodio, had been in power for nine years by the time Britain declared Northern Nigeria a protectorate in 1900. Lugard sent a Hausa translation of the protectorate declaration to the sarkin. He did not reply, but the messenger who delivered it reported that after reading the declaration, he turned to his court and, speaking in Fulfulde (which he mistakenly believed the messenger did not understand), told them: 'No letters ever brought fear like this one. I will read no more letters from these white men.'[3] The sarkin declined to reply and sent the messenger back empty-handed. This refusal to reply angered Lugard, who interpreted it as 'an insult to me and to my King'.[4] Much like Harry Johnston and Jaja of Opobo 14 years previously, the relationship between Lugard and the sarkin got off to a bad start and never recovered.

In early 1901 Lugard deposed the emirs of Bida and Kontagora without bothering to inform the sarkin in advance. The emir of

Bida had returned to power after Goldie deposed him in 1897. He reclaimed his throne after the Royal Niger Constabulary withdrew its troops. British-led troops overthrew him for the second time in four years, and Lugard reinstated Goldie's nominee, Muhammadu. The manner in which Lugard picked off the emirs one by one seemed to follow the script which Goldie had recommended to the Niger Committee five years earlier. Goldie had advised against trying to conquer the Caliphate in one war, and instead recommended a sequential conquest by isolating and overthrowing one emir after the other. Goldie's verbatim recommendation was: 'No attempt should be made to do this by a general *coup de main*. It should be done gradually, each Emir being taken in turn.'

Lugard wrote to the sarkin again on 18 March 1901 to inform him of what he had done, and invited him to nominate a successor to Emir Ibrahim of Kontagora, whom Lugard had expelled. The sarkin had three options. He could nominate a successor as Lugard asked him to, but it would be a tacit acknowledgement of the British right to depose his emirs. He could instead reply and object to what Lugard had done, but this would open hostilities with Lugard and perhaps provoke a British invasion. For the second time the sarkin declined to reply. Silence was the least unpleasant of the difficult choices before him. By now the sarkin and the emirs must have been aware of what the British were capable of. They not only knew that Britain had deposed two emirs, but also of their exploits in India and perhaps what they were doing in Southern Nigeria.

'Trouble on those who make trouble'

Later in 1901 British troops also deposed the emir of Yola. In March 1902 Lugard wrote to the sarkin for a third time to inform him that he had arrested the fugitive emir of Kontagora and had sent troops to Bauchi and Zaria. Lugard ended the letter with an ominous warning: 'Peace be with those who seek peace and trouble on those who make trouble.'[5]

In May 1902 Lugard finally received a reply from the sarkin. In view of the seismic consequences it triggered, the sarkin's letter may be the most crucial letter ever written by a Northern Nigerian ruler. Captain Abadie translated it from Arabic into English for Lugard, who then transcribed it in a report to the British government:

(Received about May, 1902) Seal indecipherable:

From us to you. I do not consent that any one from you should ever dwell with us. I will never agree with you. I will have nothing ever to do with you. Between us and you there are no dealings except as between Mussulmans and Unbelievers ('Kafiri')—War, as God Almighty has enjoined on us. There is no power or strength save in God on high. This with salutations.[6]

The letter outraged Lugard, and he interpreted it as a declaration of war and a denunciation of the treaties between Sokoto and the Royal Niger Company. The accuracy of Lugard's translation and the authenticity of this mysterious letter have been accepted in virtually every account of Northern Nigeria written by Britons and Nigerians alike during the last 117 years. The letter is of tremendous historical significance because it acted as a trigger for war. Yet at least two factors suggest that it may have been mistranslated (accidentally or deliberately) from Arabic or, at the very least, misunderstood.

For some odd reason, despite considering the letter to be of vital importance, Lugard kept its contents to himself for eight months before he bothered to bring it to the attention of the British government. The letter's aura of mystery is amplified by the fact that its original version is not available. In the archives at Kaduna, British colonial officer David Muffett later found an Arabic letter which he believed was an authentic copy of the letter written by the sarkin. The letter he found was in the same file as another letter that the sarkin wrote to Lugard. Muffett's translation of the letter is very different and far less bellicose than the one that Lugard provided:

> In the name of God, the compassionate and merciful, and the Peace of Allah be upon our Prophet, the respected one. Our entire salutations and cordial greetings, and thereafter for your information, indeed we stood upon your letter and we understood your words, but for our part, our Lord is Allah, our creator, our ruler, and in truth we are bound by what our Prophet Muhammad (peace be upon him) brought to us. As our God says in the Koran whatever the prophet brings to you, and receive, even until the end. Therefore we will not change it for anything until all is finished. Do not send anything after this.[7]

If Muffett's alternative translation of the letter is accurate, then it would seem that the British translator, Captain Abadie, mistranslated the letter from Arabic to make it sound more aggressive than it actually was, to compel Lugard to adopt a military response. Even if Muffett was wrong and Abadie's translation was accurate, there is another possible explanation for the origin of this enigmatic letter.

The sarkin supposedly wrote the letter spontaneously. Yet its tone and content are strange coming from a man who had maintained an almost monk-like silence for the previous two years. Even if Abadie's translation is accepted as accurate, unpacking the letter's mystery requires dissecting its content line by line. The first unusual thing is that it did not include its recipient's name or title. The sarkin's subsequent letter to Lugard addressed him by name and title (as we shall see). The letter's second sentence is also strange. In it the sarkin refused to 'consent that any one from you should ever dwell with us'. Why did he say such a thing? When read purposively, the letter seems to be a response to a British demand or request to place someone in the sarkin's domain. Lugard made no such request in his earlier correspondence. In fact the sarkin's letter made no reference to any of the events or matters that Lugard had addressed in his three previous letters. On closer inspection it seems that the letter was not addressed to Lugard but somehow it came into his possession. If Lugard was not the letter's intended recipient, to whom was the sarkin writing? Who had asked to place a Briton in Sokoto?

In the summer of 1901, while Lugard was away on leave, the deputy high commissioner, William Wallace, wrote to the sarkin to inform him that Britain wished to place a British official in Sokoto. This letter was delayed in transmission. It is possible that the letter did not reach the sarkin until the following year, and after receiving it at a time when the people who sent it were busy deposing his emirs, the sarkin was not favourably disposed to its contents. It seems that this opaque letter was not addressed to Lugard, but rather to his deputy, Wallace. Unfortunately, the sarkin's reply arrived at a time when the person to whom he very likely addressed it (Wallace) was away on leave. In this way the letter fell into the hands of Lugard, who did not know the context in which it was written, in the absence of Wallace to provide such context.

'You have your religion and we have ours'

Further doubts about the nature of the seemingly offensive letter arise from the next missive that the sarkin wrote to Lugard. In June 1902, he wrote in reply to Lugard's earlier letter of March 1902 in which Lugard casually informed the sarkin that he had arrested the emir of Kontagora and had sent British troops to Bauchi and Zaria. For a man who had supposedly sent a declaration of war to Lugard, the sarkin's second letter seems more sedate:

WHAT BRITAIN DID TO NIGERIA

In the name of God. To Governor Lugard.

> I have to inform you that we do not invite your administration in the
> Province of Bauchi and if you have interfered we do not want support
> from any one except from God. You have your religion and we have
> ours. We seek help from God, the best supporter, and there is no
> power except in him, the mighty and exalted. Peace. (Received about
> June, 1902).[8]

The inoffensive tone and content of this second letter make it
implausible that the sarkin could have sent another spontaneously written and aggressive letter just a few weeks earlier. It
seems, therefore, that Britain's invasion of Northern Nigeria was
built on a lie or a mistake.

Even though the letter was either mistranslated or not addressed
to Lugard, it had already set Lugard on the path to war. However,
the Colonial Office in London was reluctant to engage in another
war and would accept force only as a last resort if a negotiated
settlement was impossible, or if it was a matter of self-defence. On
19 December 1902 the undersecretary of state, Lord Onslow, sent
a telegram to Lugard in which he told him: 'as you are aware his
Majesty's government are anxious to avoid military operations in
West Africa. We have full confidence that you will not engage in
them unless absolutely necessary for defensive purposes but if in
your judgment they are necessary we leave you full discretionary
powers.'[9] Lugard needed a threat to demonstrate to the Colonial
Office that war was the only option. On 3 October 1902 events in
Keffi gave Lugard the pretext he needed to justify the use of force.
On that day, the British resident at Keffi, Captain Moloney, was
killed in murky circumstances. Lugard held the magaji (chief) of
Keffi, Dan Yamusa, responsible for the murder. Yamusa fled first
to Zaria, then to Kano, where he was allegedly received by the emir
of Kano, Aliyu. Lugard put a bounty on Yamusa's head and added
the charge of harbouring a fugitive murderer to the list of grievances against the Caliphate's rulers.

'A redoubtable slave-raider, and a man of dynamic personality'

Yet, despite Lugard's insistence that Yamusa had killed Moloney, eyewitness evidence suggested that he had pinned the murder on the wrong man. A British official described Yamusa as 'an intrepid warrior, a redoubtable slave-raider, and a man of dynamic personality'.[10] He was seen as not just the power behind the throne but more powerful than the emir of Keffi himself. After declaring a protectorate, Britain had placed Captain Moloney at Keffi. Yamusa was, according to the British, 'in obstinate opposition to the establishment of British rule'.[11] On 3 October 1902 Moloney, who 'was not a man to brook opposition',[12] went to Yamusa's residence and ordered him to come outside for 'a decisive interview'.[13] Yamusa did not trust the British, who had already arrested and killed several native chiefs, and taken over his house. Yamusa concluded that his life would be in danger if he complied with the order, so he declined to submit to arrest. When Moloney called for army reinforcements, Yamusa and his attendants panicked, rushed out of the residence, and tried to run away. As they made their escape, they fired a hail of arrows at random to deter would-be pursuers. One of those arrows struck Moloney's neck, pierced his carotid artery and killed him. A member of Moloney's personal staff testified that Yamusa did not attack or strike Moloney, that he saw Yamusa armed only with a gun, that he was not carrying a bow or arrow, and therefore could not have fired the arrow that killed Moloney. Yet Lugard still continued to declare that Yamusa had personally killed Moloney.

The sarkin's letter, Moloney's murder, and the fact that the emir of Kano gave sanctuary to Moloney's alleged killer gave Lugard the pretext he needed to use force and declare war. However, only a week after Moloney's death, Sarkin Abdurrahman died on 10 October 1902 at the age of 76 after reigning for 12 years. His nephew Muhammadu Attahiru succeeded him three days later. The change of ruler in theory opened the door to a negotiated settlement. However, for reasons best known to Lugard, he chose not to inform the British government of this potentially game-changing news. The presence of a new sarkin could bring pressure from London for Lugard to negotiate with the new ruler. However, by this time Lugard was already on the warpath and would not be dissuaded.

'An alien race detested for their misrule'

After sitting on the allegedly incendiary letter he received from the sarkin for eight months, Lugard finally made the secretary of state for the colonies aware of it. This was a very strange delay given the massive importance that Lugard attributed to the letter and that he treated it as a declaration of war. Lugard also tried to present military intervention as a war of liberation in which Britain would free the Hausa from their Fulani oppressors. He went so far as to describe the Fulani as 'an alien race detested for their misrule'.[14] To give the Colonial Office the impression that war was the only option, Lugard claimed that the emir of Kano was marching with warriors to attack the West African Frontier Force (WAFF) garrison at Zaria. The emir truly was on the march with one to two thousand horsemen, but he was not intending to attack Lugard's troops. He was, instead, hundreds of miles away travelling to Sokoto to pay homage to the new sarkin.

The Colonial Office became concerned by rumours that Lugard was assembling troops to attack Kano. Lugard's secretive and cunning nature did not escape their attention and the Colonial Office sent him a mild rebuke informing him:

> His Majesty's Government regret the necessity which has arisen for taking action against Kano. They think you should have kept them more fully informed of what was passing and that you should have

given them an earlier opportunity of considering, with the knowledge which they alone possess of the general situation in other parts of the Empire, whether it was necessary to send an expedition to Kano and whether it was expedient to do so at this time.[15]

Lugard's troops prepared to attack Kano in order to depose Emir Aliyu and capture Moloney's alleged murderer. Kano was a tough nut to crack. It was encircled by walls that were 40 feet thick at their base, and 30 to 50 feet high. The city also had ditches and cultivated farmland inside its walls which could provide food during a lengthy siege. The walls were reinforced in anticipation of the British invasion. On 29 January 1903 Colonel Morland marched out for Kano with 36 British officers and 722 soldiers. When the force reached Kano, they met little resistance. They blew a hole in the wall, stormed into the city, seized the absent emir's palace and hoisted the Union Jack on top of the city's walls. Not a single soldier on the British side was killed and only 14 were wounded. Lugard appointed the absent emir's brother as the new emir on 26 February. Sokoto was next.

'From this time and for ever a white man and soldiers will sit down in the Sokoto country'

In February 1903 Colonel Morland wrote a letter to the new sarkin, Attahiru, informing him that the British had deposed Emir Aliyu and 'are now sitting in his house'. Morland also warned him:

> We are coming to Sokoto and from this time and for ever a white man and soldiers will sit down in the Sokoto country. We have prepared for war because Abdu Sarikin Muslimin said there was nothing between us but war. But we do not want war unless you yourself seek war. If you receive us in peace, we will not enter your house, we will not harm you or any of your people. If you desire to become our friend you must not receive the *Magaji*. More, we desire you to seek

him with your utmost endeavour and place him in our hands. If you are loyal to us, you will remain in your position as Sarikin Muslimin, fear not. If you desire to be loyal to us, it is advisable for you that you should send your big messenger to meet us at Kaura (or on whatever road we follow). Then he will return to you with all our words.[16]

After leaving a garrison in Kano, British troops marched towards Sokoto without maps (there were none), but using descriptions supplied by earlier explorers. Sarkin Attahiru must have felt that the British noose was tightening around his neck. He replied to Morland to inform him that he was assembling his councillors for consultations and that he would write again to let Morland know the outcome. The Fulani rulers debated whether to negotiate, fight or flee to escape the impending British invasion. The starkness of the three choices before them led to paralysis.

'Some slaughter—much fun'

Britain fought a decisive battle with Sokoto on 14 March 1903. For some incomprehensible reason Sokoto's forces disastrously decided to concede their best advantage by leaving the protection of their walled city to face the WAFF outside in the open. The Sokoto forces fought bravely but, outside the city walls, they were target practice for the British artillery and machine guns. When two British Maxim guns jammed and over-heated, a soldier discovered that there was no water in their cooling jackets, and screamed at one of the carriers 'Here, you black bastard ... What you do with water?'[17] Two thirsty carriers who had drunk the water were given 48 flesh-stripping lashes each and made to pay for the damaged Maxim guns. On the other side, the Sokoto fighters demonstrated great acts of heroism. They took the sarkin's green flag, the symbol of his authority, into battle. Each time the man holding the flag was gunned down, another would pick it up. This continued until every flag bearer was shot dead. British forces eventually captured the flag after killing all its defenders. A British soldier described the battle as 'some slaughter—much fun'.[18] Afterwards, the mounted infantry pursued survivors who attempted to escape and, in the words of a British officer, 'We chase and kill till the area is clear of living men—and we tire of blood and bullets.'[19]

British casualties were remarkably small. Only two of their force were killed—one carrier and one soldier. Afterwards some British soldiers went onto the battlefield to kill wounded Sokoto fighters and, in the words of one of them, to 'mooch around among the dead bodies seeing if there's anything worth having on them'.[20] They hacked off arms and legs from corpses to retrieve items of value tied to them. One soldier, Charles Wells, saw what he thought was a gold anklet around the leg of one of the fallen Sokoto fighters. After ordering his assistant to use a machete to chop off the leg so he could take the anklet as a treasure of war, he got home to discover to his disappointment that it was made of brass.[21]

The sarkin Musulmi, Attahiru, survived the battle and fled. Lugard asked Sokoto officials to nominate a new sarkin. They initially nominated Umaru, the sarkin of Gobir, but then changed their minds and chose a namesake of the fugitive sarkin Musulmi, also called Attahiru. On 21 March 1903, Lugard assembled Sokoto's leading officials and read out aloud a proclamation, which his interpreter translated into Hausa at the same time and which Major Burdon, who spoke Hausa, verified word for word. Lugard promised not to interfere with the people's religion, but in his address he made it unmistakably clear that independent Fulani rule had ended:

> The old treaties are dead, you have killed them. Now these are the words which I, the High Commissioner, have to say for the future. The Fulani in old times under Dan Fodio conquered this country.

They took the right to rule over it, to levy taxes, to depose kings and to create kings. They in turn have by defeat lost their rule which has come into the hands of the British. All these things which I have said the Fulani by conquest took the right to do now pass to the British. Every Sultan and Emir and the principal officers of State will be appointed by the High Commissioner throughout all this country.

The next day, during a ceremony, Lugard appointed Attahiru II, son of a former sarkin Musulmi, Aliyu Babba, who reigned from 1842 to 1859, as the new sarkin to replace his fugitive namesake. Lugard gave Attahiru II a letter of appointment which outlined his powers, and made him swear an oath of allegiance to the British Crown. Thereafter the British started referring to the sarkin Musulmi in English as the 'sultan of Sokoto'.

Both Emir Aliyu[22] and Attahiru I were still on the run. The story of Attahiru I's eastward escape is an excellent demonstration of how dangerous it is to rely solely on Lugard's accounts as an accurate historical record. Lugard claimed that 'the mass of the people were not opposed to the overthrow of the Fulani'.[23] Yet as the fugitive Attahiru I travelled, entire villages emptied to join him. Thousands of chiefs and peasants, men and women, abandoned their homes to follow him. The tremendous support that Attahiru was able to command even after losing his position contradicts Lugard's claim that the people were relieved to see the Fulani overthrown. On the contrary, support for Attahiru was bolstered by the inciting news that the British had overthrown the head of their religion. The purpose of Attahiru's wanderings through the countryside is unclear. So long as he remained free, he posed a threat to the new sultan and the British, and could be a destabilising source of unrest. British unease about him was such that, in response to rumours that Attahiru planned to kidnap Lugard, they reinforced Lugard's security detail. Lugard and his lieutenants feared that he would lead a rural insurgency against them. Another plausible purpose for his journey was that he had decided to embark upon a *hijra* (migration) away from the infidel invaders in an attempt to reach Mecca.

As British troops pursued him, Attahiru travelled nearly 600 miles east from Sokoto to the outskirts of a town called Burmi on the fringes of the Borno Empire. The area was unknown territory for British troops. Between 22 April and 6 May, Attahiru and his supporters repelled their pursuers' attempts to capture him six times. During the fighting on 22 April, Attahiru's supporters hit two soldiers and six horses with poisoned arrows. A British soldier who saw them gave a graphic account of the gruesome agony inflicted by the poison: 'Never before have I seen men in such agony. Convulsions, tongues swollen, tearing their hair and their clothes; moaning, groaning, foaming at the mouth; the bodies swelling, the hands and feet stiffening, if this is God's way of killing people, I can't understand it, I think! But I am wrong, it isn't God's way, it's man's method!'[24] Some soldiers shot their two wounded colleagues to put them out of their misery.

The First Battle of Burmi

Soldiers led by Captain Francis Sword pursued Attahiru all the way to Burmi (in modern-day Gombe State). Thinking that Attahiru was inside the town, Sword attacked it on 13 May 1903, unaware that Attahiru had not yet arrived there. In a fierce battle, WAFF soldiers fired nearly ten thousand rounds of ammunition against the determined defenders. As the battle raged, people from nearby towns flocked to Burmi to provide reinforcements for the town's fighters. Women also came out to give food and water to the fighters. Although the WAFF killed several hundred people, including Burmi's ruler, Musa, Sword had to withdraw owing to the intensity of the resistance and the casualties to 45% of his own soldiers, two dead and 59 wounded. Sword retreated to fight another day.

Two days after the Burmi battle, Captain Hamilton-Browne continued the pursuit of Attahiru. Hamilton-Browne's soldiers came upon Attahiru's camp on 17 May and raked it with Maxim and rifle fire. Attahiru fled in haste, leaving food, baggage, 400 lb of gunpowder, guns and livestock behind. After four months on the run, Attahiru and his followers, including the fugitive magaji of Keffi, entered Burmi. Lugard believed that the town was an outpost of 'fanatical warriors'.[25] The religious fervour there was increased, not only by the presence of the former sultan, who had also been the Commander of the Believers, but also by the proclamation of a mahdi (religious reformer) in the town and the presence of members of the Tijaniyya Muslim brotherhood. It became a hornet's nest of dissidents who were willing to fight and die rather than accept British rule.

Attahiru wrote to Hamilton-Browne asking to be given safe passage to Mecca. Hamilton-Browne rejected his request and told him to surrender. Meanwhile, British reinforcements arrived to surround Burmi and cut it off from further support. Conditions inside the town deteriorated. The influx of new people into the town caused food shortages, as existing stocks were exhausted and could not be replenished with the new season's crops, which were not yet ready for harvesting. Attahiru again wrote to request safe passage to Mecca. This time he wrote to the British resident of Bauchi province, Charles Lindsey Temple. Again, his request was denied and Temple told him to surrender unconditionally. Attahiru took himself and his position as Commander of the Believers seriously. It is possible that he considered surrender to those he considered infidels tantamount to apostasy. With both sides taking inflexible and irreconcilable positions, it seemed their meeting place would be a battlefield rather than a negotiating room.

THE NORTHERN INVASION

The Second Battle of Burmi

While the WAFF fought further battles with Burmi in June and July, their encirclement of the town, their desire to capture Attahiru and his refusal to surrender meant a last stand would take place there. The most intense battle of Britain's takeover of Northern Nigeria took place not at the great Caliphate cities of Kano and Sokoto, but at a small dissident town on the fringes of the Borno Empire.

The man Britain chose to lead it into the final battle at Burmi was from a military family. He was the son of a lt-colonel, and four of his five brothers were also in the British army. Major Francis Marsh, then 37, led over 500 soldiers, including 21 British officers and 60 mounted infantry armed with artillery and machine guns, into a final battle at Burmi on 27 July 1903. The British attack began between 11 and 11.30 am. The WAFF bombarded the town with intense artillery and machine-gun fire for 30 minutes, but Burmi's fighters dug in and stayed in their trenches in front of the walls. After this initial bombardment Major Plummer advanced with troops to storm the gates. As the troops approached, the city seemed deserted and silent. When they neared the trenches and within 60 yards of the wall, they were shocked when the silence was suddenly shattered by deafening shouts of 'Allahu Akbar!' and the beating of drums, followed by a hail of poisoned arrows and gunfire from defenders on the walls. Plummer and Hamilton-Browne were wounded, and Marsh was hit on the thigh by a poisoned arrow that killed him within 20 minutes. Attahiru was praying in the mosque when the attack started and went down to the main gate to assist in the defence. Burmi's fighters demonstrated fanatical courage. Some deliberately threw themselves in front of the machine guns while others tied themselves together so they could not run away in panic. Some of the WAFF troops took fright and refused to advance as they feared the 'place was full of juju'. Lieutenants Fox and Maud led a storming party that attacked and fought close-quarter battles. They shot or bayoneted fighters to death in the trenches. Once inside the walls, the WAFF set fire to the thatched roofs of houses to force out the residents. The smoke was so thick that the WAFF had to withdraw outside the walls for a respite so as not to be overcome. The house-to-house fighting continued until just before seven in the evening.

Lugard later claimed that 'the British conquest of this vast country has been almost bloodless'.[26] How he came to this conclusion is a source of great mystery. During the second battle of Burmi alone, the WAFF fired an astonishing 32,710 rounds from small arms and piles of 700–1000 native corpses littered the town.[27] Attahiru's corpse lay with those of two of his sons among hundreds of others who chose to die trying to protect him rather than escape and live. British troops decapitated some of the ringleaders' bodies, took photos of the severed heads and then distributed them throughout the region to demonstrate that the resistance had been crushed.[28] The WAFF suffered 82 casualties: 13 dead, including their commander, Major Marsh, and 69 wounded.

The second battle of Burmi marked the end not just of Attahiru but also of the other leading members of the old Sokoto regime that had fled with him. The magaji of Keffi and many leading Sokoto officials who refused to leave Attahiru's side were among the dead. The independence of the Sokoto Caliphate ended at the smouldering ruins of Burmi several hundred miles away from its capital. British forces had subdued a century-old[29] Caliphate after only a few days of fighting. Although Lugard got the credit, he merely executed a script written by Goldie in the Niger Committee report six years previously. Goldie's plan to isolate the sultan of Sokoto by eliminating his emirs first, then leaving him till last, had worked brilliantly. Lugard was the implement that effected the plan, but Goldie was the brain behind it. The timing of the conquest also seemed to validate Usman dan Fodio's alleged prophecy that the Caliphate would last for a century.

Britain's conquest of the Caliphate added some 20 million people and 500,000 square miles to the Empire. The Caliphate's location, which had given it an advantage for the previous century, contributed to its downfall. Since it was over 250 miles inland, landlocked and insulated from European influence at both ends, it initially escaped some of the influence that Britain brought to bear on Southern Nigeria. It thus managed to maintain its cohesion and traditions undisturbed for much longer than the south. However, this isolation also proved to be a weakness when it finally encountered British soldiers in battle. Caliphate forces had also failed to learn from the only prior military contact between Caliphate and British forces, six years earlier during Bida's battle against the Royal Niger Constabulary in 1897. The defeat at Bida should have taught them that the tactics which served them so well for the previous century—cavalry charges backed by archers, lancers and a few riflemen—would not work in the open plains against the British square or their machine guns and artillery. Yet, strangely, they decided to fight to their opponent's strengths, conceded their own advantage by fighting outside their city walls, and failed to attack the WAFF column while they were marching and at their most vulnerable. They also recklessly charged the British army square and each emirate made the tactical mistake of facing the WAFF individually rather than combining their defences together.

Despite his death, Attahiru I's legacy did not end in Burmi. His *hijra* was posthumously completed. His son Mohammed Bello and 25,000 other survivors fled to Sudan and established a Fulani settlement on the Blue Nile called Mai Wurno. Their descendants still reside there. British soldiers captured Attahiru's flag and kept it as a regimental trophy. Fifty-four years later it was returned to the Caliphate on 6 November 1960 at Giginya Square in Sokoto.

13

THE SOUTH-EAST INVASION

When Britain created the Protectorate of Southern Nigeria in 1900, the people of Arochukwu, known as the Aros, (in modern-day Abia State in south-east Nigeria), exercised economic, military and spiritual supremacy among the Igbo, Ibibio, Ijaw and other neighbouring ethnic groups. The Aros were among the most well-travelled of Igbos, as they had lucrative commercial interests from trading within Igboland, with other ethnic groups, and with Europeans. They were middlemen, arms dealers, slave dealers, and providers of mercenaries. Through their alliance with martial clans, such as the Abam, Edda, and Ohafia, they were able to loan out the military services of these clans as mercenaries, and also use them as warriors for own interests. Their allies, the Abams, 'were in a state of perpetual readiness for war whenever it was made worth their while'.[1]

Children of God

A British missionary described the Aros as 'a remarkable and mysterious people'.[2] The Aros also presented themselves as agents and interlocutors of a feared deity known as *Ibini Ukpabi* (which the British called Long Juju) that resided in a secret shrine inside a cave in Aro territory. People from as far as a hundred miles away came to consult Long Juju in order to settle disputes, identify murder suspects and receive guidance on seemingly intractable problems. Long Juju also acted as a supernatural judge who adjudicated on disputes and prescribed punishment for the alleged offending party. The Aros ascribed their commercial success to their being favoured by Long Juju and also claimed that this gave them a special status. The name of their home town, Arochukwu, meant 'Spear of God' in Igbo. Their invincible aura made them one of the few groups that could travel through foreign towns and villages without attracting unwelcome enquiries. They were a threat not only on their own account but also because they wielded huge influence over neighbouring groups, whom they discouraged from dealing with the British. The Aros were held in awe throughout south-east Nigeria, and their reputation for wielding economic, military and supernatural power made them seem invulnerable. It also gave them confidence when Britain arrived in south-eastern Nigeria. At first they did not accept that the British invaders were capable of challenging their supremacy. Neighbouring ethnic groups accepted Long Juju's pre-eminence and the Aros' status as a special people, calling them *Umu Chukwu* (children of god).

The Aros believed that Long Juju gave them special protection that allowed them to deal directly with the white men, whom they portrayed to their neighbours as deadly beings only they were capable of dealing with. In order to protect their supremacy in the middleman trade, they threatened to invoke supernatural vengeance on others who dealt with Britain. They retaliated against the town of Obegu, which gave information about the Aros to British authorities, by sending the Abams to attack it on November 1901. The Abams stormed Obegu, murdered 400 people, burned the British government rest house, and destroyed water tanks installed by the district commissioner, Harold Douglas. From the British perspective, the Aros' pre-eminent position made them a threat to Britain's ambition of imposing itself as the new economic and military power in the south-east.

'They resented our appearance and were determined
to oppose us in every way'

The relationship between the Aros and the British started on the wrong foot. In 1896 British officials led by Major Arthur Glyn Leonard visited Bende to discuss free trade in areas controlled by the Aros. Before agreeing to speak with natives, Leonard was in the habit of asking them to remove their hats as a sign of respect for the British. When Leonard's interpreter asked the Aros to remove their hats before Leonard spoke, they defiantly kept them on and those without procured hats and placed them on their heads.[3] Leonard described the interpreter who relayed his message as 'a most intelligent Opobo native, who had been in England, and talked English almost perfectly'.[4] The interpreter was Albert Jaja, the son of the famous Jaja of Opobo, who had been exiled by the British eight years earlier.

Rather than building a rapport, the meeting set the Aros and British in antagonistic opposition to each other. Leonard complained:

From the very commencement the Aro people showed by their looks, gestures, and the generally-offensive attitude they adopted, that they resented our appearance and were determined to oppose us in every way. This was not only apparent by the scowls on their faces, by keeping their hats on their heads, and by many other outward mannerisms, but by the noisy disrespect they showed us, as well as by the insolent way in which they totally ignored our presence.[5]

Leonard also said that the Aros' spokesman 'denounced and vituperated the unwelcome and uncalled for advent of the interfering white men', and told them, 'The white men may have come by the sun, they may have come by the moon, or they may have come through the clouds, but the sooner they went back from where they had come, and remained there, the better.'[6] Anglo-Aro relations never recovered from this bad first meeting.

'The natives must be made to fully understand that the government is their master'

The high commissioner for Southern Nigeria, Sir Ralph Moor, began planning to attack the Aros in 1899. Moor, a former police officer, was not shy about using a military sledgehammer to deal with uncooperative natives and had masterminded the invasion of Benin in 1897. Before commencing the assault on the Aros, Moor instructed the mission's commanding officers to ensure that 'the natives must be made to fully understand that the government is their master and is determined to establish in and control their country'.[7]

The mission's stated goals were to stop the slave trade, find and destroy the Long Juju, open the country to civilisation, promote legitimate trade and introduce British currency. There was another unstated aim. The colonial authorities were concerned about the large number of weapons in native hands. Pre-colonial Igbo society was very well armed. During Leonard's visit to the Bende area in 1896, he noticed that 'not a man apparently moved except without carrying a naked sword in one hand and a rifle at full cock in the other. Even the boys—some of them not higher than an ordinary man's knee—walked about armed with bows, and pointed arrows.'[8] Although the natives mostly used their guns for hunting, and rarely in wars against each other (which were fought mainly with machetes, spears and bows and arrows), they could become very dangerous weapons if the natives ever became organised and decided to resist the British incursion.

THE SOUTH-EAST INVASION

During the Brass uprising against the Royal Niger Company in 1895, British authorities were stunned at how well armed the natives were. A British army officer admitted that during the Brass revolt,

> What the Commissioner found most difficult to understand was the Brassmen being so well equipped with rifles and percussion guns, which were prohibited under the Brussels Act. The truth was that the Protectorate Government was not in a position to undertake the somewhat formidable task of disarming the natives until about the year 1900 ... The only remedy was general disarmament.[9]

However, general disarmament was an unrealistic prospect because Britain had little intelligence or other knowledge of the ethnic groups beyond the southern coastline. After the Brass revolt, Sir John Kirk stated: 'to attempt to disarm the population by any sudden and violent action would end in failure, the ruin of trade and a general rising.'[10] Military confrontation with the Aros offered a chance to confront the problem of a heavily-armed population and eliminate a rival source of power in Southern Nigeria.

It is surprising that the Anglo-Aro war receives little coverage in Nigeria's history given the massive scale of the military deployment and the military innovations that the war featured. Both colonial and Nigerian sources have made the common mistake of dismissing the Anglo-Aro war as a one-sided British rout during which the Aros offered little or no resistance. Some Nigerian accounts even claim that Britain overcame the Aros in a single day or that the Aros refused to come out and fight. The true story was very different and involved a lengthy battle featuring tactical flexibility on the part of both the British and Aro forces.

The colonial authorities meant business. They expected heavy resistance and prepared accordingly. They assembled the largest colonial troop deployment in Nigeria's history. To supplement troops of the Southern Nigeria Regiment of the WAFF, Moor's counterpart in Northern Nigeria, Sir Frederick Lugard, loaned him 375 troops from the Northern Nigeria Regiment, and the Colony of Lagos another 300. In November 1901 more than 1,600 soldiers, 1800 porters, and 74 British officers armed with assorted weapons, including six cannons and seven machine guns, assembled at the Igbo towns of Akwete, Itu, Oguta and Unwana and marched to confront the Aros.

'Clearing volleys'

The British fighting formation of choice was the so-called 'square', in which British soldiers assembled and fought in a formation resembling a square. With the soldiers facing outwards from the square, the unit could see and fire in front, behind and to their sides, and could not be ambushed by unseen foes. However, the British military square was of limited use in environments surrounded by snipers hiding in dense forests. Yet the British had learned from their previous battles in Nigeria and other parts of West Africa and adapted their tactics. In previous campaigns they were vulnerable when marching past dense foliage on either side of the road. Rather than waiting inside their villages to be ripped apart by British machine-gun fire, native snipers often hid in the bush a few feet from the road and harassed British soldiers with musket fire as they marched past. In response, British troops developed the tactic of 'clearing volleys'—stopping periodically every 100 yards or so to fire blind volleys of machine-gun fire into the bush beside the road to clear out snipers.

However, the use of clearing volleys meant that huge amounts of ammunition had to be carried for each military campaign, and the ammunition rapidly became depleted. The volleys also became less effective because the noise of machine-gun fire gave away the position of approaching British troops, and because of the evolving tactics of the native fighters. The Aros knew that their elderly and inaccurate Dane guns were largely ineffective against the British unless they were firing at point-blank range. Thus they dug an elaborate system of trenches on either side of the road to allow them to get closer to the British troops. Aro snipers placed themselves inside these trenches and, from unseen positions, fired at advancing British troops as they marched along. The Aros also laid logs across the top of the trenches to protect their heads from return fire. About 2,500 Aros manned the trenches and 5,000 more waited half a mile away with swords and machetes to pounce on the British soldiers after the snipers in the trenches had harassed them. The British commanding officer of the operation, Colonel Arthur Forbes Montanaro, was impressed by the Aros' technical ingenuity, and noted:

> The trenches were over a quarter of a mile long with flanks thrown back; they were five feet deep and absolutely impervious to any fire we could bring against them. In addition to the trenches the enemy had constructed a small redoubt on our left flank and well advanced, the whole with good lines of retreat and all covered with bushes, so that until our troops reached the trenches nothing could be seen.[11]

The only clue that British troops had about the location of those firing at them came from the puffs of gunpowder smoke ejected into the air when the snipers fired.

'Could not have been better constructed had they been made by Europeans'

One of the commanding officers who saw the trenches said: 'The section and finish of these trenches were admirable, and their well-planned position made it difficult to believe that they were not the work of some highly trained men.'[12] In Colonel Montanaro's view, the ultimate compliment he could pay the Aros was to admit that 'these trenches could not have been better constructed had they been made by Europeans'.[13]

The system of laying ambushes in trenches worked when the British marched along footpaths, but the British then devised a new tactic to replace clearing volleys. They instead adopted flanking tactics and sent soldiers a few yards into the bush on either side of the road, telling them to march parallel to the main column of troops. The flanking troops could then find the trenches and clear out the snipers hiding in them. In addition, the British columns hired natives who had the skill to climb to the top of trees as high as 60 feet without the aid of ladders or ropes. These men would clench a knife in their teeth as they climbed (to kill any snakes they encountered in the trees), and once at the top they would scout and point out the position of Aro fighters to the British officers, who then aimed their gunfire accordingly and mowed down the Aros in that direction.

'I had no idea that savages could make such a stand'

Since the Aros could not match British firepower, they tried to slow the enemy down by setting brilliantly disguised booby traps. For example, at road intersections, they dug pits about 15 feet deep, placed dozens of sharpened stakes inside them, then disguised the traps by covering them with branches and earth so that they would not arouse the suspicion of the advancing British. When British troops stopped to rest, the Aros disturbed and attacked them. A British officer complained: 'The Aros have never left us quiet either by day or night.'[14] Colonel Montanaro conceded that 'the enemy has shown himself to be a most persistent and dogged foe ... I had no idea that savages could make such a stand.'[15]

On the afternoon of 24 December 1901, British troops raised the Union Jack over Arochukwu. Yet the Aros did not allow them to have a peaceful Christmas Eve and continued attacking British positions late into the night. The British replied and drove them back with machine-gun fire. The Aros returned to the edge of the British camp around 11 pm, attacked again, and caused the British porters to panic and stampede. British soldiers celebrated Christmas Day by building a defensive garrison with eight-foot-high walls on an elevated piece of ground. From this position, they could observe approaching Aro forces. Nonetheless, the Aros' attacks continued unabated, and they even brought out an old cannon to bombard the British positions.

On 31 December, the British discovered the position of the Long Juju oracle and blew it up with dynamite. But the military campaign continued for another four months. The absence of a centralised political authority in the south-east meant that the British could not depose one overall ruler and expect all his followers to 'fall in line'. From January until April 1902 British forces marched and re-marched over 6,000 square kilometres of Igboland, and criss-crossed the interior to attack recalcitrant villages that refused to surrender and to confiscate their guns. As troops approached, many villagers fled in fear. Since the troops had been instructed to consider any abandoned village as hostile, they often resorted to looting and burning empty villages. When British troops conquered and occupied a town or village, they would refuse to leave until its leaders and fighters came to them to surrender. This gave the conflict against the Igbo an attritional character. At the same time it allowed the British to execute the hidden part of their mission: the disarmament of Igboland. Once British forces captured a town or village, their general policy was to require it to surrender all its weapons to the British forces, who would then confiscate and destroy them. The political officer accompanying the mission, Lt-Colonel Galway, arbitrarily set a quota for the number of guns that each village had to surrender based on the number of people or houses in that village. The quota for the Aro mission was one gun for every four houses.[16]

If the village refused to surrender its weapons to the satisfaction of the political officer, the troops would either burn and destroy the village or occupy it and live off its farms and livestock until British demands were satisfied.

'The variety of rifles was amazing'

British officers were astonished at the quantity and variety of guns they recovered after the Aro war. Lt-Colonel Galway remarked: 'The variety of rifles was amazing. Among them were Brown Bess, Minié, Enfield, Winchester, Snider, and Martini-Henry.'[17] The British forces confiscated over 25,000 rifles at the end of the campaign, and Galway sent some of them to the Tower of London, where they were placed on public display.

The war also created a large refugee population. Ten thousand people fled and took refuge at the Catholic mission at Aguleri and another five thousand at the Catholic mission at Nsube. Yet the British victory over the Aros did end the confrontation between the British and the people of south-east Nigeria. There was great settling of scores after the Aro war. British officers set up military tribunals to try several Aro leaders. These included Okori Torti, who was hanged along with several others for allegedly masterminding the Obegu massacre which preceded the Aro war. On 26 January 1902, Lt-Colonel Festing, an officer of the Royal Irish Fusiliers, who had previously worked for the Royal Niger Constabulary, sentenced the Aro chief Alige to death for 'violation of parole' (his village allegedly took up arms again after surrendering). Even though death sentences could not be confirmed unless approved by a superior officer, Festing ordered Alige's execution on the same day as the verdict, for the supposed reason that he could not get in touch with a superior officer. Lieutenants Rodly and Williams also convicted and sentenced chiefs Abiakari and Ekpenyong to five years' imprisonment for not giving information to British officers and for failing to provide guides and escorts to British troops. When news of the convictions reached a legal officer at the Colonial Office, he submitted a written legal opinion declaring the trials illegal and stating that the military tribunals had no right to try them.[18]

'They still consider they are entirely their own masters and owe allegiance to no one'

Although Sir Ralph Moor claimed that the Aro war had pacified south-eastern Nigeria, it can be regarded more as the beginning of the British conquest of the area, not the end. The extreme force used, as well as the practice of punishing villages that resisted British invasion by burning and destroying them, executing their leaders, and then imposing collective fines, generated a great spirit of resistance. The acting high commissioner, Sir Leslie Probyn, admitted: 'The Aros themselves, however, were not destroyed, but, on the contrary, immediately gave further proof of their intelligence by adapting themselves to the new conditions of life.'[19] Some parts of the south-east remained no-go areas for British officials unless they were accompanied by a heavily-armed contingent. Resistance was so tenacious that at times, when overwhelmed by British troops, some villagers escaped into the bush so that they could return and live to fight another day. When villages could not resist by force, resistance took the form of a stubborn withholding of cooperation from the British administration. Some villages refused to give information and food to British officers. One officer wrote that the people 'are passively hostile and bitter, and always attempt to obstruct so far as they think they safely can. It is a pity they were never really beaten, as they still consider they are entirely their own masters and owe allegiance to no one.'[20] As a result British troops had to mount further military assaults in south-east

Nigeria over the next three years, and re-invaded the same areas as in the original Aro war in 1901–2. Between December 1901 and April 1905 British military patrols in south-east Nigeria killed around 5,000 people and seized over 100,000 guns.[21]

Placing the south-east under control and keeping it so was a constant headache for British colonial authorities. The south-east remained an area of frequent rebellion and instability. Even though Britain created Southern Nigeria in 1900, it took over twenty years of continual military operations for Britain to establish control of the south-east. During the 20-year period between 1900 and 1920, the people of south-east Nigeria fought British troops in over 300 battles.[22] Although the resistance was not coordinated, the fighting spread throughout the south-east to towns and villages such as Calabar, Ikot-Ekpene, Mbaise, Onitsha, Owerri, Umuahia and Uyo (in modern-day Cross River, Akwa Ibom, Imo, Anambra, Ebonyi, Abia and Rivers States). Neighbouring ethnic groups such as the Annang, Efik and Ibibio joined the Igbos in resisting and each village devised its own method of resistance. Many parts of the south-east were not brought under effective British control until around 1920. Yet despite the large number of battles, British casualties were remarkably few. Only four British officers were killed and 30 wounded. The Hausa troops fighting for the British bore the brunt of the south-eastern resistance: 142 of them were killed and almost 500 wounded. The massive disparity in casualties was due to the astonishing level of firepower that the British employed. During the invasion of the south-east they fired over 350,000 rounds of small arms fire and over 54, 000 cannon shells, and killed more than 10,000 people.[23]

Very little is known about these constant wars of colonial conquest between 1903 and 1920. For Britain, they were minor obstacles on the road to colonial conquest. British reports usually gloss over them by describing them with benign words such as 'expedition', 'pacification' and 'reduction'. From the native perspective, they were great battles involving mass murder and destruction. Several decades later, an elder in south-east Nigeria recalled the 'disastrous wars of the white man'.[24] What was it like to be in the vicinity of these military assaults? The British manhunt for a man named Bibi Kala in 1903 (in modern-day Bayelsa and Delta States in southern Nigeria) is worth recounting in detail for its demonstration of the brutality and collective punishments that accompanied British invasions.

'Giving him 24 lashes for daring to address the white man'

The British sought Bibi Kala, whom they described as 'a powerful Juju-man' and 'a pirate of some considerable local reputation', for the somewhat nebulous crime of 'exercising his influence on all natives in the country around the Brass river, and up to the Niger'.[25] Colonel Montanaro[26] was in charge of the manhunt. One of the other British officers on the mission, Captain Esme Gordon Lennox, recalled that 'Colonel Montanaro is determined to either capture the Juju-man or make the whole of the native population round Wilberforce Island suffer'.[27] Montanaro had been the commanding officer of the invasion of Arochukwu, and he used similar scorched-earth tactics in this manhunt. When the soldiers arrived at a village they called Ebradi (probably Egbadi), the residents and their chiefs fled in terror. However, when one villager eventually mustered enough courage to speak to the soldiers. Captain Lennox described what happened next: 'One drunken brute, displaying more courage than the others, came reeling up and asked us what we wanted. He got his answer by my knocking him down with the butt of my revolver, and then giving him 24 lashes for daring to address the white man.'[28]

While conducting the manhunt, the British officers also decided to collect an unpaid fine of £25 from Ebradi. Lennox warned the villagers:

unless they took immediate steps to pay the fine, they would have to suffer for their disobedience. The only reply I got was that the chiefs had all run away and were too frightened to return; so we decided that the first part of their payment would be done by our destroying their entire yam crop. We went down by launch to their yam fields, and having collected a plentiful supply for ourselves, destroyed all the remainder.[29]

In a society where most people were subsistence farmers, burning crops and yams was as devastating as burning their money. Afterwards, the soldiers went from one village to another, issuing ultimatums to the inhabitants, warning them that if they did not find Kala and hand him over within the deadline, their villages would be destroyed and their chiefs imprisoned. When the chiefs and residents protested that they did not know where Kala was, Colonel Montanaro 'decided that we would burn every village and farm round North Wilberforce Island and reduce the entire native population to such a state of desolation that they would be bound to give him up'.[30]

'I shudder to think how many homes we have destroyed in these two days'

On 30 September 1903 the British sailed to Amassana, where they seized 25 goats and 20 chickens, then went to Agbeni and burned half the village and left 13 soldiers behind on guard to prevent the residents returning. They then went on to Akumbri and Kabiana where they again burned half of both villages and left some soldiers behind to occupy them, before finally anchoring for the night, 'all of us tired out with this incessant incendiarism'.[31] However, the incendiarism was not complete. Around 9 pm that night:

Colonel Montanaro conceived the extraordinary idea of burning a town at night. Here was a nice game ... When the town was fully ablaze it was a magnificent sight, but as an effective method of cap-

turing Bibi Cala [*sic*] it was worse than useless. October 1st was
spent in a continuance of yesterday's incendiarism by burning every
town or farm we could see. I shudder to think how many homes we
have destroyed in these two days.[32]

When they eventually captured Kala on 3 October, he confessed that he had been living in a canoe and had never been
anywhere near the villages that the British had destroyed. The
burning and destruction served no strategic purpose for capturing
Kala and was just a game of amusement for the British officers.
The destruction and terror were as inconsequential to them as a
child kicking over anthills while playing. Kala was executed by
hanging. Afterwards, Lennox was not remorseful about the needless and extensive destruction that preceded Kala's capture but
expressed his 'wish that the capture of Bibi Cala [*sic*] had been
effected in a more sportsmanlike manner. What chance had these
wretched natives against such a heavily equipped expedition.'[33]

The brutality that accompanied Britain's conquest of the
south-east and Niger Delta had long-term consequences. The
shock and awe the indigenes experienced when encountering
high-technology violence, machine guns and white people for
the first time caused behavioural and religious shifts in the population. The destruction of Long Juju and the successful British
propaganda which declared the oracle an Aro fraud eroded
south-eastern fidelity to native religions. Natives were made to
understand that only those who demonstrated loyalty and provided support to the British invaders would avoid punishment.
For example, British authorities rewarded Nwakpuda of Old
Umuahia and Nwosuocha of Umunwanwa for providing them
with escorts and information about the Aros, by appointing
them as warrant chiefs. Such encouragement of assistance to
Britain (some might say treachery) created an association
between the acquisition of power and fidelity to the British. The
massive British display of force caused natives to begin to hold

the white man in awe and dread and to seek ways to placate him. Massive military assaults and destruction acted as a coercive inducement to convert to Christianity and learn English in an attempt to placate British authorities.

The British also exploited the natives' belief in the supernatural by making the natives believe that they were omnipresent and that their power was limitless. As a result, natives often perceived British actions against them as acts of supernatural power. For example, an elderly south-eastern woman once informed me that when the British set native cottages on fire using matches, the terrified villagers who watched the destruction from afar could not see the matches in the British officers' hands. Thus it appeared from a distance that the British were able to summon flames at will from their fingertips. If the white man was capable of such incredible feats, what else was he capable of?

PART 4

RESISTANCE

The aim of the next three chapters is to examine how indigenous communities reacted to the imposition of British authority. Colonial accounts often present narratives that give the impression that one is peering down at Britain's colonial enemies through British eyes. To some extent, a preoccupation with British actions should be expected since much of what we know about British colonialism was written by, and from the perspective of, the British. However, to continue doing so without including the contribution of Nigerians themselves risks perpetuating the existing pattern that reduces the native population to passive observers who experienced what the British did to them without being able to influence or react to it.

Anti-colonial resistance was expected. A British army officer once said: 'If I were in his [the native's] place I should object very strongly to the white man coming and subjecting me to the white man's rule, and would certainly not let him come there without some resistance.'*

* Lennox, *With the West African Frontier Force*, p. 41.

WHAT BRITAIN DID TO NIGERIA

While natives resisted Britain during the initial wars of conquest, several communities also continued doing so after these wars and after British colonial authority and institutions had been established. It is important to chronicle these acts of secondary resistance not only because British accounts tend to portray their conquest of Nigeria as a one-sided rout, but also because this secondary resistance needed more courage than was required when confronting the unknown British enemy for the first time. Secondary resistance is more impressive when one considers that it was conducted by people who were already aware of what Britain was capable of and the devastating impact of its weapons. The earth-shattering noise of British artillery, machine guns and rockets screeching through the sky terrified natives so much that some of them interpreted the British advance in an apocalyptic way as signalling the end of the world. Yet despite being confronted with high-tech warfare for the first time, some were brave enough to continue fighting back. As the various incidents of resistance against British rule are too numerous to recount, the next three chapters will illuminate the most significant rebellions.

14

THE NORTHERN RESISTANCE

St Valentine's Day Massacre: Satiru, 1906

Around 7 pm on 15 February 1906 the high commissioner for Northern Nigeria, Frederick Lugard, received an urgent telegram at his base in Zungeru stating: 'whole of C Company, Mounted Infantry, defeated and annihilated at Satiru ... Sergeant Slack, R.A., and myself and doctor only men remaining; most urgent ...'[1] The concerned Lugard replied to ask who was behind the attack, whose side the sarkin Musulmi was on, and kept the telegraph line open all night. For several days, Lugard did not know who was responsible for this attack on a West African Frontier Force (WAFF) unit.

Oral tradition claimed that on his deathbed, Usman dan Fodio predicted that the Sokoto Caliphate would last for a century, after which it would be succeeded by a foreign power for four years, followed by the arrival of the mahdi (messiah). Prophecies and millenarian beliefs had foretold that a mahdi would arise to lead the people in a struggle that would precede the end of the world. The general instability of the times, with cataclysmic societal changes such as war, violence and displacement of the Caliphate by foreigners, lent credence to the mahdi prophecies. In the early 1900s it seemed the prophecy had been partly fulfilled. Britain completed its conquest of the Sokoto Caliphate in 1903, almost exactly a hundred years after the jihad that established it had commenced. By 1906 Britain had been in power for three years. For the prophecy to be completed, the mahdi had to arrive soon.

In 1904 the chief of the village of Satiru, about 14 miles south of Sokoto, declared himself to be the mahdi and named his son Isa (Jesus). The sarkin Musulmi summoned the self-proclaimed mahdi to Sokoto but he died while awaiting trial. The mahdi's surviving followers were released after they swore an oath on the Koran not to repeat their heresy. Two years later another mahdi emerged in French-controlled Niger, north of British territory. In December 1905 and January 1906, followers of this mahdi repelled and killed French officers who tried to collect tax in their district. Their leader, a near-blind cleric named Dan Makafo, fled south into the British-controlled territory of Northern Nigeria, collecting thousands of followers as he travelled. He finally halted at Satiru and joined forces with Isa, the son of the previous self-professed mahdi of Satiru. Satiru's habit of attracting dissident clerics led Lugard to remark that it was 'well known as a hotbed of fanaticism'.[2] Despite his dismissal of the self-righteousness of the Mahdists, the irony is that both the British and the Mahdists presented themselves in a messianic way.

A curious aspect of the Satiru Mahdists is how much their movement resembled modern-day outbursts of religious dissidence in Northern Nigeria. The Satiru Mahdists attacked a neighbouring village called Tsomo, which refused to join them. Subsequent dissident Muslim groups in the north, such as those surrounding the Islamic leader Maitatsine, also had millenarian beliefs, retreated to rural areas, attacked communities that refused to join them, and had confrontations with state security forces.

In February 1906, when the resident at Sokoto, Major John Alder Burdon, travelled out of Sokoto, a 31-year-old barrister named Hillary Richard Preston-Hillary deputised for him during his absence. When Preston-Hillary heard about events in Satiru, he set off for the village on 14 February 1906 along with British army officers, mounted cavalry, 69 native WAFF soldiers, and the assistant resident, Mr Scott, who was to act as an interpreter. British accounts claimed that Preston-Hillary only wanted to talk to the Mahdists and did not want to fight them. However, to Preston-Hillary's and his colleagues' surprise, the Mahdists found it difficult to believe that a column of armed foreigners and soldiers marching in formation towards them with guns and artillery had come in peace.

When they arrived at Satiru, Preston-Hillary and Scott rode forward on their horses. The army commander, Lt Francis Blackwood, had ordered the soldiers to deploy in square formation but he became concerned that Preston-Hillary and Scott had ridden too far ahead of the soldiers accompanying them. It appears that the Mahdists had seen them coming from afar and started sprinting across 800 yards of field that separated them. Blackwood could not order his men to open fire without endangering Preston-Hillary and Scott, who were in the line of fire between the soldiers and the advancing Mahdists. He instead ordered the soldiers to move forward towards the civilians to protect them. As the soldiers moved out from their square and advanced, the Mahdists descended on them before they could re-form. The horses became alarmed and ran loose. In the ensuing melee of stampeding horses and soldiers out of formation, the Mahdists pounced on them with spears and agricultural tools such as axes and hoes, killed Preston-Hillary, Blackwood, 24

197

native soldiers, and one of the WAFF's horse attendants. They also captured one of the WAFF's Maxim guns.

With their commander dead and the chain of command disrupted, the soldiers were in disarray and started to retreat. As they did so, some of them demonstrated extraordinary courage. A native soldier, Private Moma Wurrikin, saved the medical officer, Dr Martin Ellis, who was lying on the ground after being badly wounded by a spear injury to his right shoulder, by shooting the man who had wounded Ellis, catching one of the runaway horses, and lifting Ellis onto the horse. He did the same for Scott as well, all while shooting and holding the Mahdists at bay. However, one of the Mahdists knocked Scott off his horse, and the others surrounded and killed him when he fell to the ground. Another native soldier, Private Moma Zaria, saved a British officer who had fallen off his horse by running towards the Mahdists to pick him up and rescue him.

The Mahdists chased the surviving soldiers for an hour. When the survivors returned to their base at Sokoto in disjointed groups of twos and threes, they remained vulnerable and fearful of a Mahdist attack. Moreover, the base was severely undermanned because Lugard had dispatched most of the fighting force several hundred miles away on a reprisal mission to attack the 'Munshis' (Tivs) as punishment for attacking the Royal Niger Company's depot at Abinsi. To defend the base, the survivors pre-emptively issued weapons to anyone who could handle them, even civilian staff. The British officers stayed up all night on watch in case of a Mahdist attack. They also brought the native soldiers' wives to the base in order to discourage soldiers from deserting, and replenished their stocks of food and water in case they had to withstand a siege. Had the native soldiers deserted, the British would have been at the mercy of the Mahdists.

In view of the emergency and the absence of senior officers, the resident, Major Burdon, abruptly returned from his journey and took temporary command of the base. Although he was now a political officer, Burdon had a military background; he was the last commander of the Royal Niger Constabulary before the Royal Niger Company's charter was revoked. He had fought in earlier military campaigns in Northern Nigeria, including the Constabulary's invasion of Bida and Ilorin.

On 16 February, the increasingly worried Lugard sent a telegram to the secretary of state for the colonies, Lord Elgin, expressing his concern that 'Situation of affairs gives me sufficient cause for anxiety'.[3] On 24 February Lugard sent another, more urgent telegram warning that 'Attitude of section of people Hadejia has been consistently threatening, greatly adding to anxiety in present difficulty. Consider it necessary to put a stop to this threat by arresting ringleaders. I am uncertain which side Emir likely to take.'[4] Lugard also requested reinforcements from the governor of Southern Nigeria.

Why was the usually unflappable Lugard sounding so shaky? For a start, the area was in a state of unrest and was awash with sensational rumours that the sarkin Musulmi and emirs supported the Mahdists, who had allegedly massacred the entire British expedition and left not a single man alive. In Bauchi a mallam had been preaching in favour of exterminating infidels; while another was caught trying to incite the soldiers and was hanged. Another mahdi had reportedly arisen in the northern town of Burmi, and the town of Hadejia (halfway between Kano and Borno) was refusing cooperation with the colonial government. Hadejia was so hostile to the British that they could not visit it without an armed escort, and the British accused the town's residents of killing a soldier. The WAFF that Lugard had created eight years earlier had been hitherto 'undefeated'. Yet they lost their 'unbeaten record' to a group of village farmers carrying axes and hoes. This setback was dangerous because it shattered the image of British invincibility in Northern Nigeria and demonstrated that white men also bled when cut.

WHAT BRITAIN DID TO NIGERIA

Religious revolts against British rule were rare. The fear was that if the Mahdists managed to rally the population behind a religious cause, it could set off a chain reaction of uprisings against British rule across the region. The one man with the power to effect this outcome was the sarkin Musulmi whom Lugard had appointed three years earlier, Muhammadu Attahiru II. If a native ruler whom Lugard appointed turned against him, it would also indict the policy of indirect rule. Lugard's telegram to Elgin on 24 February had revealed his apprehension about whose side Attahiru II would take. If Attahiru II chose to use religion as a means of rallying opposition to Britain, he could unite significant areas of Northern Nigeria against the British administration or even cause the Hausa soldiers to mutiny against their British commanders. Burdon also expressed his fears about what would happen if Attahiru II chose to side with the Mahdists or prevaricated over the decision:

> Had he shown the slightest indecision, I have no doubt but that the bulk of the '*talakawa*' (poor or unofficial classes) would at once have joined the enemy; many headmen would have followed suit ... and instead of an isolated fanatical outbreak we should have had to meet a general rising. Had he even procrastinated, or confined himself to promises, the result would have been the same—the probable extermination of all Europeans in the Sokoto Province.[5]

Only three years after Lugard subjugated the Sokoto Caliphate, British control over the area was under threat. It is uncertain whether Attahiru II knew that the Satiru revolt had strengthened his position or how much it had unnerved Lugard. Attahiru II made his decision known by sending his horsemen to the British fort at Sokoto instead of Satiru. When they arrived, they formed a protective screen in front of it in case the Mahdists came to attack. Attahiru II also sent instructions asking the emirs to provide warriors to help protect the surviving Britons. He voluntarily conceded his position of strength.

THE NORTHERN RESISTANCE

There are many plausible reasons to explain why Attahiru II and the emirs went to such lengths to support the British. Firstly, the revolt also potentially threatened the emirs. It seemed to be an insurrection against the established authorities, whether foreign or native. Although it is not certain that Attahiru II knew it at the time, the British claimed that most of the Mahdist corpses they saw at Satiru were Hausas and that many were slaves. This ethnic colouration could have pitted a dissident Hausa religious cult led by the *talakawa* against the ruling Fulani aristocracy led by Attahiru II. Secondly, Attahiru II owed his position to Lugard, who had killed his predecessor before installing him three years earlier. The fate of Attahiru II's predecessor was a reminder of what might happen to him if he declined to back Lugard.

With the knowledge that the native leadership was backing them, the WAFF started regrouping. Major Burdon acted as de facto interim leader of both the political and military administrations. He offered a £10 reward for the return of each corpse of the white officers killed at Satiru, and a £1 reward for the return of each native soldier's corpse.[6] The fact that Burdon considered a native soldier's life to be worth a tenth of a white man's should have hammered home to the native soldiers how little their employers valued them.

Burdon agreed to allow Sokoto forces under the marafa Muhammadu Maiturare to launch a raid on the Mahdists on 17 February, despite his initial reservations that natives protecting and fighting Britain's battles would lower British prestige. However, the Mahdists repelled them and they fled in disarray. The marafa was nearly killed. For the second time in three days, Privates Wurrikin and Zaria were again the heroes and saved the marafa's life. However, the Mahdists had won a second successive battle in only three days, and had humiliated both the British and Sokoto armies.

WHAT BRITAIN DID TO NIGERIA

Vengeance in Satiru

Lugard and Burdon were determined to have a rematch with the Mahdists and to punish them. Their desire to inflict revenge was so great that Attahiru II and other emirs sent horsemen and warriors to occupy the neighbouring villages around Satiru to block the Mahdists from dispersing, and to keep them at Satiru until Lugard could send reinforcements. They essentially made the Mahdists a static target. In their dispatches to the Colonial Office, Burdon and Lugard repeatedly stressed their desire to reinstate Britain's damaged 'prestige'. This desire stemmed from Lugard's conviction that an overwhelmingly disproportionate act of vengeance was required to re-establish British deterrence and discourage further religious rebellions, and that Preston-Hillary's 'anxiety to avoid bloodshed'[7] was responsible for the defeat on 14 February. British officials had also been incited by exaggerated accounts by locals who claimed that the slain British officers were tortured before being killed and that their corpses were mutilated after they died.

'The most bloodthirsty expedition in the history
of British military operations in Northern Nigeria'

Artillery officer Major Goodwin was given command of the revenge mission. Even though he had 'every confidence that with my present force I should defeat the enemy with heavy loss', he decided to wait for reinforcements because 'it was desirable that so dangerous a body of fanatics should be completely defeated'.[8] Troop reinforcements arrived from Zungeru, Lokoja and Kontagora. On 10 March 1906 Goodwin marched out to subdue the Mahdists with 517 soldiers and thousands of cavalrymen provided by Attahiru II and the emirs. Lugard admitted that the Mahdists were 'an almost unarmed rabble'.[9] There was little doubt about who was most likely to win a fight between a village group armed only with farming implements and an experienced, modern, trained professional army with machine guns and mounted cavalry, who had been drilled to fight in formation. Given the tremendous disparity of weaponry, what happened next can only be described as a ruthless massacre. A British historian has called it as 'the most bloodthirsty expedition in the history of British military operations in Northern Nigeria'.[10]

Goodwin wanted to entice the Mahdists en masse into the open where they would be cannon fodder for the Maxim guns. He ordered the infantrymen to form a square in the same field where their colleagues had been killed a month earlier. Goodwin then sent out Lt Fendall as bait to draw out the Mahdists. When they saw him, Fendall turned around and walked slowly back to the square without firing a shot. The Mahdists fell for the trap and emerged. Goodwin confessed that the Mahdists 'to my disappointment, did not come on in the dense masses I had hoped for, but in a loose straggling crowd'.[11] Goodwin let a group of about one hundred Mahdists advance to within 150 yards of the square, then ordered the Maxim guns to open fire. After mowing down this first group, the square moved on and cut down another group of Mahdists before moving to the east side of Satiru, which had been set ablaze by shell fire. The mounted infantry moved to the west side of Satiru, while Captain Gallagher (who had been wounded by an arrow that hit his elbow) led soldiers to the south side, where they went from house to house, charging in with bayonets and killing the occupants. Goodwin was pleased with their work and later said that Gallagher and his men 'went at the enemy with a dash which I have not seen equalled in this country'.[12]

With the village ablaze and soldiers conducting house-to-house mopping-up operations, some villagers fled, but Goodwin ordered his men to pursue them. The mounted infantry and the sarkin Musulmi's horsemen chased them wherever they went—in some cases five to ten miles outside Satiru. The seek-and-destroy chase went on for five hours from early morning until mid-afternoon. They dragged out those they found from their hiding places in the bush and killed them. To deal with any survivors they could not locate, they opened fire into the bush.

The killing was accompanied by extreme brutality on the part of both the WAFF and the native warriors that Attahiru II and his lieutenants supplied. They impaled some of the Mahdists on stakes and sliced off some women's breasts.[13] When the slaughter was over, approximately two thousand Satiru residents lay dead.

The WAFF and Sokoto cavalry took surviving women and children into custody and handed them over to Attahiru II 'for subsequent disposal'[14] (a euphemism for the likely distribution of the women as concubines). They also recovered the (unmutilated) corpses of the three British officers killed and buried them with full military honours, and retrieved the Maxim gun and rifles that the Mahdists had captured. Before leaving, they removed all animals[15] from Satiru, then burned and destroyed the village. Burdon reported that the day after the battle, 'All of Sokoto went out ... to inspect the battlefield and to raze Satiru to the ground. No wall or tree left standing.'[16] It was a biblical scene of death and destruction. Attahiru II cursed Satiru and issued an edict forbidding anyone to rebuild the village or undertake farming there. Over 116 years later, the land where Satiru once stood is now a forest. Satiru was wiped off the map.

The WAFF handed over the Mahdist leader, Dan Makafo (who had been shot and wounded in the leg), for trial before an Islamic court in Sokoto.[17] This was a deliberate measure to extract political capital from the fact that Makafo would be condemned by fellow Muslims and, in Lugard's view, 'to show the people how fully the native chiefs are identified with us'.[18] Makafo and some of his supporters were executed by hanging in the Sokoto market place. The executions became so enthusiastic that Lugard ordered a halt to further ones without his approval.

On 12 March, Attahiru II and other emirs attended a massive durbar. Lugard sent a note of gratitude which was read on his behalf. Britain rewarded Attahiru II the CMG for his services and loyalty in suppressing the revolt. The Companions of the Order of St Michael and St George seemed a strange honour to bestow upon a Muslim ruler. The soldiers who took part in the mission were also rewarded. Goodwin was promoted to brevet-major (local lieutenant-colonel), Captains Gallagher and MacDonnell and Lt Fendall of the Mounted Infantry were awarded the Distinguished Service Order, and Sergeants Maynard and Slack were awarded the Meritorious Service Medal. Native soldiers Sergeant Major Aliyu Arfam, Sergeant Awudu, Birnin Kano, Corporal Fajenyo and Private Nomad Bamba were awarded Distinguished Conduct Medals. Those who sent men and horses to support the British were also rewarded. Every single sarkin Musulmi for the next 32 years after the Satiru uprising was a man who supported the British assault on Satiru. These include Muhammadu Maiturare, who succeeded Attahiru II as sarkin Musulmi in 1915, Maiturare's son who succeeded him, and Hassan, who handed Dan Makafo over into British custody, and who became sarkin Musulmi in 1931.

They killed every living thing before them

Lugard carefully edited his reports to the Colonial Office to under-emphasise the extent of the atrocities. However, Lugard's letter to his wife, in which he freely admitted to his desire to 'annihilate' the Mahdists and remarked that 'the slaughter of these poor wretches has been terrible',[19] left no doubt as to his intent and awareness regarding what happened. Nonetheless, Lugard's successor as high commissioner, William Wallace, investigated events at Satiru and found that 'killing was very free, not to say slaughter ... they killed every living thing before them' and that fields were 'running with blood'.[20] The atrocities also came to the attention of Lugard's younger brother Edward, who was his trusted confidant and assistant. Edward Lugard, Wallace and other officials 'buried' the investigation and withheld it from Parliament and the public. However, events did not escape the attention of the undersecretary of state for the colonies, Winston Churchill, who did not take pleasure from 'this extermination of an almost unarmed rabble' and asked, 'How long is this sort of thing going to escape Parliamentary attention and what will happen when it attracts it?'[21]

After eliminating Satiru, Lugard went on to settle other scores. Lugard alleged that before being executed, Makafo claimed that the emir of Gwandu had promised to support him. As a result Lugard ordered the emir to be arrested and deposed. Lugard also did not forget the passive resistance of the town of Hadejia. In April 1906 he delivered an ultimatum to the emir, ordering him to arrest and hand over eight people who were the alleged fomenters of anti-British hostility in the town, to demolish part of the town's defensive wall, and to ensure that the town's residents surrendered all their weapons. Lugard also offered the emir the choice of going into exile at Katagum if he was unable to comply with the demands. The emir had one day to reply. Lugard must have been spoiling for a fight and knew that the emir could not agree to such humiliating terms. Even if he wanted to agree to Lugard's terms, he could hardly do so without risking a revolt or assassination at the hands of his own people. The emir declined to do Lugard's bidding and replied that if the British wanted to make arrests, they should do it themselves. Lugard also alleged that the emir slapped the messenger who delivered the ultimatum. Lugard thus got what he wanted: an excuse to attack the emir. He dispatched Lt-Colonel

Lowry-Cole, who marched into Hadejia with soldiers and, after five hours of raids, killed the emir and three of his sons. Lowry-Cole's men then destroyed a 150-yard section of the town's walls. Hadejia was the last of the Fulani emirates to fall into British hands. Lugard installed a new emir and moved the emirate's headquarters to Katagum.

The comprehensive root-and-branch destruction of the Mahdists does not diminish the significance of their rebellion in Nigeria's history. It was simultaneously a portent of further religious radicalism in Northern Nigeria, a missed opportunity for the region's rulers to test the strength of British rule, and a close shave for the British. After the utter devastation at Satiru, uprisings against British rule became rare in Northern Nigeria. British supremacy had been restored and greatly amplified. Notable exceptions to this were the Tiv, who were restive and menaced the British with mysterious poisoned arrows that killed those who were struck within a few hours. The British found it difficult to identify the source of the poison despite conducting toxicology tests on the arrows. But there was also another innovative but largely overlooked rebellion in the north-east area of Northern Nigeria.

'The small Chibbuk tribe of savages'

Another notable act of resistance in 1906–7 was that of people who dwelt in the area around the Chibok Hills of the north-east. These hill dwellers incurred the wrath of the British by coming down and raiding trading routes on the plains below. The ethnicity of the raiders is uncertain because British reports described them as 'the small Chibbuk tribe of savages'.[22] The 'Chibbuk' people that the British referred to were from the Chibok area, home to the Kibaku and Marghi ethnic groups. Either one or both of them could have been responsible. For ease of reference I will refer to them as the Chibok.

WHAT BRITAIN DID TO NIGERIA

The British did not seem to know much about the cave- and hill-dwelling ethnic groups that successfully escaped or resisted the Fulani jihad. The dwellers of the Chibok Hills had fled to high ground in the 18th and 19th centuries to resist both the jihad of Usman dan Fodio and the Kanem-Borno Empire. They still remained independent of both empires and also managed to avoid control by the British administration.

In late November 1906, 170 WAFF horsemen and foot soldiers commanded by Lieutenants Chapman and Chaytor headed for the hills to deal with the Chibok. As the WAFF tried to clear the Chibok, the latter ensconced themselves inside an elaborate maze of tunnels and caves in the hills where they had stored food and water.

'Conditions extraordinarily difficult and nerve trying'

Every time the WAFF tried to take the hills, they suffered casualties as the Chibok shot poisoned arrows at them through holes in the cave walls. After eleven days of intense fighting, 10 WAFF soldiers lay dead and another 40 were wounded. The British resident in the area reported:

> a series of the most stubborn fighting for 11 days, in which our troops met with such determined resistance as has seldom, if ever, been seen in the Protectorate; and I venture to state my deliberate opinion that no military operations have taken place during the last seven years in which the troops engaged had such genuine fighting to do under conditions extraordinarily difficult and nerve trying.[23]

After the mission, Lt Chaytor saved 15 arrows that the hillsmen had fired at them and donated them to the British Museum. The resident at Borno promised the Chibok that if they surrendered and accepted colonial rule, Britain would bring development to their area. They rejected such assurances and refused to surrender. The high commissioner for Northern Nigeria,

William Wallace, admitted that 'our troops met the most determined lot of fighters'.[24]

In mid-December 1906, another WAFF detachment of 80 soldiers commanded by Lt Wolseley tried to expel the Chibok from their caves. Wolseley was familiar with the hills, but when his men attacked, a soldier was killed and another 12 were wounded. After taking poisoned arrow shots 'from unseen foes, in passages to which daylight did not penetrate',[25] Wolseley abandoned the idea of trying to capture the caves. He instead decided to lay siege to them and 'starve out' the Chibok by waiting until their food and water supply ran out. However, the Chibok were experienced cave fighters, were prepared for a siege and had stored enough food and water to sustain them until the next rainy season. WAFF officers became concerned that 'if the hillsmen had held the caves and tunnels no force on earth without artillery could have removed them'.[26]

However, the WAFF had a lucky break when they inadvertently stumbled upon the Chibok's natural water supply in the centre of the hill. By cutting the Chibok off from their water supply, the WAFF made them vulnerable, and after three months of arduous and attritional fighting, in February 1907 the hillsmen dispersed to the surrounding countryside. However, the matter did not end there. The Chibok were determined to continue fighting wherever they went and they maintained their resistance from their new village locations. A Briton who travelled through nearby areas reported: 'some of the more turbulent spirits had escaped from the rocks and found refuge in the villages around, whose foolish inhabitants they were again stirring up to hostility against their British masters'.[27]

Major Alder Burdon
and Hausa soldiers.

A Hausa village in
the 1800s.

Sir George Taubman Goldie.

A Nupe man in the late 1800s.

A Fulani man in the late 1800s.

Lord Frederick Lugard.

Flora Shaw
(Lady Lugard).

House of the British Resident at Zaria, early 1900s.

Britain installing a new Emir of Zaria after deposing the previous Emir, 1903.

A compound in Zaria, Northern Nigeria, early 1900s.

Location in Lokoja where the Royal Niger Company's flag was lowered and
replaced with the Union Jack on 1 January, 1900.

An Igbo woman's hairstyle –
early 1900s.

Members of an Igbo masquerade.

Soldiers of the Royal Niger
Constabulary in the late 1800s.

Overami, the Oba of Benin.

Captain Alan Boisragon (right) – commandant of the Niger Coast Protectorate Force, and Ralph Locke (district commissioner of Warri), both of whom survived the Benin Massacre of 1897.

Ologbosere with his hands and legs chained after being arrested by British troops in 1899.

King Jaja of Opobo.

King Jaja's palace in Opobo.

Horsemen riding to meet Lugard.

Mary Slessor's adopted daughter,
Janie, holding babies.

Mary Slessor and a young
Nigerian boy she is
caring for, 1910.

Alake of Egbaland.

Bishop Ajayi Crowther and members of his clergy in the 1800s.

A group of Yoruba women in the late 1800s.

A group of women and children from Opobo in the late 1800s.

15

EKUMEKU

THE SILENT ONES

Indigenous resistance against Britain was not limited to force or armed opposition. Nigerians also adopted other methods such as supernatural and spiritual protection, misinformation and manipulation ('psy-ops' or 'psychological warfare' in modern terms) and civil disobedience. South-eastern Nigeria deployed all three methods. Resistance against British colonial rule in south-eastern Nigeria was so widespread that an entire book could be devoted to it.

Spiritual and Supernatural Resistance

Following the Aro war of 1902 and British alarm about the large number of guns that natives possessed, Britain forbade the importation of guns, weapons and materials that could be used to make weapons. Whenever Britain subdued a community, they also adopted the routine practice of disarming it and destroying all of its weapons. It may have appeared to the British that such communities had been 'pacified' or were 'loyal'. However, the natives often resorted to insidious resistance such as spiritual and supernatural warfare. In a perverse way, resorting to such practices increased the risk of the British using force against them. For instance, when communities invoked supernatural intervention by sacrificing animals or humans, practices the British abhorred, these would be used by the British as a justification for the use of force. Yet supernatural invocation continued.

'The Haunted Rest House'

In south-eastern Nigeria, the Igbos consulted *dibia* (native doctors and supernatural practitioners) for help against the British. The belief in the effectiveness of such supernatural practices was not limited to the natives. The British district officer Frank Hives once had a terrifying time at a government rest house in the Bende district which was built on a site cursed by a *dibia*. Hives was so distraught by his night in the house that he burned it down and built a new one in a different location. Afterwards he wrote an account of it, which he prefaced by saying: 'I can only say that I am relating exactly what I saw. I attempt no explanation—for to me the thing is unexplainable.'[1] Hives' account of his experience at what he called 'the Haunted Rest House' is worth recounting in his own words:

> [I] could not get away from the feeling that something was watching me ... as I looked—the chair was drawn back to the wall, so that the leg rest fell with a clatter to the hard mud floor ... What could have caused the chair to move? Nothing was visible ... Then the table was suddenly moved to one side as though some invisible hand had dragged it, and the chair toppled right over! ... At the same time the eerie feeling returned, together with what I might describe as a sense of some impending horror that sent cold shivers down my spine. My scalp felt as though it was being loosened, and my teeth chattered with cold. I sat there petrified, utterly unable to move

hand or foot, in expectant terror ... I saw something move just outside the opening in the veranda wall, where the stench was coming from ... The first thing I saw was what I took to be the head of a very old native. Then the rest of the body appeared, crawling very slowly on hands and knees and not making a sound. Presently the creature came within the radius of the lamplight so that I could see it more clearly. A more horrible sight I have never seen, a more loathsome thing I hope never to see ... Then I fired two shots in rapid succession at point-blank range, expecting to see the body fall. But nothing happened. The creature continued to climb, eventually reaching the rafters, trailing the rope behind, but making absolutely no sound. I then stood up, reached out until the muzzle of the revolver was only three or four feet from the mark, and fired again. Still nothing happened, and the figure continued to climb. I knew then that it could not be human.[2]

Later, when Hives travelled to the Efik-speaking area (in modern Cross River State), he met an aggrieved woman who blamed him for her son's imprisonment. The woman cursed Hives, and he admitted that she hypnotised him and placed a snake curse on him. In the next three days he unaccountably encountered fifteen different snakes, including a five-feet-long snake in his bed and others that appeared in his boots and stationery rack, and wherever he went. Hives admitted that after the woman's curse, 'snakes seemed to follow me round'.[3]

In another example, when the military barracks at Abakaliki were destroyed by fire, the local people attributed the misfortune to supernatural causes.[4] After spending two decades among the Efik people of south-eastern Nigeria, the Scottish missionary Mary Slessor began to believe in the efficacy of some native medicine. A British historian was equally convinced of its effectiveness:

I think that it is possible that Igboland's *dibia* were developing real skills—or sciences—in the sphere of what we would now call extrasensory perception. The imposition of colonial rule has basically put an end to these skills, and deflected Igbo intellectual energies into such 'modern' spheres as medicine or physics. It is possible that in doing so it cut off a real and original advance of the human mind, and impoverished the total development of human knowledge.[5]

'Much injustice and oppression has been unwittingly done by our forces'

After the natives realised that the British forces had far better weapons than they did, they learned to manipulate Britain's superior firepower and weaponry to their own advantage. Colonialism was not just a binary conflict between Britain and the natives. The latter had their own mutual grievances and squabbles, and when they realised that the new foreigners in their midst had power that eclipsed all of them, they tried to leverage that power to settle old scores. Some communities accused their enemies of things that they knew would turn the colonial authorities against them. One example is the conflict in the early 20th century between the two warring Igbo towns of Akokwa and Obodo. When they heard of the British destruction of the seemingly indestructible Aro Long Juju shrine, each side sought British intervention on its behalf. The Akokwa people sent a representative, Ukachukwu, to Bende to invite British intervention to help them to conquer Obodo. As a result Akokwa was the only town in the area not to be conquered, while the neighbouring towns were destroyed during British military raids in 1907. Britain subsequently appointed Ukachukwu as a warrant chief. It is likely that a great deal of unnecessary blood was spilled as a result of such manipulation. Even Lugard became concerned that British troops were being used unwittingly as a proxy force in native conflicts. He stated: 'it is my conviction that throughout Africa—East and West—much injustice and oppression has been unwittingly done by our forces acting on a crude information, and accusations of slaver-raiding, brought by enemies of the accused to procure their destruction.'[6]

In addition to the surreptitious acts of resistance described above, some communities were determined to confront the British with weapons despite the risk to themselves. This was particularly so in the Niger Delta area, which has a long history of instability and rebellion. In modern times the area has been known for insurgent activity connected to Nigeria's petroleum industry. Yet rebellion against authority in that part of West Africa did not start in 1966 with Isaac Adaka Boro's declared secession of the Niger Delta, or in 2003 with the insurgency waged by the Movement for the Emancipation of the Niger Delta. Subversive activity against authorities in the area began over a hundred years earlier. It was the location of the Nembe people's attack on the Royal Niger Company's factory at Akassa in 1895, and of the most intense and long-running resistance to the British presence in Nigeria's history.

The Silent Ones

The land that the Igbos of south-eastern Nigeria inhabit is bisected into western and eastern segments by the River Niger. Igbos living in the western part are often referred to in modern times as Anioma, Ika-Igbo or Ikwerre. They live in an area lying between their fellow Igbos to the eastern side of the river and the historical lands of the great Benin kingdom to their west. Men from a shadowy organisation in this part of Igboland waged the most ferocious and longest organised insurgency against the British presence in Nigeria.

'A peculiarly venomous native secret society'

Over a dozen previously disunited communities spread over an area of 800 square miles overcame their mutual antagonisms and joined forces to oppose British invasion of their lands and attempts to abolish their culture and religion.[7] For 13 years between the late 19th and early 20th centuries, a group of mysterious insurgents attacked, burned and destroyed British court buildings, government rest houses, mission stations, and the houses and livestock of natives who assisted the British. The insurgency so menaced the colonial authorities that in some areas around the town of Asaba in the Niger Delta, British officials dared not venture out into villages without armed escorts. The British struggled to understand the shadowy insurgents who operated in silence, only at night, and who were never seen during the day. They used several unflattering descriptions to refer to them, including 'a peculiarly venomous native secret society',[8] 'bands of raiders ... responsible for a vast amount of havoc in the districts where they operated',[9] and an 'anti-foreign secret society'.[10] The insurgents preferred to make their intentions known by actions rather than words. Their modus operandi of moving and fighting in complete silence earned them the nickname of 'the Silent Ones'.

Who were the insurgents? Many African societies have or had secret sodalities that predated the British arrival. Their purpose varied from one society to another. Some prepared and initiated youths into adulthood, acted as educational institutions for the transmission of knowledge from adults to children, while others emerged only at times of public celebration and pageantry. Examples of significant West African secret societies include the Poro and Sande of the Mande people of Liberia and Sierra Leone. Owing to their tendency to dismiss these sodalities as nothing more than superstitious cults, the British blinded themselves to their importance, and allowed an insurgency to take them by surprise. In a community without a professional standing army, the natives surreptitiously converted a secret society into a guerrilla opposition movement to confront the British.

The Igbos also had secret societies. In Nigeria's documented history, the names of British explorers, soldiers and colonial officers are frequently referred to. Yet the names of those they conquered or killed, or those who opposed them are rarely mentioned. Even when they are, they are usually given anonymously in casualty statistics. However, the names of a group of warriors who resisted the British still lives on in the oral traditions and history of their communities in the western part of Igboland, who recall them in tales of nostalgic valour similar to that which the British have for Richard the Lionheart, or the French for Napoleon. Its leaders included King Nzekwe of Ogwashi-Uku; Dunkwu, Elumelu and Chiejina of Onitsha-Olona; and Idegwu, Mordi (a renowned marksman) and Nwoko from Ubulu-Uku. These men belonged to a deadly and feared secret society known as *Ekwumekwu* (or 'Ekumeku').

The name Ekumeku has a complex and disputed etymology. According to one historian, 'The word ... in its indigenous meaning is onomatopoeic, conveying the idea of a whirlwind or something fast, devastating, invisible and yet forcefully real.'[11] While the name has no direct English translation, another academic says that it is synonymous with words such as 'hurricane', 'invincible' or 'whirlwind'.[12] A plausible explanation for the origin of the group's name is that it is a corrupted, anglicised transliteration of the Igbo phrase '*Ekwuna okwu*' ('do not speak' or 'be silent'). The disputed nature of the group's name added to its attraction and mystique, creating much gossip and rumour among villagers, and a mythological sense of their omnipresence. A British missionary who resided in Igboland reported that 'they went here, there and everywhere, swiftly and silently'.[13]

'The most formidable confederation in the country'

Despite the opaque origin of its name, it is undisputed that, for 13 years between 1898 and 1911, the group operated a guerrilla army that one Briton admitted was 'the most formidable confederation in the country lying between Asaba and Benin' (in Delta and Edo States in modern Nigeria).[14] Ekumeku emerged in, and capitalised on, the mutinous climate of opinion against the British in Asaba and surrounding areas to mount opposition against British attempts to force cultural, political and religious changes on the community. The people of the area had become extremely bitter after losing the right to trade in their own homelands to the Royal Niger Company, and seeing their towns and villages continually bombarded by the company's gunboats or burned to the ground by its Constabulary. In 1882 HMS *Flirt* shelled and destroyed Asaba and its neighbouring towns in retaliation for a native attack that destroyed the company's store in Asaba. In 1888 the company again destroyed half of Asaba in an attempt to force its residents to stop slavery and the practice of sacrificing humans to commemorate the burial of prominent chiefs.

Ekumeku was a nocturnal organisation. Their habit of meeting and attacking only at night and in complete silence unnerved British army officers and the Hausa troops under their command. The group's members maintained the utmost secrecy regarding their leaders, initiation rites, operational locations, and members. They swore lifelong oaths of allegiance and secrecy to each other, and adopted several methods to maintain that secrecy. Communication between members was usually conducted by non-verbal means such as gesticulation using signals that could be recognised only by other members. Examples included covert finger gestures intelligible only to members, or the shaking of bullet containers in a manner that signalled the time of their meetings.[15] They also employed a trumpeter who blew his horn to convey coded messages about battle plans and the location of British troops. They used emissaries to pass on messages between their members in different villages. While fighting and moving at night, they prevented death from 'friendly fire' by covering their bodies with white chalk, which served as their 'uniform'.

Although a Briton claimed that 'The king of Issele-Ukwu was the accredited head of the whole society',[16] it is unlikely that Ekumeku had a single, paramount leader. The intensity of its activities in Issele-Ukwu (in modern-day Delta State) may have given others the impression that this town was the unofficial 'capital' of the Ekumeku. They were more akin to a federation or a franchise. However, their members included or were supported by prominent local chiefs, who had good reasons to support Ekumeku. Native courts and British-appointed warrant chiefs had stripped them of their power, and Christian missionaries who preached the equality of all men and the evil of human sacrifice also threatened the interests of wealthy chiefs and slave owners. From the chiefs' perspective, such doctrines incited their slaves to rebellion.

Ekumeku directed resistance at four manifestations of British authority in their lands: British soldiers, Christian missionaries, the Royal Niger Company and, later, the British colonial administration, which succeeded the company. Ekumeku tended to conflate all four groups and see them as one and the same emanation of the British presence. This was not necessarily a mistake given the extraordinary level of collusion and cooperation between the four groups. For example, one of the incidents that ignited the insurgency involved cooperation between the Church, the Royal Niger Company and British troops. The company's chief justice, Sir James Marshall, who was a clergyman and regarded the Niger Delta area as a 'devil's stronghold',[17] invited an Italian Roman Catholic priest, Father Carlo Zappa, to establish a Catholic mission in Asaba, from where Zappa and other Catholic priests proselytised and converted many natives to Christianity. Relations between Zappa and the Royal Niger Company were so cordial that they gave him a gold watch as a gift. British army officers also gave him a gold-mounted revolver.[18] When Obi Egbuna, a native chief of Issele-Ukwu, converted to Christianity, he also gave land to Roman Catholic missionaries, allowed them to build a mission there, manumitted over a hundred of his slaves, and forbade certain religious practices. The last action splintered Issele-Ukwu society between those who supported the obi—mainly Christian converts and freed slaves—and those who were outraged that a prominent man in society not only abandoned the religion of his community, but also tried to force the foreigners' religion on them. Zappa appealed to the Royal Niger Company to intervene. In response, 300 of the company's Constabulary troops under the command of Major Arthur Festing entered the area in January 1898 to burn and destroy anti-missionary villages. Six weeks of intense fighting ensued between the Constabulary and Ekumeku.

Although Ekumeku attacks were sporadic, the most intense fighting occurred in 1898, 1902, 1904, 1906 and 1910. The conflict settled into a pendulum pattern, with Ekumeku attacks followed by British collective punishment, followed by more uprisings in response to the punishment, followed by even more severe punishment.

'Every man from youth up carries a gun, and knows how to use it'

A British army officer who faced the Igbos in combat claimed that Igbos were 'constitutionally lazy and treacherous', yet in the next sentence he acknowledged that they 'spend most of their time hunting. Every man from youth up carries a gun, and knows how to use it.'[19] Many Igbo men were hunters and accurate marksmen. They gained experience of shooting at moving targets from a distance while hunting animals. Some Igbo communities also had a strong martial tradition that accorded honour to warriors who proved their valour in battle. Many of them had acquired battle experience during the frequent fights between Igbo villages. Such warriors were given privileges in life, and honorific burials when they died. The residents of many Igbo villages were also related to each other by blood or marriage. Igbo villages thus sometimes operated almost as one large extended family with strong bonds of social affinity. Consequently, a British attack on an Igbo village may have been interpreted as an attack on an entire family. British bombardment and harassment was unlikely to produce peaceful results when the communities targeted were unaccustomed to centralised political control, but had many able-bodied young men who carried weapons, knew how to shoot, and had experience of battle.

British Responses to Ekumeku

The British regarded Ekumeku as a bandit organisation and employed three methods to crush the insurgency: collective punishment, ruthless military force, and the recruitment of collaborators and informants from the indigenous population. In 1902, a British provincial commissioner, Widenham Fosbery, toured the Asaba areas. When he arrived in Okpanam, he ordered local chiefs to provide 30 carriers to assist British troops. When the chiefs mustered only 12 carriers, he warned them that they themselves would be conscripted as carriers if they did not provide more. Younger chiefs fled in response to Fosbery's ultimatum, but troops arrested five elderly chiefs who were too frail to flee and refused to release them until the requisite number of carriers had been provided.[20] The knowledge that openly assisting the British made one a candidate for elimination by Ekumeku may have made the Okpanam chiefs reluctant to help the British. Ekumeku often sent messengers to warn people to stop cooperating with the British, and attacked those who refused to heed the warning. For example, in 1902 residents of the village of Oko-Okwe attacked a policeman who came to the village and tore his uniform to shreds. They then burned down the house of the resident who had made the original complaint that brought the policeman to the village and butchered his livestock.[21]

British troops launched a military crackdown against Ekumeku and villages where the group was suspected of operating from or those deemed uncooperative in delivering suspected Ekumeku members into British custody. Throughout the entire month of December 1902, troops launched military assaults against villages in the Asaba area such as Onitsha-Olona and Ogwashi-Ukwu. They burned houses to the ground and destroyed entire villages. They also refused to allow the residents to rebuild their houses until the Ekumeku leaders surrendered. However, this military crackdown failed to crush the rebellion. British interrogation of natives had limited effect because Ekumeku members swore to maintain the group's secrets. The movement's internal rules made the disclosure of information about the group to non-members an immense sacrilege punishable by death. Meanwhile, those who were not members could not provide much useful information, even if they wanted to, about a nocturnal group they knew only from rumour and folk tales.

Resistance also manifested itself in civil disobedience. Some Igbo communities withdrew cooperation with British authorities. For example, when Mr Boyle, the district commissioner of Asaba, tried to visit Ubulu-Uku in 1903, he was turned back and warned that the residents would not allow any government representative to enter their town. Residents of Issele-Ukwu and Ogwashi-Ukwu boycotted native courts, ignored their summonses, and refused to appear before them.

'Fighting against an enemy who is never visible'

In January 1904 Ekumeku attacked and destroyed four different Christian Missionary Society stations, a Roman Catholic mission and two native courthouses. They also murdered an Issele-Ukwu chief who was friendly with missionaries and the British. In response, British troops under Captain Ian Hogg marched out on 17 January 1904 with 225[22] troops and attacked 17 different towns. Severe fighting with Ekumeku ensued. Hogg complained that 'fighting against an enemy who is never visible ... and whose position can only be determined by the smoke from his gun hanging round the dense undergrowth, is trying to the nerves of any troops'.[23] When his troops camped, Ekumeku harassed them with rifle fire and shot dead any sentries or troops who strayed even a few yards outside the camp's outskirts. To move outside the range of sniper fire, Hogg had to clear the bush surrounding the camp 'for a greater distance than in any previous camp I have known owing to the strong charges of the snipers here'.[24] The Ekumeku resistance was so considerable that Hogg called for reinforcements on 11 February. The decisive battle was fought in the town of Ubulu-Uku where Hogg's troops destroyed the chief's compound. After three months of fighting the British imposed fines on 12 towns for sheltering Ekumeku members, arrested and imprisoned over 250 Ekumeku supporters, and ordered them to pay compensation to towns and the families of those killed, and to rebuild all mission stations and courthouses they had destroyed. Yet such punishments did not end the insurgency.

Ekumeku's reputation became so fearsome that it was automatically blamed for any attack against British citizens or facilities, whether or not they were in fact responsible. One example involves the tyrannical district commissioner for the Agbor region, Oswald Crewe-Read. Crewe-Read was not a popular man among the natives. He was in the habit of conscripting them for unpaid forced labour and ordering chiefs who offended him to be flogged in public. On 8 June 1906 Crewe-Read summoned all the chiefs of the village of Owa for a meeting. When the chiefs did not appear at the time he demanded, Crewe-Read sent police officers to arrest one of them, Ekuti. Ekuti's supporters resisted his arrest and drove the officers away. However, the act of an already unpopular colonial commissioner ordering the physical manhandling of a chief outraged the community, and some of Ekuti's supporters shot and killed Crewe-Read. Missionaries and the colonial government automatically held Ekumeku responsible for his murder, even though this seemed to be a spontaneous act of revenge by the Owa community rather than a premeditated Ekumeku attack.

'The most severe fighting which has occurred in the country'

In reaction, 200 soldiers under the command of Captain E.W. Rudkin of the Royal Field Artillery were deployed to carry out the usual punitive reprisal. However, this encounter would be different and turned into a military quagmire for the British troops. Trying to punish the Owa people precipitated what a British officer described as 'the most severe fighting which has occurred in the country'.[25] Although it is not certain that Ekumeku was involved in the ensuing conflict, the episode is worth recounting in depth because the tactics and intensity of the defenders were reminiscent of them. The native fighters included not only Ika-Igbos but also fighters from neighbouring ethnic groups such as the Afenmai and Esan.

Constant exposure to British military assaults actually improved the natives' battle proficiency and fire discipline when using their rifles. Having become accustomed to British military methods, they adjusted their tactics accordingly and also demonstrated great improvisation against a better-trained and armed enemy. When he encountered the native fighters, Captain Rudkin noticed enhancements in their aptitude:

> They have learnt that a gun aimed from the shoulder at twenty yards is more effective than one fired from the hip at fifty or a hundred. They realise that bloodcurdling yells are not a necessary accompaniment, but a waste of breath, and have neither the effect of making a gun shoot straight nor of making the white man turn tail.[26]

They also adapted their tactics to the topography of the land by concealing themselves in trenches dug inside thick bush where they placed snipers and shot at the advancing British troops. Another of their favoured tactics was to slow down British troops by setting booby traps along footpaths where they marched. A common trap consisting of digging trenches, placing poisoned stakes inside them, then concealing the trench with earth and tree branches. In 1896, one of these booby traps badly injured a native officer in the Niger Coast Protectorate Force, Lt Daniels, who fell into a trap and sustained a nasty injury when a stake drove through his thigh.

'One could not help admiring their tenacity and the stout resistance'

To clear the snipers from their hiding places, Rudkin's troops tried charging into the bush, but abandoned this tactic when they kept losing three or four soldiers to enemy fire each time. Rudkin realised that 'this was going to be a much bigger thing than we had anticipated' and admitted that 'the position was extremely critical now, and we could not gain a yard for two hours'.[27] For the next three months, the native fighters engaged in attritional bush warfare during which the British troops twice called in reinforcements of 110 and 130 soldiers in June and July respectively (more than doubling the number of soldiers on the mission to 434)[28] and more ammunition. Forty per cent of men in two British army companies were killed or wounded.[29] The fighting continued until August 1906 when the British troops captured the towns of Owa and Agbor, and killed Ekuti in the latter. The British lost 19 soldiers and at least another 113[30] were wounded during the battles. Rudkin was awarded the Distinguished Service Order medal after the battle, and 15 native soldiers were given commendations. Rudkin was full of admiration for his adversaries, whom he described as 'a bold and well-trained enemy ... One could not help admiring their tenacity and the stout resistance they showed.'[31] Five of the ringleaders were publicly executed by hanging at Agbor and the rest were imprisoned.

Fence-sitters were caught between the rock and hard place choices of constant collective punishment meted out by the British and reprisals by Ekumeku for collaboration. The British destroyed the entire village or town of anyone who harboured or cooperated with Ekumeku members, while those who helped the British rendered themselves liable to being attacked by the movement. The severity of British collective punishment created pressure on residents to turn informant and allowed British authorities to infiltrate the group. Those with incentives to become British informants included warrant chiefs, Christian converts and slaves who gained their freedom because of the activities of missionaries. Each of these categories owed its status to the British to some extent. Some Christian converts whom Ekumeku attacked took refuge at Christian missions for their own safety. Thereafter Christian missionaries gained a curious level of knowledge about Ekumeku. For example, a decade after the insurgency, a British missionary drafted a surprisingly detailed description of Ekumeku operations.[32] The fact that British authorities held so many Ekumeku members and others from their community as prisoners also provided them with vital sources of intelligence. Somehow the British learned that in some areas Ekumeku members who had killed in battle tied a special ribbon around their wrist. Such knowledge that allowed them to identify and apprehend other Ekumeku members was very unlikely to have been obtained without the testimony of an Ekumeku informant. There have also been allegations about the source of these leaks. Chief Onwudiaju Okpabu of Issele-Asagba was allegedly 'considered to be the greatest traitor of the *Ekumeku* resistance movement and most visible informant to the British officials. He was reported to have sabotaged the movement,'[33] by divulging its secrets and strategies to the British. Another alleged British collaborator was Obi Egbuna of Issele-Ukwu, whose conversion to Christianity and abolition of traditional indigenous religious practices was one of the causes of the insurgency.

Ekumeku also made a mistake that aided the British. They changed their tactics. Instead of using guerrilla attacks, as they had done before, they began to garrison themselves inside their towns and villages. This robbed them of the element of omnipresence and surprise that had so unnerved their enemies. By remaining in fixed locations, the British could confront them by invading one village after another.

British authorities also took other stern measures to eliminate the group. They established night-time patrols, enacted laws that forbade night-time travel without the carrying of a lantern or torch for identification, prohibited the carrying of weapons and knives unless one was going to and from a farm during the day, and in October 1910 enacted the Unlawful Society Ordinance, which classified and banned Ekumeku as an illegal organisation and made membership of it a crime. The combination of penal legislation, collective punishment of Ekumeku-supporting communities, and leaks from collaborators chiselled away at the movement. The group made a last stand in 1910 after which many of its leaders were arrested and subjected to mass trial, execution, imprisonment or exile in October 1911. Two hundred were imprisoned in Calabar where several of the inmates committed suicide or died of disease. Only five of the 200 prisoners were still alive a year later.[34]

Destruction and fines economically devastated the towns and villages where Ekumeku operated. Some men divorced their wives, as they were no longer able to maintain large households and pay the fines imposed. The crushing of the insurgency not only eliminated Ekumeku's threat, but also consolidated British power in the Igbo-speaking areas of the Niger Delta, weakened Igbo chiefs, and reinforced the power of the warrant chiefs appointed by Britain.

The area where Ekumeku emerged remained a military hotspot in Nigeria's history. Okpanam, near Asaba, is the ancestral home of the most prominent figure behind Nigeria's first military coup in January 1966, Major Chukwuma Kaduna Nzeogwu. People from the Asaba area still recall Ekumeku with nostalgic reverence and some proudly claim to be descended from its warriors. A memorial statue of Ekumeku warriors still stands in Asaba to this day.

16

THE WOMEN'S WARS

Armed resistance to British rule in south-east Nigeria substantially decreased in the 1920s after Britain disarmed the native population. However, protest movements did not entirely disappear but instead took on a different form. Protest became characterised by civil rights and civil disobedience campaigns. Because so many of the British administrators in Nigeria, and the local rulers who acted as their political proxies, were men, it is tempting to dismiss the role of women in colonial Nigeria as one of passive witnesses. Although not characterised by the spectacular violence of men's protests, women's protests played an influential role in altering the contours of colonial rule.

Arguably the most impactful and prominent of these was a protest movement staged by women in south-eastern Nigeria. These events have taken on near-legendary proportions and are still fondly recalled in Igboland as *Ogu Umunwanyi* (the Women's War). As often happens, what started as an innocuous misunderstanding between two individuals snowballed far beyond the intention of its protagonists. It began as a protest against the manhandling of a woman, and escalated into a protest against taxation, then into a protest against the excesses of warrant chiefs, and eventually into a protest against the entire colonial system. Although like the other uprisings discussed in this book, it represented an attempt to turn back time and restore south-eastern society to its pre-British form, this rebellion was also different from the others because it was spontaneous and was led and carried out exclusively by women. It also changed the traditional narrative of pre-colonial African women, which presented them as passive and powerless agents in a patriarchal society.

It is important to give the broader context of the history and structure of taxation in Nigeria so that what happened next is not viewed in isolation. Britain's policy of making its colonies generate their own revenue to finance the cost of colonial administration led to the introduction of new taxes on the natives. These taxes created new sources of friction between the British authorities and the natives. The background to the Women's War lies in the government's decision in 1928 to extend direct taxation to the south-eastern provinces. Britain had already introduced taxation in Northern Nigeria in 1906, and in the Yoruba areas of the south-west in 1916 and 1917. It could be applied in those areas as a logical extension of the pre-colonial practice of giving 'tributes' in the form of gifts to emirs and obas. However, taxation was a difficult concept to implement in the Niger Delta and south-east, which did not have the tax collection precedents and structures that existed in northern and south-western Nigeria. Even when south-eastern communities pooled funds, they usually did so on a village-by-village basis, and not region-wide, as the British envisaged. Concerns about introducing taxation to the south-east led Britain to postpone its implementation until 1926. But taxation could not be deferred forever. To British administrators it was simple logic. The rest of Nigeria paid taxes, and it was inequitable for the south-east to be exempt from a taxation scheme that applied elsewhere. In 1927 the government conducted a census of men, after which men in the south-east were ordered to pay tax. However, another tactlessly implemented census in 1929 created unsettling anxiety and rumours that taxation would be extended to women, in a society in which men traditionally bore primary economic responsibility. This time women (and not only men) would be counted.

'Was your mother counted?'

In 1929 the assistant district officer for Owerri province, Captain John Cook, instructed the warrant chiefs to re-count people in the district in order to update the existing tax records. On Saturday 23 November 1929 a census enumerator named Mark Emeruwa arrived at a compound in the village of Oloko to count its occupants. In the compound Emeruwa encountered a woman from the Ngwa Igbo clan called Nwanyeruwa as she was processing palm oil. His questions to her about the number of women, cattle (which were usually owned by women), and children in the compound displeased Nwanyeruwa, who was mourning the death of her daughter-in-law at the time. In a community that values children and fertility, such questions are often viewed as sinister and unduly inquisitive. Nwanyeruwa objected to Emeruwa's enquiry by sarcastically asking him, 'Was your mother counted?' A physical altercation ensued between the two, with each blaming the other and claiming that they acted in self-defence. Emeruwa complained that Nwanyeruwa used her oil-stained hands to grab him and soil his uniform, and she alleged that Emeruwa grabbed her by the neck.

'Sitting on' the Men

Nwanyeruwa immediately passed on news of her contretemps with Emeruwa to other women in the community. They all agreed that, Emeruwa's interest in counting women was confirmation that the census was being conducted with an ulterior motive and that the day they dreaded, when taxation would be extended to women, had arrived. To them it was a replay of the previous census that was used to levy taxes on men. Nwanyeruwa and her colleagues sent emissaries carrying palm fronds to neighbouring villages and towns to mobilise other women to join them. The distribution of palm fronds was a cultural and symbolic distress call for help and solidarity and it had an incendiary effect.

The day after the altercation, women marched to the local warrant chief Okugo's residence to protest and 'sit on' his compound. The action of 'sitting on' is a literal translation from Igbo; it is a cultural metaphor for how Igbo women traditionally responded to, and sought redress from, men who had wronged them. This was usually done by besieging the home of the alleged offender, singing songs with lyrics detailing their grievances, and refusing to leave until he made amends. The closest modern equivalent would be a sit-down protest. Another physical altercation ensued during which Okugo's attendants and the compound residents drove the women away and injured three of them. The news of women being injured at Okugo's compound raised the temperature of an already volatile atmosphere. The women took their complaint to the district officer, Captain Hill, and both Emeruwa and Okugo were convicted of assault and sentenced to imprisonment terms of three months and two years respectively. Three thousand women came to watch Okugo's trial. Hill also accepted the women's demand for him to surrender Okugo's cap of office to them.

Emeruwa's and Okugo's convictions gave an electric charge to the protest. Within a few days news of the altercation between Emeruwa and Nwanyeruwa quickly spread, and over ten thousand women arrived from faraway towns such as Aba, Calabar,

Ikot-Ekpene and Umuahia to join the protests in and around
Oloko. Although the women assembled in Igbo-speaking areas,
many of them were from other ethnic groups such as the Efik
and Ibibio. They assembled outside the houses of detested warrant chiefs and ridiculed, shamed and taunted them in symbolic
ways, such as demanding that they hand over their red caps in
what was a symbolic stripping of their authority. They also
'occupied' roads that had been constructed by British colonial
authorities. The protests spread over an area of 6,000 square
miles. Warrant chiefs, native courts, factories, British-built
roads—their targets had an obvious correlation. All were agents
or products of the new order that British colonial authorities
had implemented.

The protests had at least four remarkable aspects: the speed
with which they spread, the fact that virtually all of the protesters were women, their impressive organisation, and their multi-
ethnic nature. The pace with which the women mobilised people
and resources was remarkable. They split responsibilities between
themselves, cooked food to sustain their comrades from other
villages, and appointed three women known as 'the Oloko trio'—
Ikonnia, Nwannedia and Nwugo—as their leaders and spokes-
women. The Oloko trio used their authority to urge the women
to keep the protests peaceful and exercised an extraordinary level
of control over them. For example, on 4 December, Captain Hill
summoned the trio and complained that women were obstructing trade at European factories in Umuahia. Although they
promised to speak to their comrades, Hill nonetheless expected
trouble and headed to Umuahia with 18 police officers. By the
time he arrived in Umuahia the next day he was astonished to
discover that 'there was scarcely a woman to be seen in the town'
and that 'the town was perfectly quiet and business proceeded as
usual'.[1] The protesters had dispersed on the orders of their leaders. This astonishing level of organisation, which allowed women

to assemble and disperse so rapidly, gives an indication of some intrinsic characteristics of female life in south-eastern Nigeria that made the protests possible and successful.

The women had certain pre-existing economic and social networks into which they tapped in order to organise the protests. For example, married women had a special social status in Igbo society. When a woman married, she not only automatically became a member of her husband's family and village, but also maintained familial links with her *umunna* (paternal relations) and *umunne* (maternal relations). Moreover, the post-partum Igbo tradition of *omugwo* whereby a woman would visit and stay with her daughters and daughters-in-law shortly after they gave birth, do household chores, and help nurse the newborn babies also created social bonds between mothers and the villages and communities where their daughters and sons resided. Thus one woman could simultaneously have familial and social affinities with several different communities. Many of the women were also so-called 'market women'—petty traders who sold food and vegetables in local markets. These market women usually belonged to women's market-trading clubs, which operated as unofficial trade unions, and to village associations. These clubs and associations had their own internal rules of membership and organisation, sanctions against members who violated the rules, and protocols that placed mandatory social obligations between their members. They also had a leadership hierarchy and zonal branches. As these groups transcended generations, grandmothers, mothers and daughters from the same family were often united in the same protests. Participation in the protest became a source of pride for the women.

'We did not think soldiers would fire at us'

The protests commenced largely in a non-violent, festive and almost playful manner. Protests consisted mainly of women

marching unarmed with palm fronds tied to their waists, dancing, and chanting songs to embarrass male warrant chiefs whom
they accused of corruption. However, an incident in Aba changed
the nature of the protests. When a large group of Ngwa women
assembled on the Aba–Owerrinta road on 11 December 1929
and refused to disperse to let cars pass, a medical doctor, William
Hunter, knocked down and seriously injured at least two women.
Hunter claimed that he did so out of concern for the safety of a
female European nurse who was a passenger in his car. While
Hunter presented it as an accident, the women claimed that he
deliberately accelerated and hit them in order to clear them from
the road. After the hit-and-run incident, Hunter took refuge at
a factory belonging to the United African Company. The inflic-
tion of casualties on the women made the protests become more
militant. After some women saw that a trading company was
harbouring Hunter, they started looting and vandalising
European factories elsewhere, and attacked and burned native
courts. These actions allowed the authorities to present the protests in unflattering terms as the 'Aba riots', which connoted
disorder and lawlessness.

Previous accounts usually gloss over or omit the extent of force
and violence that the security forces used against the women.
However, it is useful to consider whether the women really were
an objective threat to law and order and to the survival of the
government, as the British authorities claimed. There was a
strange discordance between the protesters' and the authorities'
assessments of the threat they posed to each other. The women
seemed unconcerned about their safety perhaps because of a mis-
placed confidence in stereotypes of British chivalry and gentlemanly behaviour towards women. They had heard, and naively
believed, that white men did not kill women. A woman named
Emena Okpopo said: 'We did not think soldiers would fire at
us.'[2] Conversely, at every opportunity British army and police

officers and administrators portrayed the women as threatening and wild, often described them as 'a mob', kept emphasising that the women were 'armed with sticks', and repeatedly warned of the danger of 'mobs of women in various degrees of frenzy armed with sticks and cudgels'.[3] The sticks the women were 'armed' with were palm leaf stems, which they used as symbols of solidarity rather than as weapons. This was the dynamic in a confrontation between unarmed women who were not afraid of armed police officers and soldiers, and British officers who walked around with revolvers but presented themselves as being in mortal danger from village women carrying leaves.

The protesters' stereotypes about British gentlemanly behaviour to women were rudely shattered in mid-December 1929. On 14 December, at Abak in the Annang-speaking areas, police tried to disperse protesters by charging them with rifle butts and bayonets, after which Captains Blackburne, Ford and James, and police constables opened fire at the area where the women were congregated. The police fired about 120 rounds.[4] Blackburne, who claimed that he fired warning shots at the women's feet to scare them, later admitted that he saw a group of elderly women in front of the protesters but concluded, 'I think I was over-lenient in not firing into the crowd.'[5]

Utu Etim Ekpo

Matters escalated the next day at Utu Etim Ekpo. Protesters there damaged a native court building and factory. This allowed security forces to present a stunningly exaggerated impression of the women's threat. They were preoccupied by the fear that the women would disarm trained infantry soldiers, take their weapons, and turn them against the British. Captain James of the police and Lt Browning of the army seemed particularly bellicose. James said, 'I feared that if the troops got involved in a hand to hand struggle with these mad women it was possible that some sort of reverse would have been sustained and the whole country would have been up.'[6] Such fears are difficult to rationalise. Although the women were vociferous, most of their attacks were against buildings. On the few occasions when they physically attacked people, their targets were African warrant chiefs, not the British. Not a single Briton was killed during the protests. Even the British-appointed commission of inquiry admitted that 'never once did they [protesters] succeed in inflicting upon them [the police and army] an injury more serious than a bruise, a scratch, or in one case only, a cut on the arm'.[7]

These mad women

Browning felt he knew the best way of dealing with natives: 'In my opinion when dealing with natives, to use half-hearted measures is hopeless; they get more confident and look on leniency and hesitation as weakness.'[8] When James and Browning saw the protesters walking along a road, James asked Browning to open fire on them. Browning brought out the Lewis machine gun, and he and the other soldiers opened fire with the machine gun and their rifles. They gave no verbal warnings before they started shooting. James and Browning claimed that the women were 'armed' with sticks and continued charging at them after they opened fire. So they kept shooting, killing 18 women and wounding many others. The women retreated, carrying their wounded with them as the soldiers followed them, stepping over corpses lying on the ground. The victims included the wife of a local chief named Akpan Umo, who had actually tried to help the police pacify the protesters. Two of Umo's other wives were also wounded. To James, the death of one of Umo's wives and the wounding of two others was not sufficient punishment. He ordered Umo's compound to be burned as a punishment for his failure to restrain the protesters, and also ordered other compounds to be burned until the protesters surrendered themselves and came in to 'submit'.[9]

Opobo, 16 December 1929

In another incident, at Opobo on 16 December 1929, thousands of women assembled outside a Native Administration office building and demanded assurances that they would not be taxed. The district officer, Arthur Whitman, saw women 'wearing short loin cloths and palm fronds, which he interpreted as a sign of solidarity and of hostile intention'.[10] Lt Hill of the 3rd Battalion, Nigeria Regiment, arrived from Uyo with 30 soldiers in a lorry. Before leaving Uyo, the resident at Calabar, Edward Morris Falk, with the approval of Hill's commander, Captain Drake-Brockman, gave Hill the following instructions: 'Do not hesitate to use ball cartridge in the defence of life and property; you must not allow any hostile crowd to get embroiled with the troops so that they could take their arms from them.'[11]

Sons of pigs

Quite why Falk and Drake-Brockman had to get Hill 'fired up', as if he was going to confront a dangerous group of warriors rather than elderly women and housewives singing and dancing, is perplexing. It is possible that the constant threat warnings about 'these mad women', 'frenzied mobs' and the possibility of soldiers being disarmed had prepared Hill mentally for battle. Hill walked up and down the fence separating the women from the building and told them to be quiet. Hill, who did not speak Annang, Ibibio or Igbo, claimed that he heard the women verbally abuse him and other soldiers by calling them 'sons of pigs'[12] and taunt them by saying they knew the soldiers would not shoot them—which was a strange conclusion to draw given that many of the women were already aware that soldiers had shot and killed women the day before at Utu Etim Ekpo.

As the large crowd pressed against the fence, it collapsed. Hill drew his pistol and shot one of the women in her face. Hill then ordered the soldiers to open fire on the women. They then fired 61 shots in addition to his and killed at least 32 women protesters and a male passer-by, who was hit by a stray bullet. As the women panicked and tried to flee, a further eight of them accidentally fell into a nearby river in the stampede and drowned.

Afterwards Hill claimed that the women continued to surge forward towards him and his troops after the first volley of rifle fire. Yet, oddly, no corpses were recovered from the side of the fence where he was standing. All the bodies were on the side outside the compound. The coroner, Dr Crawford, examined the corpses of 25 of the women killed at Opobo and found that nearly three-quarters of them died from gunshots fired at close range that hit the women in the back or on the sides of their bodies.[13] Unless the women were charging at Hill and his men while running backwards with their backs turned towards them, the pattern of gunshot wounds strongly suggested that they were facing away from the soldiers and trying to run away when they were shot. Hill also claimed that he saw a group of 30 or 40 men behind the women 'armed with machetes'. Of the 485 witnesses who gave evidence, Hill was the only one who saw or mentioned the presence of armed men among the women. He also failed to mention the presence of these armed men in his written report of the incident that he sent to his commanding officer. Strangely no machetes were recovered from the scene. Hill was not the only British officer to give puzzling evidence. Captain Harvey initially stated that the shooting was preceded by soldiers hitting the women with rifle butts to disperse them. When he was reminded of this fact and that it was in a written copy of a statement he had made, Harvey retracted the reference to hitting women with rifle butts and claimed it was a mistake.[14]

The protests continued into January 1930, by which time at least 55 women had been killed and another 50 wounded. One woman, Rosanah Ogwe, testified that soldiers stripped naked and sexually assaulted some women, and that she and others tried to rescue a woman they witnessed being gang-raped by three or four soldiers.[15]

The government implemented its Collective Punishment Ordinance by ordering 33 towns and villages to pay fines because their residents had participated in the protests. They were also forced to pay for repairs to the buildings that protesters damaged. These fines were accompanied by the usual destruction and burning of houses and villages deemed to have supported the protesters. None of the British army and police officers who shot women or ordered compounds and villages to be burned were prosecuted (in contrast to natives such as Emeruwa, who was imprisoned for grabbing one of the women).

The government set up a commission of inquiry at which the women protesters, warrant chiefs, and other witnesses including Nwanyeruwa and Emeruwa, whose argument triggered the protest movement, testified. The women chose a schoolteacher in Umuocha, Mary Okezie,[16] an Igbo woman of the Ngwa clan, to draft and submit a memorandum to the commission on their behalf. Although Okezie did not participate in the protests, she was chosen for this role because she was literate and was the first Ngwa woman to gain a Western education.

Some of the testimony at the inquiry was important for its revelation of the extent of dissatisfaction with colonial rule in the south-east, and for the women's aspirations to restore their society to its pre-colonial condition. The fact that the women made such comments *after* more than fifty of their comrades had been killed, and in a public arena at a commission presided over by white

British men, demonstrated the unpopularity of British rule in the south-east. The commission's conclusions were simultaneously painstaking and farcical. Even though hundreds of natives gave evidence, its conclusions about the violence and killing of protesters were based almost entirely on the testimony of the British perpetrators who did the killing. The British accounts—even when contradictory, far-fetched and self-serving in justifying the use of excessive force—were presented as fact, and rarely did the commission present in its conclusions the testimony of women about the force used against them and the killing of their comrades.

Despite not being weaponised, the Women's War ironically stimulated more change than the violent insurgencies waged by men that preceded it. The men's campaigns tended to result in massive British reprisals that devastated the protesting communities and placed them in a worse position than before the uprising. Although the Women's War led to the penalisation of the protesting communities, it also caused British colonial authorities to reappraise the political system they had imposed on the south-east.

After the inquiry the government implemented reforms of the governing system of south-eastern Nigeria. It assured women that they would not have to pay tax, investigated warrant chiefs and dismissed some of them, reformed the native court system, and created a new Native Administration, made up of traditional chiefs, to exist alongside the native courts. This led to a decentralisation of power away from the autocratic warrant chiefs and to power sharing between native courts and community elders and lineage leaders. This created a separation of powers, with the Native Authority functioning as the executive branch of government and the native courts as the judicial branch.

To some extent, each side got what it wanted. Natives got more representation in government and Britain was able to implement the system of indirect rule more fully by delegating authority and including more natives in government. The protests also acted as a stimulus for women's education in south-eastern Nigeria. The corruption and abuse of power by warrant chiefs sensitised women to the value of literacy and Western education. Several warrant chiefs were literate and most of the women were not. Warrant chiefs derived much of their power from the simple fact that they could speak English and knew how to read and write. For example, Emeruwa, whose argument with Nwanyeruwa triggered the mass protests, was a school-teacher. Gaining Western education would allow women to learn what the warrant chiefs and British administrators knew, make them less vulnerable to their manipulation, and permit them to better understand the political system that Britain imposed on their region.

To some extent the Women's War also represented a symbolic point of no return. It was the last mass organised protest in south-eastern Nigeria that sought to return to the pre-British status quo. After it, governance and public administration passed into the hands of the Western-educated elites, who continued to set the agenda for national development.

Tax Revolts in Yorubaland

The Women's War was not the only large protest movement by women against colonial taxation. Taxation was one of the biggest sources of discord between the natives and British colonial authorities. After the governor-general, Sir Frederick Lugard, introduced taxation into the Yoruba areas of Southern Nigeria in 1916 and 1917, trouble ensued.

The Adubi War

Taxation of Abeokuta (just outside Lagos in south-west Nigeria) residents became effective on 1 January 1918, and each adult male was required to pay a minimum of five shillings. Many people protested that the tax was too large and refused to pay it. There was also a perception that the taxes collected would end up in the private pockets of those who were collecting them. Protests and riots erupted, and culminated in the so-called Adubi War of 1918.

Protesters sang abusive songs in public that criticised the tax collectors, the British, and the government secretary, Adegboyega Edun. When the lieutenant-governor of Southern Nigeria, Sir Alexander George Boyle, toured the area with Edun and the traditional ruler, the alake, protesters greeted the trio with insults. In one instance someone brandished a gun in Boyle's presence. Boyle told Edun and the alake to end the crisis themselves, otherwise he would summon the police to end it by force. Protesters reacted before Boyle had a chance to carry out his threat. On 13 June 1918, thirty thousand protesters, many of whom were armed with rifles, destroyed railway lines and telegraph lines south of Abeokuta, and set railway stations on fire. The protest had a military character as demobilised soldiers joined the protesters, including Yorubas from the neighbouring French colony of Dahomey. In Dahomey the Yoruba had been protesting and fighting the French government over colonial policies such as forced recruitment to the army during World War I. Military deserters joined the anti-tax protest, during which protesters killed a European trading agent and a high-ranking Egba chief. European shopkeepers fled in fear, and the alake left his palace and sheltered at a Catholic mission.

As the protest occurred during World War I, there were many trained soldiers who could be used to confront the protesters. The colonial government mobilised almost 3,000 soldiers to suppress the revolt, after which around 1,000 Egba people and 100 soldiers lay dead.[17] The use of force against the protesters was so extreme that leaders of the Church Missionary Society protested and some individuals in Nigeria and Britain called for an inquiry into the causes of the protest and the government response to it. However, simmering resentment against colonial taxes continued for decades and re-emerged in a new guise in a campaign led by women in Abeokuta.

The Egba Women's Tax Revolt

In 1945 a group of Egba Yoruba women in the town of Abeokuta formed an organisation called the Abeokuta Ladies Club (renamed the Abeokuta Women's Union (AWU) in 1946). The AWU's original members were mostly upper-middle-class women who were either educated or married to educated men, and its initial aims were focused on addressing community problems and teaching middle-class etiquette to young women. However, a mix of events in the broader society and the dynamic personalities in its membership cadre transformed it into a vehicle for opposing British policies.

During its first meeting on 15 March 1945, the club elected a slender, charismatic, fast-talking schoolteacher named Funmilayo Ransome-Kuti as its president. Mrs Ransome-Kuti was descended from a Saro family who were not strangers to activism. Her husband was a clergyman named Israel Oludotun Ransome-Kuti, who was a founding member of the Nigerian Union of Teachers. The Ransome-Kutis had several sons who later became prominent in Nigeria. One son, Olufela, later became one of the most famous and successful African musicians of all time.[18] Mrs Ransome-Kuti's sister-in-law, Grace Eniola Soyinka (her husband's sister), was also an AWU founding member. Grace's son Oluwole later became a famous writer and Africa's first Nobel laureate.

The AWU relaxed its initially selective upper-middle-class membership and became more socio-economically diverse by including weavers, farmers, market traders, illiterates as well as literates, Christians, Muslims and animists. Despite its cosmopolitan membership, the AWU found a common rallying cause in the issue of taxation. Its objectives transcended matters such as encouraging mass education among women and became increasingly political and anti-colonial. The taxation of women became one of its grievances. The AWU claimed that flat-rate taxes of two shillings and sixpence on women were burdensome since women had to pay them whether or not they had an income, and they also objected to the tactless manner in which tax collectors went about their duties. Since women had to start paying taxes at 15, some tax collectors stripped teenagers naked to 'prove' that they had developed breasts and were old enough to pay tax.

As indirect rule required local rulers to collect tax on Britain's behalf, the alake of Abeokuta, Ladapo Ademola, bore the brunt of the anti-tax hostility. Several times in 1946 and 1947, Ransome-Kuti led delegations of women to the alake's palace to protest against tax increases and collection practices. The AWU hired a lawyer to represent them and an accountant to audit the records of the Sole Native Authority for evidence of corruption. They sent several petitions demanding the repeal of the flat-rate tax and advocating tax reforms. From 29 to 30 November 1947, ten thousand women staged a 24-hour sit-down protest outside the alake's palace. Although their physical demonstrations were directed against the alake, their real target was the British colonial government and the taxes that it forced the alake to collect on its behalf. The protests turned into a critique of women's position under colonial rule. Ransome-Kuti and many other women refused to pay their taxes, and the AWU hired lawyers to defend them after they were arrested and charged in court.

The protesters argued that there should be no 'taxation without representation' and pointed out that they were being taxed even though women were not members of the native governing authorities. They also argued that their taxes should be used to fund services that improved women's lives, such as health care and education. Ransome-Kuti's fluent command of English and Yoruba allowed her to simultaneously articulate the women's grievances to the alake and British officers. When discussing with British officers, she instantly translated the dialogue into Yoruba for the women protesters, so they could follow the progress of their petitions. She said: 'all Egbas both men and women in every nook and corner of Abeokuta town and District pay tax, it does not matter how small the village maybe, the villages would be fished out and their taxes collected, but won't they get in return? Nothing whatever!'[19]

The women were not a disorganised mob. Ransome-Kuti held 'practice sessions' at her house and tutored the women on how to behave and react during their demonstrations. For instance, she instructed them on how to cover their eyes, mouths and noses with cloth if the police fired tear gas at them, and even told them to pick up tear gas canisters and throw them back at the police. When they could not secure demonstration permits to march, the women would euphemistically agree to meet for a 'picnic', and then thousands of women would arrive at the picnic-cum-demonstration. When several protesters were arrested, over ten thousand women held another sit-down demonstration at the alake's palace. This time they stayed even longer (for 48 hours from 8 to 10 December) and refused to leave until their comrades were released. Just like the south-eastern women before them, they sang protest songs that mocked those who aggrieved them (the alake in this instance).

The circumstances in which the women led anti-tax revolts arose in the south-east and south-west were remarkably similar. In both instances, clumsily implemented colonial tax policies triggered opposition from women. The protest groups in the two regions were also very similar. Both comprised an intergenerational and diverse group of women who tapped into pre-existing female kinship groups such as women's trading associations as rallying points for solidarity and to transmit their grievances as a group. Both protest movements also had strong and charismatic leadership—the Oloko trio in the south-east and Ransome-Kuti in the south-west—and were marked by civil disobedience campaigns.

Just like the south-eastern women twenty years before them, the Egba women extracted meaningful concessions from the colonial authorities, including the abolition of the flat-rate tax and representation for women in Abeokuta's governing council. The alake resigned in 1949. Having achieved these gains, the AWU expanded and developed into a pan-national organisation known from 1949 as the Nigerian Women's Union. It became a major force in the greater Nigerian nationalist movement during the 1950s.

PART 5

CULTURAL, POLITICAL
AND RELIGIOUS CHANGES

By 1900 the indigenes of the River Niger area were no longer dealing with a trading company but rather with an imperial foreign government that had conquered their land by force. The concluding five chapters of this book will examine how British rule radically changed Nigeria's cultural, educational and religious identity. After decades of war and resistance, Nigerians had to navigate a path between keeping their pre-colonial lifestyles and discarding it to adopt the coloniser's identity. This cultural movement caused a radical educational and religious revolution. Britain transplanted to Nigeria its own cultural and religious complexities, and Nigeria became a convergence point for multiple cultural, economic and ethnic interests and rivalries.

17

THE CRESCENT AND THE CROSS

In the Beginning

Nigeria is unique in terms of its religious composition. It is the only country in the world with its population equally split between Christians and Muslims.[1] The changes that brought about this religious pattern occurred in the 19th and 20th centuries and were among the most rapid and remarkable mass religious conversions in the history of humankind. Why did Nigerians convert to religions brought by foreigners and invaders?

Mass religious conversion was possible for several reasons. Although British historical accounts accused Nigerians of 'rank heathenism'[2] or of being 'pagan tribes, addicted to every kind of vile customs',[3] they had their own religions before the British arrived. Apart from Islam, other deities and religions existed. For example the Igbos and Yorubas believed in supreme beings called Chukwu and Olodunmare respectively, who created the universe. In addition to these supreme beings, people also worshipped subsidiary deities and spirits who had power over demarcated areas or phenomena such as the weather or fertility. In pre-colonial cosmology, very little was presumed to be the product of coincidence. People's fluctuating daily fortunes were not attributed to concepts such as luck or chance. Rather, various deities and spirits were often given the credit (or the blame) for blessings and ills such as plentiful farm yields, drought, marriages, births, infertility, sickness and unsuccessful business deals. Daily life for many Nigerians involved worship and sacrifice to maintain good relations with benevolent spirits that could confer blessings, and to placate evil spirits that could bring misfortune.

The Crescent

Africa was the first place in the world to practise Islam outside the Arabian Peninsula. Islam first came to Africa with sixteen early followers (twelve men and four women) of the Prophet Mohammed who fled Mecca to escape persecution and travelled to Abyssinia (ancient Ethiopia) around 615 AD, where the Christian King of Aksum received them and granted them refuge. Islam infiltrated Nigeria in two directions: firstly, from east to west when it entered the north-east, and then from west to east when it entered from the lands to Nigeria's west (such as Mali) into the north-west and south-west of Nigeria.

Traders and migrants brought Islam to the Kanem-Borno Empire on Nigeria's north-eastern frontier (in the modern-day Borno area) in the 11th and 12th centuries, and it arrived in Hausaland (to the west of Borno) in the 14th century. Some sources claim that Islam was a religion of the Hausa kings and elites, while the peasantry remained animist. To be sure, the arrival of the new religion did not entirely displace old animist beliefs, which continued to coexist alongside Islam. For example, in Hausaland, the *maguzawa* declined to adopt Islam and continued with their old belief systems.

THE CRESCENT AND THE CROSS

Although in modern times Islam is regarded as the religion of Northern Nigeria, it coexisted in the south and north for centuries. By the mid-18th century it had diffused through the northern part of Yorubaland in south-west Nigeria and was originally known as *Esin Imale* (the Malian religion), which gives a clue about the people who introduced it into Yorubaland.

The Cross

Christian missionaries were probably the most effective catalysts of social change in colonial Nigeria. They became interested in West Africa because the early accounts of traders and explorers they read contained exaggerated descriptions of the people 'dwelling in the coast regions [as] heathens, drunkards, robbers, murderers, and cannibals'[4] or as 'for the most part degraded savages, worshippers of devils, and participators in horrible fetiche [*sic*] rites' living in a 'mass of dark humanity'.[5] Such accounts convinced them that the area was full of miserable heathens who had to be converted to Christianity in order to save them from their own immorality. Some missionaries also went to Nigeria on humanitarian grounds to abolish practices such as slavery, human sacrifice, twin immolation, and other customs which they regarded as contrary to the word of God.

Portuguese traders introduced Christianity to the Benin area in the 15th century. However, it remained dormant and did not gain traction. The origins of modern Nigerian Christianity can be traced to the 19th century when missionaries from the Church of England's Church Missionary Society (CMS) arrived at Badagry on the outskirts of Lagos in 1842. Four years later missionary activity spread to the nearby town of Abeokuta, and then to Calabar when Presbyterian missionaries began working in the far south-eastern corner of what later became Southern Nigeria. In 1857 the CMS established its first mission in Igboland in the town of Onitsha. Yet despite the missionary presence and proselytising, conversion to Christianity was a spectacular failure in its early stages. After thirty years of missionary presence in Onitsha, the church congregation was around 400 people out of a population of between ten and fifteen thousand. The mission at Asaba on the west side of the River Niger baptised only 20 people in the first six years of its existence, and at Osomari the mission baptised 10 adults in its first decade of work.[6]

Rather than advancing Christianity, the missionaries seemed instead to accelerate the advance of Islam. In the first half-century of colonial rule, the Muslim population of West Africa doubled and acquired more converts than it had done in the preceding thousand years.[7] By the late 1920s it was estimated that conversions to Islam outnumbered those to Christianity by a ratio of 10:1,[8] and by the early 1950s 34 per cent of West Africa's population was estimated to be Muslim, compared with only 4.5% Christian.[9] Why were Nigerians initially resistant to Christianity but attracted to Islam? Since Christian converts spoke the invader's language, wore his clothing, and bore Anglo-Christian names, Islam could be presented as an indigenous religion (even though it came from abroad), whereas Christianity was viewed as the white man's religion. The two Abrahamic religions could be seen in these diametrically opposed ways because Christianity was so closely associated with the British coloniser. Its proselytisers were citizens of the coloniser and it was transmitted through the English language.

From the Nigerian perspective, Christianity had many disadvantages that made it difficult to adopt. Christianity's inflexible insistence on monogamy was an incomprehensible assault on the economic and family sensibilities of married Nigerians. The requirement of monogamy disqualified polygamous people from Christianity. To circumvent this obstacle, missionaries devised the 'solution' of requiring male converts to divorce all their wives except their first. Some of the wives they divorced and sent away were still nursing their babies. This caused a sudden rise in single mothers, divorcees and unmarried women in societies where being married was a valued status. Monogamy was also problematic in Igboland where women observed a post-partum custom of not having sex with their husbands for years after giving birth. A man wishing to become a Christian had first to divorce all but one of his wives, tear his family apart, resign from the secret societies he belonged to, free his slaves, and make himself an outcast in his own community. A British army officer was extremely pessimistic about the chances of converting Nigerians to Christianity. He said:

> You will never Christianize these natives ... As long as polygamy and domestic slavery exist, it will be an impossibility to attempt to Christianize the native. Do these missionaries expect a chief to discard twenty-nine of his thirty wives, and to free all his domestic slaves in order to become a Christian? Not a bit of it—he won't.[10]

In contrast, Islam did not require polygamous people to destroy their family lives by divorcing. Conversion to Christianity was also much more complicated and lengthier than the equivalent process in Islam. Repeating the simple *Shahada* affirmation that 'There is no god but God, and Mohammed is his messenger' in front of Muslim witnesses was sufficient for someone to be accepted as a Muslim. Yet, the process of converting to Christianity was a bewildering and cumbersome process for Nigerians. Although missionaries had humanitarian aims, they also had a superiority complex that viewed their religion and way of life as limitlessly superior to that of the Nigerian societies they encountered. For missionaries, conversion to Christianity was not merely spiritual but also required the convert to declare war on their indigenous religions and culture. Only after invalidating their pre-existing beliefs, culture, clothing and lifestyle could they be accepted as Christians.

Missionaries sought to abolish pre-existing African religious practices and condemned most facets of African culture as anti-Christian. They also required converts to reject and abandon their previous way of life and replace it with the culture of the missionaries, learn the missionaries' language, and dress identically to the missionaries. Before admitting prospective converts to Christianity, missionaries subjected them to arduous teaching and spiritual preparation which would continue until the missionary was satisfied that the converts had totally abandoned their old way of life. Christian converts were not only required to change their faith but often had to publicly renounce their prior religions. For example, an Igbo woman informed me that when her grandmother converted to Christianity, she was required to bring out the carved wooden statues representing the deities she had previously worshipped, and publicly burn them in the presence of the entire community and the missionaries, who supervised the burning. Such public obliterations of predominant and pre-existing worship systems must have been considered sacrilegious to many.

The missionaries also made their jobs harder (and further confused potential converts) by bringing with them the myriad sectarian cleavages that existed in Europe. Thus Nigerians were bewildered by the different Anglican, Presbyterian, Roman Catholic and other church denominations that arrived and proselytised, yet professed to be messengers of the same God. For example, twelve different Christian denominations were present in Ibadan in 1951. In addition, missionaries had to convince sceptical natives that they were not representatives of the dreaded Royal Niger Company, which had inflicted so much misery.

With these challenges, how did Christianity manage to get a foothold in so many parts of Nigeria? At least five trends assisted Christianity's advance. Firstly, many Nigerian communities associated the missionaries with the colonial authorities and their power. They tended to conflate all British people. For example, in areas of south-eastern Nigeria where colonial authorities pulverised villages into submission with ruthless military assaults, the locals used Christianity as a way to get on the good side of the British authorities. Secondly, Christianity's teaching of the equality of all men and women was attractive to those who sought upward social mobility. As a result, many early converts were slaves or social outcasts. Becoming a Christian allowed a slave to look upon his former master as an equal or even to look down on him as a pagan. Thirdly, many missionaries had medical expertise, and their treatment and curing of native diseases won the affection and trust of communities where they operated. The missionaries' ability to treat illnesses not only won the confidence of Nigerians, but was often interpreted as a sign of the power of the god they served. Fourthly, Nigerians had good reasons to question the efficacy of their animist religions. After all, their deities had failed to stop the British from conquering and subjugating them, burning down their towns and villages at will, destroying their crops, or evicting them from their homes. The animist deities also had no answer to Britain's military superiority represented by long-range weapons that could fire countless high-velocity projectiles of death at those Nigerians who resisted.

Christianity's most potent weapons were education and literacy. Education was fundamental to the propagation of Christianity, as it enabled converts to read the Bible. To Nigerians, their colonisers seemed to store the secrets of their knowledge and technology inside a source that had hitherto been incomprehensible to them: books written in English. Since missionaries also set up mission schools to teach Nigerians to speak, read and write in English, conversion to Christianity carried the related benefit of Western education, which could teach Nigerians the secrets of the white man's power and technology.

WHAT BRITAIN DID TO NIGERIA

Missionaries and Indigenous Languages

Missionaries valued being multilingual as it allowed them to spread Christianity to different people around the world. One of the greatest challenges that missionaries encountered in Nigeria was the bewildering number of languages and dialects they found there. Nothing short of superhuman linguistic skills could help them when they were trying to convert people in a country that had over 500 indigenous languages. They responded by trying to undo the Tower of Babel they found by combining different languages and dialects into new 'standard' languages. The translation of the Bible into Yoruba and Igbo offers excellent demonstrations of the massive changes that such linguistic consolidation brought to Nigerian society.

'Yoruba Proper' and 'Union Igbo'

Missionaries heavily influenced the emergence of modern Yoruba and Igbo ethnic identities and languages. Even though they shared cultural affinities and a similar language, albeit with multiple differences in cadence, grammar and pronunciation, the people of south-west Nigeria were fragmented into at least 12 different kingdoms and did not regard themselves as members of the same ethnic group, nor did they collectively identity as Yoruba. Outside Oyo, the people of these kingdoms instead identified themselves by the name of their kingdom or home town, such as Egba, Ekiti, Ijebu or Ijesha. In Sierra Leone, freed slaves who originated from the area were called 'Aku' rather than Yoruba. The Igboland area of south-east Nigeria had similar linguistic variation. In 1919 a government anthropologist estimated that there were at least 20 different Igbo dialects.[11] The people did not consider these to be dialects, but instead regarded each of them as a separate, independent language in its own right. However, the missionaries remained convinced that what they spoke were simply derivatives of the same language. They set about linguistic unification by producing 'standardised' texts of these 'dialects' which would combine them into a single 'parent' language.

The missionaries used Nigerian interlocutors, whom they hired, educated in English, and converted to Christianity, and who then helped them to translate the Bible into standardised versions of Nigerian languages. For example, after rescuing a young boy named Samuel Ajayi Crowther from a transatlantic slave ship, British missionaries educated him at a mission school in Sierra Leone and he became a key evangeliser in south-west Nigeria. In 1889 he produced the first Yoruba translation of the Bible. Since Crowther was from Oyo and believed that his language was 'Yoruba proper', the translation was based on his Oyo language (with some modifications to include Egba and grammar spoken in the coastal areas near Lagos).

'His extraordinary powers of gesticulation'

The origin of the modern-day 'Union Igbo' language spoken in Nigeria's urban centres also lies in missionary translation work. An Anglican clergyman from Sussex, Thomas John Dennis, believed that the different languages spoken in south-east Nigeria were merely different dialects of the same Igbo language. Dennis's siblings Edward ('Ted'), Ellen ('Nellie') and Frances ('Fanny') also worked as missionaries in Nigeria. Dennis regarded the Igbo language as deficient in grammatical discipline and claimed that the Igbo,

> being a born orator and mimic, depends quite as much upon his extraordinary powers of gesticulation, facial contusion, mimicry, voice modulation, and of producing imitative sounds, as upon his articulate utterances to make plain his meaning. In speaking he will,

in all probability, jerk out his words with a sublime disregard for such trifles as tense form or conjunctions.[12]

Convinced that Igbo had a 'parent' dialect, Dennis set about producing a 'Union Igbo' translation of the Bible in a version of Igbo that would be understood by all people in what is now Igboland. Since Dennis was based near Owerri, he believed that the Owerri language was this parent dialect, and that 'the Igbo people of Owerri speak as pure a form of the language as any in the country'.[13] Dennis and his team completed the Union Igbo Bible in 1913 and printed it in a new dialect that was not actually spoken by any Igbo group. The translation included editorial discretion such as carefully translating God as 'Chineke' (the god of creation) rather than 'Chukwu' (the pre-colonial Igbo name for God). This was in order to avoid conflating the Christian God with the Aro people, who were called *Umu Chukwu* (children of God) and whose myth of invincibility had been shattered when British troops detonated their deity with dynamite a few years earlier. Some Igbo groups rejected the Union Igbo Bible for being written in a foreign language, and they found it difficult to read because of the presence of new and unfamiliar words, phrases, characters and tenses.

Nonetheless, the Yoruba and Union Igbo translations of the Bible overcame these initial challenges. Both transcended their religious purpose and became important catalysts for the unification of the modern Yoruba and Igbo people and their languages. The ability to read and speak the new 'parent' languages became a badge of access to Western education, a prerequisite for baptismal candidates and participation in church, and an umbrella for pan-Yoruba and pan-Igbo identity. In 1913 the government made Union Igbo the standard for its official Igbo language exams. By constant repetition and dissemination, these new parent languages eventually became comprehensible by most Yorubas and Igbos. The new parent languages also led their speakers in the south-west and south-east to stop identifying themselves as Egba, Ekiti, Ijebu or Ijesha, or as Aro, Bende or Ngwa, and instead as Yoruba or Igbo respectively.

Yet the missionaries did not succeed in transforming all of Nigeria. While they operated freely in the south, their activities were restricted in Northern Nigeria, and they could not proselytise there in a Muslim area without the emir's consent. Missionaries started evangelising in Northern Nigeria in 1841. Almost sixty years later they had managed to establish only two mission schools in the whole of the area. Owing to understandable Muslim concern, missionary activity was limited to areas that British authorities called 'pagan' in the non-Muslim parts of the north. The work of missionaries in the south caused a religious revolution, and their restricted activity in the north insulated Islam from Christian encroachment. Rapid educational and theological change in the south was accompanied by the preservation of pre-colonial educational and theological values in the north. This amplified the differences between the two regions in a way that can still be seen today.

Missionary work transcended religion and generated profound educational and societal changes. The missionaries were arguably the most significant agents of change in colonial Nigerian society. Their humanitarian work is often overlooked, and they caused more radical societal changes than the British colonial government. Although they can be blamed for destroying African religious and traditional practices, missionaries can also be credited for contributing to the development of written text in native languages. In their attempts to spread the word of God, they undertook serious studies of indigenous languages and developed new systems of orthography in order to translate the Bible into native languages. By 1925 they had translated the entire Bible into Yoruba, Igbo, Efik and Hausa, and portions of it into 45 other Nigerian languages.[14]

WHAT BRITAIN DID TO NIGERIA

Their work caused the emergence of new ethnic groups and systems of orthography, and the written recording of the histories of some Nigerian ethnic groups for the first time (although some communities such as the Hausa States had written histories that predated the British arrival by over 700 years). In their attempt to understand the people they were trying to convert, missionaries became front-line anthropologists and historians. They conducted anthropological and historical research, and much of what we now know about pre-colonial Nigerian society came from the research and written work of missionaries and the Nigerians they converted. The multilingual skills, literacy and mission school education of the native converts enabled them to use Roman orthography to translate secular literature, such as histories, poems and stories, into dozens of Nigerian languages including Hausa, Igbo, Yoruba, Efik, Nupe and Fulfulde.

Although colonial accounts doubtless exaggerated the barbarity of pre-colonial Nigerian societies, there were practices such as slavery, twin infanticide and human sacrifice which caused severe misery and needless death. In the Edo and Efik areas, a powerful chief's death also endangered the lives of his servants, who were sometimes killed and buried with him to continue serving him in the next world. Twin abandonment was also present in some parts of Efik and Igboland. Twin births were regarded as the outcome of evil spirits and an abomination which distorted the natural order of humanity to propagate by single births. The mothers who gave birth to twins were consequently ostracised from their communities. Twin births were so feared that sometimes entire villages would evacuate in fear of the evil spirit that gave rise to them. A puzzling aspect of the taboo about twins is why communities in the same area sometimes had completely different attitudes to them. For example, the Ekoi people, who live close to the Efik, rejoiced at twin births, celebrated them with pageantry and rejoicing, and gave gifts to the parents.

The Briton most associated with ending twin abandonment is the Scottish Presbyterian missionary Mary Slessor. She was born in Aberdeen as the second of seven children in a poor family, the daughter of an alcoholic father with a volcanic temper and a mother who was a devout Christian. After the death of her father, she took a job in a factory and worked 12 hours a day to help her widowed mother and siblings. After the Scottish missionary David Livingstone died, she decided to follow in his footsteps and dedicated her life to spreading Christianity in Africa. She came to the Calabar area of south-east Nigeria in 1876 at the age of 28, never married, and devoted her life to adopting abandoned twins, looking after their outcast mothers, healing the sick, and preventing human sacrifices alongside chiefs' burials. She nursed the twins she adopted as if they were her own children, and named one of the twins she adopted 'Janie' after her own sister. She learned to speak the local Efik language, ate the local food and lived among the Efik people. She died in Nigeria in 1915, one year after the country's formation.

Although Nigerian schoolchildren are widely taught that Slessor ended twin abandonment by herself, the process of its abolition began when she was still an infant in Scotland. In 1851 King Eyo Honesty of Creek Town issued an edict to forbid twin infanticide. Slessor was only three years old at this time. Despite friction and opposition, some communities reached a compromise by handing twins over to missionaries. Slessor's role in opposing twin infanticide cannot be understated but, although she made a huge contribution to ending it, she was not the sole cause. However, she was a very important actor in a process that began a quarter of a century before she arrived in the Calabar region.

If any British group can claim to have spread 'civilisation' in Nigeria, it is the missionaries, not the colonial government. The missionary introduction of Western education and Christianity caused the most dramatic cultural and social changes to Nigeria. Yet missionaries also destroyed several cultural rituals of pre-colonial Nigerian life. Christianity's insistence that converts had to renounce their old way of life required them to abandon key native customs such as secret societies and initiation ceremonies (which were a crucial part of the indigenous rite of passage to adulthood), pageants and masquerades (which were integral parts of entertainment and social life), traditional names and funeral ceremonies. Christian principles such as the equality of all before God also assaulted some foundational tenets of traditional African society, such as respect for elders and obedience to traditional authorities. As a result, much of pre-colonial Nigerian culture was lost and will never be recovered.

18

PEOPLE OF THE BOOK

Perhaps the greatest legacy of Christian missionaries to Nigeria was in the area of education. In the first fifty years of Nigeria's existence there were very few literate Nigerians who did not receive a mission school education. While missionaries were keen to educate Nigerians to advance their own agenda, the colonial government was less enthusiastic. The latter tried to design an educational system that would discourage Nigerian aspirations for upward social mobility, and instead teach Nigerians to know and accept their place at the bottom of the colonial system. The lack of a common, nationwide colonial educational policy also increased the cultural differences between north and south by transforming the culture of one region, while preserving that of the other.

Pre-colonial African Education

There is a common misconception that Nigerians did not have education or writing skills and were illiterate before the British arrived. Yet many Nigerian communities had centuries-old pre-colonial indigenous educational and writing systems. Many Muslims in northern and south-western Nigeria could read and write Hausa, Fulfulde, Kanuri and Yoruba in a script called *Ajami*. In southern Nigeria, the Efik, Igbo and Ibibio had developed a system of writing called *Nsibidi*, which used visual pictograms. *Nsibidi* is not widely known but came to recent prominence when images from it briefly appeared in the blockbuster film *Black Panther*.

The British incorrectly regarded Nigerians as uneducated because indigenous methods of educational instruction were unfamiliar or invisible to them. For example, the *Nsibidi* script was developed as a code to allow secret society members to communicate with each other. Its deliberate restriction among a select few prevented it from being widely learned by outsiders. In Northern Nigeria education was largely Koranic, and many mosques used their courtyards as Koranic schools. By 1914 there were at least 25,000 Koranic schools in Nigeria with 218,000 pupils, who were taught to recite the Koran from memory and to read and write in Arabic.[1]

Indigenous educational systems that did not incorporate reading and writing did not necessarily prevent people from transacting in the modern world. In societies where reading and writing were absent, other forms of tutelage existed. In such societies, the illiterate compensated by developing high levels of verbal and visual memory and recognition, and transmitted knowledge through oral traditions. In many pre-colonial Nigerian societies, knowledge was usually transmitted to children through folktales, poetry, proverbs, riddles and other forms of oral literature. This education covered a wide range of fields, such as agriculture, art, construction, hunting, trading, religion, music, pottery and soldiery. Such traditional education also acted as an important vehicle for preparing children for adulthood.

Mission Schools and Western Education

Western education represented one of the most revolutionary influences that Britain had on Nigeria. It came hand in glove with the missionaries as they evangelised and sought converts to Christianity. Missionaries had a virtual monopoly on education and the establishment of schools in Nigeria for nearly a hundred years. Until 1898 all Western education in Nigeria was controlled by Christian missionaries, and as late as 1942 missionaries controlled 99 per cent of all schools in the country.[2]

Since the colonial government showed little interest in education, mission schools served a dual purpose as educational institutions and as a means for converting the natives to Christianity. Whereas adults may have been irrevocably devoted to animist religions, children were more malleable targets for conversion. To gain Christian converts, missionaries encouraged natives to send their children to mission schools. Missionaries boosted school enrolment and aided Christian conversion by often admitting children to their schools free of charge. School education provided a stepladder to Christianity because it taught pupils to read and write in English, which in turn made it easier for them to understand the proselytising of Christian evangelisers and to read the Bible. As a result, the schoolteacher functioned both as a tutor and as a Christian evangelist.

A serious problem that arose for the government was that after having left education in the hands of missionaries for so long, the quality of education that pupils received was dependent on the preferences and idiosyncrasies of the teacher or the mission school. There was no common syllabus or examination system. Students at different schools learned from different textbooks, and there were no common inspectorates or standards. Yet for several decades the government made little effort to take control of education or to prioritise the provision of Western education to Nigerians. The government's lack of interest in implementing an educational policy did not significantly change until it realised that it was cheaper to educate and hire literate Nigerians than it was to hire expatriate Europeans, West Indians or Sierra Leoneans to fill positions in the colonial administration. The first government secondary school in Nigeria, King's College in Lagos, was not founded until 1909—some 67 years after missionaries had opened Nigeria's first primary school and 50 years after they opened Nigeria's first secondary school.

In the south, parents' initial reluctance to send their children to school dissipated when they realised that school offered the opportunity for economic and social elevation. Education and its twin sibling, Christianity, also provided tools that Nigerians could use to understand the white man. To many Nigerians, their British colonisers seemingly stored the secrets of their knowledge and technology inside their books. Thus conversion to Christianity and school attendance allowed Nigerians to learn the secrets of his the coloniser's power and technology by reading his books, and to communicate with him by learning his language. For example, in south-eastern Nigeria education was seen as an antidote to the excesses of the colonial administrators and their detested local collaborators and allies, the warrant chiefs. People noted that those who were literate were favoured by the British and were appointed to positions of influence as warrant chiefs or to clerical positions in the colonial administration. Education also made people less vulnerable to the manipulation of native colonial staff, who often used written instructions on paper (purportedly from British officials) to defraud and intimidate illiterate rural residents.

Schools not only allowed Nigerians to get closer to their British colonisers, but also acted as factories for the production of British clones. Missionaries and teachers saw the moral improvement of the natives as part of their mission, and many of them believed that their pupils' character would be corrupted and they would relapse into bad habits if they were allowed to return to their communities at the end of school every day. Mission schools tried therefore to isolate pupils from their community by keeping them in boarding schools where they could supervise them around the clock. This had the effect of separating students from indigenous cultural influences and making them outliers among their own people. For school-teachers, civilising their Nigerian students involved a deliberate campaign of drilling students to emulate European behaviour and imbibe European culture. School subjects imitated those of British students. Nigerian students learned about English kings and queens rather than their own, learned to read and write in English, Greek and Latin, and studied Shakespeare. This type of education produced an educated class who were more versed in the traditions of the British coloniser than their own. By learning the coloniser's language, religion, history and man-ners, schools indoctrinated young Nigerians to become like their colonisers. A British-style education also made them venerate the coloniser and look down on their own culture and people. This created a strange situation whereby educated Nigerians could effortlessly recite the names of English kings, queens and cities but knew little about their own people's cul-ture, history, poetry and great historical figures.

Yet despite the Europeanising effect of education, Southern Nigerian parents sent their children to school because they rec-ognised that educational achievement had become a prized status symbol that offered upward economic and social mobility. Passing school exams became a barometer of achievement, and acquiring a British educational certificate provided a school-educated Nigerian with a qualification that proved they were as capable as the British colonisers. So great was the appeal by par-ents for missions to establish schools in their communities that missionaries could not keep up with the demand for new schools and applications from prospective pupils.

Education in Northern Nigeria

Before colonialism, the north had been far ahead of the south in written education, history and literature. The north had established educational and judicial systems and trained scholars. The British presence in Nigeria inverted the educational development of the north and south. Within fifty years of Britain establishing its first colony in what later became Nigeria, the north, which for centuries had led the south in literary and educational accomplishment, fell far behind the south. Even though Northern Nigeria possessed over 50 per cent of the population of the country, by 1947 only 2.5 per cent of the total number of secondary school students in the country were northerners.[3] How did this happen?

Since Western education was introduced in the south long before the north, there was a geographical pattern to the establishment of schools and education that mirrored the historical trajectory of Britain's entry into Nigeria. Educational enrolment peaked in the south, while the further north one went, the lower the levels of Western educational access and impact. By the time Britain conquered Northern Nigeria in 1903, southerners had been receiving Western education for sixty years. Additionally, the association of Western education with Christianity made northern Muslims reluctant to adopt it. For many Muslims, schools and churches were synonymous. Missionary determination to use schools as a vehicle for Christian evangelisation was matched by Muslim determination to resist them. Resistance to Western education in some parts of the north was so substantial that it became almost a virtue among northerners. The association between Christianity and schools generated a long-standing

scepticism towards Western education and created two contend-
ing forms of *ilimi* (education) in the north. These were *ilimin
boko* (Western education) and *ilimin Islamiyya* (Koranic education). Many Muslim northerners preferred Koranic education
and resisted government campaigns to increase Western education school enrolment in the north. Some considered *ilimin boko*
to be inauthentic and inferior to *ilimin Islamiyya*. The fact that
ilimin boko was taught in a strange language (English) and was
brought by European colonisers and by missionaries who converted their neighbours to Christianity intensified the reputation
of *ilimin boko* as an alien and untrustworthy medium of instruction. The complex etymology of the word 'boko' in Northern
Nigeria further demonstrates what many northerners really
thought of *ilimin boko*. In Hausa boko refers not only to Western
education, but to Western culture in general. The word is also
used to refer to something that is fake or fraudulent.

The colonial government shared the Muslim northerners'
lukewarm attitude to Western education. Initially, Lugard and
the emirs permitted only very limited numbers of Western
schools in the north. Christian missionaries first travelled to the
north in 1841. Nearly sixty years later they had been allowed to
establish only two schools in the whole of Northern Nigeria, at
Gbede and Lokoja. Even then the emirs kept the mission schools
out of Muslim areas and restricted their activities to the so-called
'pagan' districts outside major Muslim population centres.
Lugard was also reluctant to establish schools in the north, as he
did not want to provoke religious opposition to the British colonial government by giving Muslim northerners the impression
that the government was an advocate for the propagation of
Christianity in the Muslim north. Since the missionaries who
operated mission schools were British and Christian, there was
an ever-present danger that northerners might perceive the colonial government and missionaries to be in alliance to Christianise
and change the northern way of life.

Many of the early northern schools were 'home schools' for emancipated slaves and their children. After the colonial government abolished slavery in Northern Nigeria for all children born after 1 April 1901, it established a home for freed slave children at Zungeru. The children were given rudimentary schooling in English; the girls were taught needlework, cooking and washing, and the boys were taught a trade. Since the pupils learned to speak English and converted to Christianity, it became difficult for them to find spouses in the mainly Muslim north.

'The self-assurance and importance of these anglicised blacks is beyond calculation'

Lugard's lack of enthusiasm for native schooling in the north was not only due to a concern about generating religious unrest. Just as slave-holding states in America blocked slaves from receiving education because it gave them critical thinking and an aspiration for freedom, Lugard and some other British colonial administrators disliked the effect education had on Nigerians. They abhorred the confidence that education gave Nigerians and the assumption among educated Nigerians that their educational credentials and ability to speak English placed them in a position of equality with their white colonial masters. Lugard wrote with great irritation in his diary that 'the self-assurance and importance of these anglicised blacks is beyond calculation'.[4] He was also appalled to discover on one occasion that educated Africans were actually allowed 'a tent and some Europeans stores'.[5] Lugard was prone to making sweeping generalisations about Africans based on pseudo-science. For example, he believed that education made Africans 'less fertile, more susceptible to lung trouble and to other diseases, and to defective dentition'.[6] His brother Edward held similar views and also disliked the 'civilised trouser negro'. Unsurprisingly, men holding such views had a very narrow vision of education for Africans. In the north, Lugard envisaged a limited form of education that would produce an educated class to fill subordinate roles within the colonial administration. In 1906, he proposed the opening of a school for mallams (Koranic teachers) at which they would be taught to write Hausa in Roman script, and the establishment of a boarding school for the sons of emirs which would train them in patriotism, honesty and loyalty.

'The European can never do manual work in West Africa'

Another concern of British administrators was that education made Nigerians aspire to clerical work rather than manual labour. Some claimed that educated Nigerians looked down on manual labour, and believed that their education conferred a special social status on them.[7] Nigerian career aspirations for something more than physical labour would seriously disrupt the system of colonial labour in Nigeria, which was entirely reliant on (unpaid) indigenous labour. According to a British expatriate: 'The European can never do manual work in West Africa, therefore the execution of all work, whether government or commercial, depends on native labour.'[8] If education were to dry up the indigenous manual labour pool, it may also have raised the completely wild and unfathomable possibility that white Britons in Nigeria would have do to manual labour themselves: carrying their own bags, walking without being carried and washing their own clothes. As a result, the colonial government and missionaries established vocational schools in order to disabuse Nigerians of the view that it was more prestigious to work in an office than to earn a living by manual labour. The Hope Waddell Training Institution was founded in Calabar in 1895, and mission schools began to add vocational training to the curriculum in areas such as agriculture, brick-laying and carpentry.

Unlike in the south, where mission schools deliberately tried to produce carbon copies of educated Britons, education in the north was adapted to the region's cultural and religious sensitivities. When the Church Missionary Society (CMS) opened schools at Bida in 1903 and Zaria in 1905, Lugard insisted that the school at Bida had to be secular. The Bida school was established mainly to teach and encourage mallams to write Hausa and Nupe in Roman script. Its purpose was not really to produce an educated class, but rather to facilitate easier communication between emirs and British colonial officers by training mallams, who in turn could teach emirs how to read Roman script. Although the Bida school experiment largely failed, the CMS secured its first Hausa Christian convert in Mallam Fati, who helped Lugard's friend Dr Walter Miller, a medical doctor turned CMS evangelist, to translate many texts into Hausa. One of the graduates from the Bida school taught the emir of Zaria how to read Hausa in Roman script. Miller also devised a plan to create a boys' boarding school for the sons of emirs. He suggested that each emir should be asked to send two of his children to the school. In 1909 Hans Visscher, a Swiss who was granted British nationality in order to allow him to work for the British colonial administration, opened a school in Kano for the sons of emirs.

Effects of Western Education

Western education produced striking differences in the north and south of Nigeria. Overall it widened the cultural and religious divisions between the north and south. In the south it generated and encouraged upward social mobility, whereas in the north its initial effect was to preserve and amplify the differences between the elite and the ordinary people.

Although it was not its intent, Western education created a 'Nigerian dream' in the south that provided an avenue for lower social classes to move up within society. Ironically, many of the first recipients of Western education in the south were slaves and social outcasts. However, many of the newly educated Nigerians also absorbed the attitudes of cultural and intellectual superiority towards the non-literate that the British had. Being able to speak, read and write the white man's language, and performing clerical jobs that were only previously performed by Westerners, imbued some Western educated Nigerians with a sense of intellectual and social superiority to their uneducated compatriots. In many parts of the south, to be called 'illiterate' became a grave insult. Those with fresh educational qualifications could look down on their illiterate countrymen as unsophisticated and backward heathens, much as the British did.

However, the governor-general of Nigeria, Sir Hugh Clifford, was not complimentary about southern education and perceived the region's education as providing quantity over quality. Although he acknowledged that 'the children are themselves curiously eager to attend school', he claimed in 1922:

> In the southern provinces, education is at the present time in even worse case than it is in the northern provinces. There is a great deal more of it; but the general standard to which it attains is far lower than any with which service in other tropical dependencies of the Crown has familiarised me ... there is throughout the southern provinces an abundance of schools but very little genuine education.[9]

'They were alert to protect their culture from infidel communications'

In the north, Western education helped to preserve and reinforce the region's societal cleavages and social structure. The different colonial educational systems in the north and south also helped the former to emerge from colonialism with a great deal of its cultural and religious heritage intact, in contrast to the south, where education encouraged students to discard much of their African identity and many of their customs and replace them with those of their British teachers. In the south, education was in the hands of missionaries for almost a hundred years, whereas in the north the indigenous authorities were able to influence and shape the trajectory of education in the region. While many southerners copied British manners, customs and clothing, northerners rejected them. Dame Margery Perham noted: 'When we turn to the north it is a widely different situation. They wanted none of our instruction. They were alert to protect their culture from infidel communications and were well satisfied with their 25,000 Koranic schools where in courtyards under trees little boys in shrill repetition learned a few Arabic texts.'[10]

In the north, the colonial government's concern to avoid antagonising Muslims led it to create an educational system that sought to avoid unduly disrupting the local culture. The northern school curriculum included religion, Arabic instruction, native modes of dress, behaviour, sanitation and local customs. As a result, education did not have such a transformative effect on northern society as it did in the south.

The north's educational problem was the opposite of that in the south. The north's schools were better in quality but not enough pupils were enrolled in them. Despite the establishment of an embryonic Western educational system, the north was always playing numerical catch-up with the south. Protecting the north from outside influences came at a price. Northern schools may have provided higher-quality tuition than their southern counterparts since they hired expatriate professional teachers, but they taught fewer students. At end of 1914, the year Nigeria was amalgamated, over 97 per cent of students enrolled in Nigerian schools were southerners, and more than 95 per cent of Nigeria's schools were located in the south.[11] In that year alone, an additional 13,399 southern pupils enrolled at school. The number of southern pupils who started school for the first time that year was approximately twelve times greater than the total aggregate number of northern pupils attending school in all class years.

In 1922 Sir Hugh Clifford gave a damning indictment of the state of Western education in the north:

> After two decades of British occupation, the northern provinces have not yet produced a single native of these provinces who is sufficiently educated to enable him to fill the most minor clerical post in the office of any government department; while the African staff of these offices throughout the northern provinces are therefore manned by men from the Gold Coast, Sierra Leone, and from the southern provinces of Nigeria; and while the men belonging to the northern provinces, who obtain work as artisans in the railway workshops at Offa or at Minna, are so ill-educated that they are unable to compete on even terms with men of a similar class drawn from other parts of Nigeria; education in the north has been practically confined to the vernacular and to Arabic, has been allowed to become the almost exclusive perquisite of the children of the ruling classes.[12]

Clifford had a solution for this problem. He created Katsina College (later Barewa College) in 1921 as a training school for the sons of emirs along the lines of similar colleges in British India. Such elite schools modelled on private schools in England such as Eton and Epsom, produced graduates from the elite segments of northern society. By establishing elite schools, Britain allowed the sons of northern royalty and the elite to add Western education to their credentials, and to place themselves at the front of the queue of those who would inherit power from Britain when independence came. In Nigeria's first independence government, the federal prime minister, premier and governor of the Northern Region, the minister of finance, minister of education, three other federal ministers, the speaker of the Northern Region House of Assembly, and the leader of the opposition in the north were all alumni of Barewa College in

Zaria. Barewa College has produced more heads of government than any other school in Nigeria's history. Forty-two per cent of Nigeria's post-independence heads of government were Barewa College alumni. As a result, the north's educated elite became even more distanced from the *talakawa*.

The separate educational systems also produced differences among the northern and southern elites. Many of the northern elite were members of the region's aristocracy, and education simply provided additional credentials to their already elevated status. Conversely, in the south, educational achievement, rather than membership of royal houses, was a credential that gave people access to the elite. For example, the rise to prominence of southerners such as Obafemi Awolowo and Nnamdi Azikiwe was partially due to their academic success. Azikiwe was one of Nigeria's first PhD holders. Part of his electrifying charisma among his people was based on his exceptional command of English and his 'special gift for oratory, characterised by lavish use of long, technical, unusual and foreign-sounding words'.[13]

As independence approached, education became a crucial commodity because regions that had the most educated people also had the chance to inherit the economic and political power of the outgoing British colonial authorities. The north's lack of a large Western-educated workforce placed it in a vulnerable position vis-à-vis the south. Demand and supply in respect of educated people was inverted in the north and south. In the south the supply of educated school-leavers far outstripped the demand for them, whereas it was the other way round in the north. When British expatriate workers in the north departed, the vacancies created by their departure were filled not by northerners but instead by educated southerners. Thousands of southerners, especially Igbos, migrated north to perform jobs that required an education. This migration contributed to the series of tensions that eventually resulted in the mass bloodshed of

1966 and the Nigerian civil war of 1967–70. Igbo migration to the north and their entry into administrative, clerical and technical jobs created apprehension among northerners. The Igbo presence alarmed northerners for at least two primary reasons. Firstly, they were an economic threat. From the northern perspective, wherever they turned, Igbos were schoolteachers, business owners and landlords. Secondly, the Igbo adoption of Christianity and Western school education made them identifiable as an alien presence in the north. Igbos wore the British invader's clothing, spoke his language, and practised his religion. This enabled many northerners to view Igbos as poor caricatures of the British who had copied the white man's attire, education and religion. Northern prioritisation of Western education belatedly emerged as a reaction to the arrival of southerners in the region and from an apprehension that the north would not be able to compete with the south for economic opportunities when colonialism ended.

While colonial authorities can be blamed for disruptive educational policies, both the north and south also contributed to the destabilising effects of Western education in their regions. The north was at least a partial architect of its educational disadvantage. By rejecting Western education outright, it handicapped itself when it could have used its influence over educational development in the region to insist that Western education had to be secular and provided on a mass scale. The south also missed a chance to create an educational system customised to local needs, such as the north had. In the 1930s the government suggested changing the curriculum to base it on an African rather than an English standard. Had southerners demonstrated enthusiasm for this proposal, the south could have created an educational system with less disruption to the south's culture. However, educated Nigerians strongly opposed these changes. They feared that an Africanised educational system would be regarded as inferior to the British system and would perpetuate their subordinate status. They were also apprehensive that not possessing a British educational qualification would bar them from clerical job appointments.[14]

The cultural, historical and religious differences between the north and south probably made it impossible to conduct colonial education in the same manner nationwide. Yet despite the differences, education closed the linguistic distance between the two regions. Using English as the language of educational instruction transformed it into the language of the elite nationwide. While this facilitated inter-regional access and communication among the elite, it made that elite even more inaccessible to the uneducated, and widened the gap between the educated and illiterate. While 'proper' English remained the language of the elite, its pidgin version became the language of the urban working class.

Although this was not intentional, education was the British import that left the most indelible mark on Nigeria. It gave Nigeria a new national language, a new religion practised by half of its citizens, and a new cultural and societal ethos for advancement. In 1952 only 8.5 per cent of Nigerians could read and write in English. By 2010, 76 per cent of Nigerians aged 15–24 were literate.[15] Educational achievement in Nigeria has been so rapid that less than seventy years later, Nigeria now has more English speakers and English literate people than Britain has.

19

INDIRECT RULE

Britain's colonial rule was distinguished by economy in its provision of staff and resources, and by the massive disparity in numbers between the colonial rulers and those they governed. By 1925 there were only 200 British administrators in Nigeria for a population estimated at 20 million,[1] or one administrator for every 100,000 Nigerians. Why did Britain employ so few personnel in a foreign colony?

'They would rather be misgoverned by their own people than be governed by the very best of our officials'

According to some, it was wise to limit the number of British colonial personnel in Nigeria in order to limit disruption to native governing institutions, and because the natives would rather be misruled by one of their own than be ruled by foreigners. Sir George Goldie said: 'It is certain that the population of Nigeria, whether Mohammedan or pagan ... would rather be misgoverned by their own people than be governed by the very best of our officials.'[2] Was indirect rule purely a device to give natives a stake in colonial governance?

WHAT BRITAIN DID TO NIGERIA

'A land in which Europeans cannot permanently dwell'

Despite what Goldie said, there were other practical and pecuniary reasons for the limited British presence in Nigeria. Britain simply did not have enough personnel. In 1902 Lugard said of Nigeria: 'Nor have we the means at present to administer so vast a country.'[3] Even if it wanted to, Britain could not send many colonial administrators to Nigeria because of the high mortality rate. The heat, humidity and mosquitoes made it a hazardous place for British health. Between 1895 and 1900, about 7.5–10 per cent of British people living in Nigeria died every year.[4] Medical care for the British in Nigeria was not yet advanced enough to risk establishing a large permanent staff there. Even the amount of staff available was periodically depleted by their frequent trips back to Britain to recuperate. As late as 1929, a British colonial officer asserted: 'It is doubtful whether Europeans could ever live permanently in Nigeria and rear their children. The effect of the sun, the absence of suitable nourishing food, and the humidity that exist in certain parts of the country, combine to make it a land in which Europeans cannot permanently dwell.'[5]

'West Africa had a bad name'

The high mortality rate meant that Nigeria was not a popular destination for the British. It could not become a settler colony like South Africa or Zimbabwe. British people needed to be given a good reason to go there to work. British officials usually expected high salaries, perks and frequent holidays back in England in exchange for agreeing to work in Nigeria. The former commandant of the West African Frontier Force, Brigadier-General Sir James Willcocks, said: 'West Africa had a bad name, and many white men only went there because the pay was good and the life one of comparative freedom.'[6] However, the British government was not a charity and the colonial budget was finite. This presented the problem of how only a few Britons could rule a country with an indigenous population of several millions. The British had little choice other than to rely on indigenous agents to rule on their behalf. Fortunately, Britain had a tried and tested solution that it had already used in other colonies such as India and Uganda: it was called 'indirect rule'.

Indirect rule operated by co-opting the pre-colonial local rulers into the British colonial system by appointing them as Britain's proxy rulers. Britain superimposed its authority on top of the colony's pre-existing system of indigenous rule, placed it under British 'supervision', and delegated to the native rulers the day-to-day responsibility of carrying out British edicts and governing in accordance with British instructions.

Indirect Rule in Northern Nigeria

'It is our task to regenerate this capable race'

Colonial Northern Nigeria has been heralded as a classic example of indirect rule in practice. In Northern Nigeria, the Fulani emirs stood on the highest rung of the indigenous ladder. In their usual casual typecasting of native ethnic groups, many British administrators believed that the Fulani were a superior and more intelligent race of Africans and born rulers. For example, a British visitor to Nigeria wrote: 'The Fulani was a great organizer, a born governor, an astute Statesman, and an intrepid soldier.'[7] Sir Frederick Lugard, whose name is most closely associated with indirect rule, said: 'The Fulani of Northern Nigeria are ... more capable of rule than the indigenous races.'[8] In his view, they were a superior ruling race who had gone astray but he believed that they could recover their lost glory under British supervision.

WHAT BRITAIN DID TO NIGERIA

I believe myself that the future of the virile races of the protectorate lies largely in the regeneration of the Fulani. Their ceremonial, their coloured skins, their mode of life and habits of thought, appeal more to the native populations than the prosaic rule of the Anglo-Saxon can ever do. It is our task to regenerate this capable race, to mould them to ideas of justice and mercy, so that in a future generation, if not in this, they may become worthy instruments of rule under British supervision.[9]

Despite Lugard's customary ethnic typecasting, the Fulani really did have sophisticated political and judicial systems already in place by the time Britain arrived. Those pre-colonial systems were sufficiently developed and long-standing for Britain to utilise them without major overhaul. As the rulers of a Muslim theocracy, the emirs already had a judicial system with alkalis (judges), a revenue generation system and several titled officials. The Sokoto Caliphate's sophistication ironically rendered it ideal for indirect rule.

Britain allowed the system of selecting emirs to continue—subject to confirmation by the colonial government (which informed the kingmakers of its preferred candidate). The colonial government gave letters of appointment to the emirs and required them to swear an oath of allegiance to the British Crown. Britain also retained the Caliphate's judicial system; albeit with modifications. Indirect rule offered Britain the convenience of being able to divest itself of responsibility for the most unpopular features of colonialism, such as tax collection, and delegate them to native rulers. Since the budget for running the native colonial administration and paying the emirs' salaries came from the taxes they collected, the emirs were incentivised to become tax collectors on behalf of the British. Taxation could be superimposed on the colonial Caliphate as an extension of the pre-colonial tradition of paying tributes to emirs.

Although this account makes indirect rule in Northern Nigeria appear seamless, there were some knotty issues behind the facade of continuity. For example, British changes to the criminal justice system of Northern Nigeria merit discussion because the legacy of those changes are relevant to the controversy about Sharia law, which still rages in Nigeria today. Although the British colonial government permitted the Caliphate to continue implementing Sharia law and prescribe penal punishments as sanctioned by the Koran, it abolished punishments which in Britain's view were 'repugnant to humanity' or which contravened 'the observance of the fundamental laws of humanity and justice'. As a result the colonial government abolished punishments such as amputations for theft, *diya* (blood money as a settlement for murder), retaliation for personal injury, and death by stoning for adultery.

'If an Emir proves unamenable to persuasion or threats ... he is deposed'

Britain also had the power to depose an emir. Lugard admitted: 'If an *Emir* proves unamenable to persuasion or threats ... he is deposed.'[10] Given that the threat of dismissal hung over any emir who displeased the British, how much independence did the emirs really have? Dame Margery Perham said that the 'Emir retains nearly all his powers in theory while in practice, behind the curtain, he is checked and propelled, not by a ministry, still less by a democracy, but by an unobtrusive, kindly, middle-aged Englishman who derives his authority from the military power and wealth of Great Britain.'[11] In colonial Northern Nigeria, the 'unobtrusive, kindly, middle-aged Englishman' that Perham described was called a 'resident'. The resident was Britain's colonial representative and his job was to 'advise' the emir in his district. The resident also acted as an invisible hand to prod and guide the emir towards outcomes favourable to Britain. Despite the image of the resident playing a non-interventionist role, Captain Orr, a former resident in Northern Nigeria, declared:

the Resident does far more than advise. He has power to arrest, try, and sentence natives in his own court, without referring to any of the native rulers. With regard to taxation, he conveys precise orders from the Governor as to the amounts to be collected, mode of assessing and collection and so on ... and generally carries out a direct interference in all the internal affairs of the State.[12]

'Henceforth they must be our puppets and adopt our methods and rules'

In some respects the power of the emirs was diluted to mirror that of the British constitutional monarch today. Both were *de jure* heads of government but had their de facto powers encumbered by the bureaucracy of non-royal administrators. This raises the question of whether the emirs really ruled or whether they were merely ceremonial agents of the colonial power. On this point Lugard was explicit: 'I wish to try whether we can succeed in ruling the country through the Fulani *not by the Fulani* ... Henceforth they must be our puppets and adopt our methods and rules.'[13]

For Lugard, indirect rule was a success in Northern Nigeria. It allowed Britain to operate a leanly staffed colonial regime on a low budget. He was so pleased with the success of indirect rule in the north that he attempted to apply it to Southern Nigeria using the model that worked for him in the north. Despite some challenges, indirect rule could be implemented in south-west Nigeria, which had several indigenous pre-colonial chiefs that could be incorporated into the colonial system. However, in the south-east in particular, it produced a wildly different and destabilising outcome.

Indirect Rule in South-Eastern Nigeria

A key ingredient of the effective operation of indirect rule was the preservation of the pre-existing indigenous governing structures.

However, in south-east Nigeria, indirect rule had the opposite effect. Rather than preserving and utilising pre-colonial indigenous institutions, it dismantled them and replaced them with new ones.

If British colonialism in Nigeria had a blind spot, it was in the south-east. Indirect rule operated on the mistaken British assumption that all Africans had chiefs or rulers. This assumption failed miserably in south-east Nigeria where the primary ethnic groups such as the Igbo, Ibibio, Efik, Ekoi and Ogoni did not have large kingdoms, nor did any of them recognise any one person as their ruler. South-eastern Nigerian society instead consisted of small, politically autonomous villages. This was a problem for the colonial government. How could indirect rule work in communities that did not have powerful indigenous rulers on whom Britain could rely? However, the colonial government devised a solution for this problem. If it could not find chiefs, it would simply manufacture them.

The Warrant Chiefs

In areas where the British colonial government could not find a chief, it found someone who it presumed was powerful or had leadership qualities and appointed him a chief by giving him a certificate known as a 'warrant'. Such appointees were called 'warrant chiefs'. The warrant chief system threw south-eastern Nigeria into political turmoil from which it may not yet have recovered. It was one of the most controversial and bitterly resented legacies of colonial rule in the region. The warrant chief system does not have a shortage of critics. It has been described as a 'disaster for traditional leadership in Igboland',[14] while some of the warrant chiefs themselves have been denounced as 'careerists and rascals'[15] and 'mere upstarts and non-entities'.[16]

There were at least four great problems with the warrant chief system. Firstly, warrant chiefs were a resented and alien creation in societies that did not have paramount rulers. The British government granted the warrant chiefs powers that no one had ever exercised in south-eastern Nigeria. This inevitably led to abuses. Secondly, there was no ordered process of selecting warrant chiefs. This lack of selectivity set a low bar for eligibility and there were not sufficient checks to ensure that only those fit for power got to exercise it. Thirdly, it created a new source of internal friction in indigenous communities. The bitter resentment about the creation of warrant chiefs created turmoil between the warrant chiefs and those they were supposed to govern. Fourthly, the enormous and unprecedented powers that warrant chiefs exercised enabled new types of extortion and fraud to arise in south-eastern Nigeria. The first three of these problems were caused by the British colonial administration, and the last by south-easterners themselves.

Britain gave unprecedented new powers and responsibilities to the warrant chiefs. Warrant chiefs were also tax collectors, could forcibly conscript people to become labourers on colonial projects, and also had judicial powers. In pre-colonial south-eastern society, such autocratic powers were not vested in one person and had previously been shared among various individuals and groups in society.

'Indirect rule was making puppets of African chiefs'

Britain put the warrant chiefs in a difficult position with their own people. Being empowered by the British made them seem like stooges of the colonial invader. Their communities did not respect a warrant chief simply because he had a letter of appointment and wore a red cap given by the British. During a discussion of indirect rule held by the African Society and the Royal Society of Arts in 1934, one of the attendees remarked:

> Indirect rule was making puppets of African chiefs ... they were
> chiefs in name only. If the chiefs were called agents it would be a

better name because they were carrying out the orders of the British Government. The chiefs represented the people no longer, and the Africans did not want their chiefs to sell the people to the British. That was what indirect rule was doing.[17]

The method (if one existed) by which warrant chiefs were appointed was also problematic. There did not seem to be any systematic criteria for appointment as a warrant chief and selection seemed arbitrary. The British often gave someone a warrant as a reward for services rendered to the British government, such as giving information about anti-British insurgents or for providing carriers for a British military operation. This method of awarding warrants led to the emergence of one of the most fascinating indigenous leaders in colonial Nigeria. Ahebi Ugbabe was the only female warrant chief in the history of colonial Nigeria. She was born in Igboland but fled as a young girl and spent 20 years in Igala-land. During her exile she became a prostitute, befriended the *attah Igala* (Igala king), and had sexual relationships with British colonial officers and other powerful men. She learned to speak Igala, pidgin English and Nupe in the course of her interaction with the Igala elite, British officers and soldiers. Her polyglot skills and knowledge of local routes made her a valuable asset to the British military. She acted as a guide and informant for them, and provided them with information on routes to reach and conquer her home town of Enugu-Ezike. She was appointed as a warrant chief in reward for her services to the British. Using warrant chief appointments in this way had the effect of rewarding colonial collaborators. For example, Nwakpuda of Old Umuahia and Nwosuocha of Umunwanwa acted as guides for British military operations in the early 1900s and were appointed warrant chiefs as a reward for their services.

Tragi-comic outcomes also emerged on the occasions when the colonial government consulted with natives before appointing a warrant chief. Owing to the extreme violence that accompanied colonial conquest and incidents of Britain kidnapping and exiling chiefs it considered uncooperative, the natives severely distrusted the British. When Lt-Colonel Galway travelled to Ibibio-land, several people refused to attend meetings with him. He admitted: 'The practice of calling chiefs to meetings and then seizing them, and of calling in guns to mark and then destroying them, has resulted in general distrust of the government and its policy.'[18] Many assumed that becoming a chief working for Britain was a ruse and a one-way ticket to slavery, exile or death. As a result, those who were fit for leadership refused to volunteer, and some communities put forward unqualified candidates whom they would not miss. Sometimes they press-ganged social outcasts or those they deemed expendable to become warrant chiefs. For example, in one incident in Umuariam in Obowo, the locals tried to get rid of a social misfit in the village by putting forward his name to the British. When soldiers led him away, the locals thought they would never see him again. To their horror, the man returned with a warrant from the colonial government announcing that he was now their chief.[19] In other similarly comic episodes, British officials mistook men who had a commanding presence or who 'looked' like leaders and appointed them as warrant chiefs.[20] For example, a town crier was mistaken as a man of influence and selected as a warrant chief because villagers responded to his drumbeat to attend meetings.

'To grow fat an insect must feed on fellow insects'

When people realised that becoming a warrant chief was not, as they initially feared, a condemnation to slavery, exile or death, but instead offered a gateway to enormous power and wealth, they started scrambling for the position. This caused a plethora of chiefs to emerge in Igboland. By 1915 there were more than 900 warrant chiefs in the Owerri province alone.[21]

The colonial government also established a series of Native Courts over which the warrant chiefs presided. Although they employed court clerks and messengers, Native Courts were more than judicial courts. In addition to their judicial functions, they acted as the seat of local government and had executive powers. Being a warrant chief also offered the opportunity to become rich. Some warrant chiefs aspired to, and copied, the lifestyles of British district officers, who were Southern Nigeria's equivalent of Northern Nigeria's residents. Some bought hammocks and demanded to be carried from place to place in them, just like British district officers. The humble ones bought bicycles or motorcycles, then graduated to motor cars in which they would ostentatiously arrive for meetings, or built large palatial concrete houses with corrugated-iron roofs which overshadowed the more modest houses of other village residents. When one warrant chief was asked how he got so rich, he replied, 'To grow fat an insect must feed on fellow insects,' and declined to elaborate further.[22]

'Inspired fear and respect as well as hatred'

According to a former warrant chief, court messengers 'inspired fear and respect as well as hatred'.[23] A former court messenger went further and revealed that 'in remote villages court messengers were regarded as the incarnation of the government'.[24] He also admitted that he had once thrown a man who needed his services out of his house for not offering him a 'bottle of English wine' as a bribe, and refused to cooperate until the man knelt down before him, called him 'master', and promised to bring the wine to him.

The fact that the colonial treasury in the south-east, which paid the salaries of warrant chiefs and Native Court personnel, was initially financed from fees and fines levied by Native Courts gave the warrant chiefs and their staff an incentive to keep the courts 'busy'. Large avenues for the abuse of power and corruption emerged since Native Courts and their personnel were often unsupervised by British officials. British colonial officials rarely learned to speak south-eastern languages and did not frequently attend Native Court sessions. As a result they were completely beholden to, and subject to, the version of events given by their interpreters, court clerks and messengers. Since the interpreters, court clerks and messengers conveyed instructions between the British district officers and the warrant chiefs, they often used this power to manipulate information flows and shape narratives for their own benefit. Some warrant chiefs and court clerks colluded to enrich themselves by elaborate fraudulent schemes. For example, since clerks could issue summonses and arrest warrants, they contrived a fraudulent practice known as *akwukwo nnunnu* (bird summons). These bogus or frivolous summonses were issued to arrest and imprison their enemies or seize the property of innocent people. Sometimes the innocent party would not be able to regain their freedom or property until they had paid a bribe. Even where a legitimate case existed, some court clerks 'sold' the verdict to the highest bidder. Some warrant chiefs also abused their right to conscript people to work on bogus colonial work projects 'for the white man'. Realising that people dared not refuse work ordered by British colonial officers, an offence that carried punishments such as flogging and the destruction of one's village, warrant chiefs duped unsuspecting villagers into working on their farms and on their own personal projects.

Legacy of Indirect Rule

The British colonial government arguably had no option but to implement indirect rule since it did not have enough staff and money to govern directly. From Britain's perspective, indirect rule was advantageous and successful. It reduced the costs of colonial administration and saved many British lives by doing away with the need for a constant British presence in every corner of Nigeria.

As with so many British colonial policies, indirect rule produced different results in the north and south. Indirect rule can be considered at least a qualified success in Northern Nigeria. Although it made the northern emirs subordinate agents of the colonial government, it preserved much of their power over their subjects. Not only did indirect rule preserve the emirs' power over the communities they already ruled, but it also extended their power to new communities they did not previously control and that were not part of the pre-colonial Sokoto Caliphate. For example, the Hausa state of Kebbi had spent a century resisting invasion and control by the Caliphate, and did not officially accept incorporation into the Caliphate until British troops occupied it.

Indirect rule also provided a buffer that kept the coloniser at a safe distance from the people they ruled. Britain maintained constant vigilance and trod carefully to avoid taking measures that would provoke a revolt. A British academic who travelled through colonial Northern Nigeria cautioned that 'the risk of a local or general insurrection, of a fanatical or emotional character, is a possibility for which for many generations their European masters must be prepared'.[25] The Satiru rebellion of 1906 illustrated that this was not a theoretical threat, and the ruthless and excessive use of force used to suppress it was to some extent an emotional over-reaction to that concern. British avoidance of a sustained revolt in Northern Nigeria was partially due to avoiding such drastic measures as abolishing the emirates and replacing them with a different system of governance.

An argument can also be made that colonial rule transformed most British-recognised colonial chiefs in Nigeria into warrant chiefs. The practice of giving letters of appointment to indigenous chiefs created new chiefs where none existed in the south-east, but also turned pre-colonial chiefs into *de jure* warrant chiefs (at least during the period of colonial rule) since their appointments and authority were ratified by and derived from letters of appointment from the colonial government.

In the south-east and Niger Delta, the creation of warrant chiefs produced disastrous effects. Although these areas had few paramount rulers in the pre-colonial era, Britain exacerbated the problem by overthrowing and exiling the few powerful rulers from those areas such as Jaja of Opobo, the oba of Benin, and Nana Olomu. By the time Britain implemented indirect rule, it had already made the task difficult by creating a political power vacuum after removing pre-colonial rulers. The only way to implement indirect rule in these areas was to create new power centres and a new ruling elite.

The warrant chief system created new 'Big Men' in south-eastern Nigeria and inverted the social power pyramid by empowering younger members of society who had warrants. It also added a new currency of power: money. The new power holders did not have to rely on age seniority since they could instead mobilise followers and resources by using money.

One of the most ironic legacies of the warrant chief system is that it created and entrenched a plethora of 'chiefs' in the part of Nigeria with no pre-colonial history of large kingdoms or chiefs. Nigeria is now awash with thousands of titled men who demand to be addressed as 'his royal majesty', HRH, and 'royal father', and who claim to be 'traditional rulers' of 'kingdoms' that never existed before colonial rule. Rulership titles such as *eze*, *igwe* and *obi* have proliferated in parts of south-east Nigeria where such titles did not exist before British rule. By the late 1980s, there were 820 government-recognised traditional rulers in Igboland alone.[26] Yet the overwhelming majority of them had no pre-colonial existence. Although south-eastern Nigeria has been the focus of this section, similar problems also arose in non-Muslim areas of Northern Nigeria that did not have paramount rulers, such as the Tiv and Idoma. For example, the tor Tiv and ochi Idoma are the present-day 'paramount rulers' of the Tiv and Idoma ethnic groups respectively. Yet these rulership positions did not exist before colonial rule.

Many of Nigeria's present chiefs are descendants of warrant chiefs and have turned the position, a colonial administrative position issued with a piece of paper and a red cap, into a hereditary title. Some people with three generations of descent from a warrant chief claim to be 'royalty'. Even though such chiefs earned their titles from the colonial warrant chief system rather than from an ancient royal line, their success has been hereditary. Since being literate helped warrant chiefs to understand the intricacies of Native Court procedure, those who went to school had an advantage. The wealth that warrant chiefs acquired also allowed them to send their children to elite schools. Many of south-east Nigeria's first-generation educated elite were the children of warrant chiefs. For example, the first Nigerian judge at the International Court of Justice, Charles Onyeama, was the son of one of the most famous warrant chiefs, Onyeama of Eke. Many of Nigeria's current elite are also descendants of warrant chiefs. For example, the British Labour MP Chi Onwurah is the great-granddaughter of a warrant chief in Awka in south-east Nigeria. Nigeria's minister for foreign affairs Geoffrey Onyeama is the grandson of warrant chief Onyeama of Eke. The minister of the Niger Delta (and former senator, and former governor of Akwa Ibom State) Godswill Akpabio is the son of Udo Okuku Akpabio, a former warrant chief in Ikot-Ekpene; and Senator (and former Abia State governor) Theodore Orji is the son of former warrant chief Tom Ikoro Orji. This pattern is not limited to the south-east. The former governor of Kwara State Adamu Attah (an Ebira) was the son of warrant chief Ibrahim Attah.[27]

The warrant chief system nonetheless produced a positive outcome by encouraging education and literacy in south-east Nigeria. Education and being able to read and write in English reduced people's vulnerability to fraudulent manipulation by Native Court personnel and the incomprehensible bureaucratic procedures surrounding the courts.

An outstanding question that merits discussion is who can be regarded as the architect of indirect rule. Thanks to his large propaganda team, including his wife, who was a writer, and his other writer friends such as Margery Perham, Lugard (as usual) is credited with being the originator of indirect rule. However, one should note that Sir George Goldie laid down the ideological template for indirect rule in Nigeria six years before it commenced. According to Goldie:

> even an imperfect and tyrannical native African administration, if its extreme excesses were controlled by European supervision, would be, in the early stages, productive of far less discomfort to its subjects than well-intentioned but ill-directed efforts of European magistrates, often young and headstrong, and not invariably gifted with sympathy and introspective powers. If the welfare of the native races is to be considered, if dangerous revolts are to be obviated, the general policy of ruling on African principles through native rulers must be followed for the present.[28]

Goldie put these ideas into practice in 1897 after his Royal Nigeria Company invaded Bida and Ilorin, deposed their emirs and replaced them with new emirs of his choosing. Although he did not realise it at the time, his actions provided the ideological foundation that Britain used to rule Northern Nigeria for almost sixty years. Goldie's adroit use of amenable local rulers to govern on his behalf would later be given a name—indirect rule.

Nigeria's traditional rulers remained ensconced in the indirect rule system even after the country gained independence. Rather than playing subordinate roles within a British colonial system, they moved into playing subordinate roles in Nigeria's post-colonial governments and never recovered the powers they had prior to colonialism. A native of Ghana provided a fitting epitaph for indirect rule when he said:

> The introduction of indirect rule into Africa ... had resulted in the divorcement of the people from their chiefs and elders. The sacredness of the Stools, and the sanctity of the person occupying them were losing their sway. If ever there was anything which the pure African would never forgive the European for, it was that act of defiling the sacredness of the Stools ... it diminished the prestige of an African paramount chief, sub-chief or elder, to be nominated as an agent of the British. That was one of the results of indirect rule.[29]

20

COLONIAL LIFE

While the prior chapters have chronicled the tectonic changes caused by British invasion and conquest, this one will focus on the day-to-day social and political life of colonialism. What was it like being a British person or a Nigerian in colonial Nigeria?

'To have his servant watch him like a dog, evidently noticing nothing but the needs of the new master'

The first question to address is: why did British people volunteer or agree to work in colonial Nigeria? The reasons varied. For some such as Goldie and Lugard, travelling far away from home offered them a chance to escape the entanglements of their wrecked personal lives and start afresh. For the soldiers, it was a sense of adventure: going to Nigeria offered them a chance to serve their country, fight, and hunt game in a new environment. For the missionaries, going to West Africa was a divine mission to spread the word of God and civilisation. For the vast majority, the reason was economic. Colonialism allowed Britons to gain in Nigeria a level of material comfort they would never have in their home country. The pay was good and they could experience a life of freedom in an environment where their social position was elevated, and where they would be attended to by their own personal retinue of Nigerian servants and guards. They had Nigerian servants to cook their food, wash and fold their clothes, clean their houses, and carry their bags. Some did not even have to walk as they hired Nigerians to carry them in hammocks on their journeys. An Englishman who travelled through Nigeria said:

> For the first time in his life the middle-class [British] man knows what it is to be waited on hand and foot, to have his servant watch him like a dog, evidently noticing nothing but the needs of the new master ... He finds his bed, bad as it is, better made than it was last night, and that the lad really does understand the 'palaver' of the mosquito-net, how to hang it up and how to tuck it in. He finds he likes having his clothes quietly taken from his hands one by one as he stands behind the funnel getting ready for the night, and he falls asleep feeling that his new life is beginning in earnest.[1]

Segregation

Although Nigeria was not a settler colony, British personnel there usually segregated themselves physically by living in separate neighbourhoods from Nigerians. They did so ostensibly for health reasons, believing that prolonged contact with, or living close to, Nigerians was hazardous to their health and sanitation. A colonial officer said:

> As most of the inhabitants of Nigeria are infected with malaria, one of the methods adopted for preserving the health of Europeans is segregation. Separate residential areas are laid out, where this is possible, for Europeans and Africans ... By this arrangement ... a higher standard of sanitation can be insisted on for the European reservation than would be possible in a 'mixed' neighbourhood ... moreover, [it] allows them to enjoy in peace the drumming and noisy laughter so dear to the Negro heart and so irritating to the European.[2]

British colonial staff usually lived inside spacious compounds in separate neighbourhoods called Government Reservation Areas (GRA). While the British lived in large houses in the compound, their Nigerian servants lived in separate, smaller bungalows in a different section of the compound called the 'boys' quarters'. The lifestyle of colonial officers created a new standard for material wealth among Nigerians. Wealthy Nigerians tried to emulate the lifestyles and material possessions of the colonial officers living in the GRA. They aspired to have a car, servants, a large house, and a walled compound like the district officer. The architectural design and influence of colonial housing can still be seen in Nigerian housing today. Many middle-class and upper-middle-class Nigerians still follow the segregated colonial housing pattern to this day: they live in a main house, while their personal staff of cleaners, cooks, drivers and nannies live in the 'boys' quarters'.

Interracial Relationships

'The satisfaction, with which I began to survey the negro beauties'

When it came to having sexual relations with Nigerians, some British expatriates and colonial officials suddenly became less concerned about segregated housing and the purported health risks of close contact with Nigerians. For early British travellers, Nigeria also offered sexual opportunities. The 19th-century explorer Hugh Clapperton spent considerable time writing in his journals about the 'satisfaction, with which I began to survey the negro beauties',[3] and about a trader who took him 'to show me the best looking slaves in Mandara. He had three, all under sixteen, yet quite women, for negresses, they were the most pleasing and perfectly formed I had ever seen.'[4] His journals were full of references to late-night visits he received from native women. On one occasion he cheekily proposed to (an already married) 'buxom young girl of fifteen'.[5]

British colonialism in Nigeria was a largely male enterprise. Owing to the hot and humid climate, and the alarming British mortality rate, women were considered too 'fragile' to be posted there. In 1921, only 10% of Europeans living in Nigeria were women.[6] Most of the early colonial officials were either bachelors or were unaccompanied married men, having left their wives behind in Britain. Lugard was still a bachelor when he first came to Nigeria, and even after he married, his wife never lived permanently with him in Nigeria. Being thousands of miles away from home without female partners offered the men plenty of opportunity to fraternise with Nigerian women. Such relationships are rarely mentioned in accounts of colonial Nigeria written by Britons or Nigerians, and are almost taboo. They were a source of embarrassment to colonial officials, who, on the rare occasions they mentioned them, did so only to register their disapproval. An Englishman wrote: 'I will not offend my readers by discussing the black mistress. Concubinage is a degrading relationship be the mistress black or white, and apart from the sexual morality it entails the telling of many lies. But the African half-caste procreated from such connections is a stout race.'[7]

Although interracial relationships were rarely mentioned in the colonial reports, which focus on dry statistics, such relationships (especially between British men and Nigerian women) were common. Lugard's secretary admitted: 'There is no use ignoring the fact that such irregular unions do exist, and in the past they were almost universal.' He supported the presence of British wives in Nigeria because it would 'reduce the number of cases of white men who live with black mistresses'.[8] In the early colonial days, the Foreign Office nagged George Goldie 'to take action about the various liaisons some of his agents on the coast were having with the local honey-coloured nut brown beauties'.[9]

Goldie replied that he was unable to act unless the government wanted him to replace the energetic young men in his company with grey-haired old men. There may have been another reason for his reluctance to confront his staff on the matter. One of Goldie's friends wrote: 'He was very fond of women, and no man admitted it more frankly. Reports of his personal relationships certainly reached the ears of Queen Victoria.'[10] Goldie fathered at least three children with local women in the Niger Delta area, and he may have had more children. He could not reprimand his staff for having relationships with native women without drawing attention to his own.

Unlike the French, who encouraged their colonial officers to live with native paramours in their colonies, Britain frowned upon 'miscegenation'. British authorities responded to interracial relationships by either 'burying' evidence of them or penalising officials who were in such relationships that could not be kept quiet. Official British concern and disapproval led Lugard to issue 'Secret Circular B' to forbid British officials from engaging in interracial relationships. This document was circulated in a highly restricted way. We may never know its exact contents as it was subsequently withdrawn and all copies of it were destroyed. However, clues as to its contents emerge from the less-filtered memoirs of British military officers who tended to be more forthright than their circumspect civilian colleagues. In his memoirs, Brigadier-General Frank Crozier cited a memorandum which read: 'It is forbidden for European officials to keep native women. Any officer, British N.C.O. or civilian official contracting V.D. [venereal disease] will forfeit pay and allowances when under treatment.'[11] While we do not know if this is Lugard's Secret Circular B, it does reveal official awareness of interracial relationships. Despite the government's disapproval, British officials nonetheless continued these relationships clandestinely.

WHAT BRITAIN DID TO NIGERIA

'He kept a woman in Africa and a wife in Wales'

British army officers in the Northern Nigeria Regiment (NNR) had a system of procuring young Hausa and Fulani girls for themselves. A soldier named Burnham 'bought' a young Hausa girl for £1, disguised her as a boy and kept her with him as a sex slave when the NNR went to invade Sokoto.[12] Even a British Christian missionary in Northern Nigeria, one Fuller, 'kept a woman in Africa and a wife in Wales'[13] and contracted venereal disease. When locals realised that some British officers had a predilection for local women, they tried to exploit this by offering women as bribes. In an effort to convince then Lieutenant Crozier to become his adviser, the emir of Katsina offered him Fulani women. Crozier recalled the emir taking him to see 'beautiful Fulani girls walk, quite nude, in front of big merchants who select in strict secrecy'.[14]

Taking young girls as sex slaves was so widespread in the NNR that an aggrieved father from Sokoto complained that a British officer named Bellamy had seduced his young daughter and taken her away. According to another British officer, 'she is below the age, even in native law'.[15] Given that fathers in Northern Nigeria allowed their daughters to marry at ages as young as 12, she must have been very young indeed. The British resident ('Ash')[16] hushed up the scandal by promising that 'I'll fix the compensation and try to keep it quiet'.[17] Captain Sword of the NNR was also sent home prematurely before his tour of duty in Nigeria ended because of 'his association with the native women of the country'.[18]

Stanhope White, a colonial officer in Northern Nigeria, discovered a file regarding a British trader at Kano who had been imprisoned for sodomy. Rather than denying the accusation of homosexuality against him, the trader instead protested against his punishment 'by alleging that such practices were common amongst Government Officers, and were condoned'.[19] White prevented further inquiry into the veracity of the trader's allegation by destroying the file with the approval of the British resident at Kano. Soon after his conviction, the trader committed suicide.

Another case involved a British education officer, Dr Rupert East, who was an esteemed scholar of Hausa literature. A young girl from Adamawa, Maimunatu 'Dada Sare' Abdullahi, was kidnapped at the age of 11 or 12 and given as a sex slave to a British officer. After impregnating her, the officer completed his tour of duty and returned to England. Maimunatu later met Dr East and started a relationship with him. Unlike other interracial affairs of that era, East did not hide his relationship with Maimunatu. The couple lived together and she often attended social events at which he hosted other British expatriates. Later, East left Maimunatu behind in Nigeria and returned to England, where he married an Englishwoman.

Being used and left behind in this way did not please Nigerian women. A celebrated relationship that ended tragically involved a 22-year-old Igbo woman named Ada Ocha Ntu ('Esther Johnson') and a middle-aged expatriate British railway worker, Mark Hall. In the course of their relationship Hall asked Ada to loan him £400. Shortly after receiving the money, Hall travelled to England on holiday. When he returned to Nigeria in 1953 he gave three surprising pieces of news to Ada. Firstly, he was unable to repay the £400 loan; secondly, he had married a woman in England; and thirdly, he had used the £400 she lent him to buy a car for his new wife so she could use it to start a taxi business. To Hall's surprise, Ada did not respond well to the news he delivered. She flew into a rage and stabbed him to death with a pair of scissors. She was sentenced to death, but Nigeria's first indigenous governor-general, Nnamdi Azikiwe, pardoned her in 1961 shortly after Nigeria's independence.

British and Nigerian accounts of these relationships differ. The British accounts tend to portray them as casual, transient or transactional, by describing the Nigerian women as 'concubines' or 'mistresses'. In contrast, Nigerians portray them as committed relationships. For example, a Nigerian man I interviewed, a grandson of a union between a Nigerian woman and a British colonial officer, tried to give his grandmother's relationship respectability by describing her as the 'wife' of the British man.

Colonial Officers

'The [British] officials in general are honourable, honest gentlemen'

Having examined the romantic encounters between British officials and Nigerians, we can now turn to the political relations between them. In their accounts of their stewardship, British colonial administrators almost always portrayed themselves as affable, kind and dedicated to uplifting the welfare of the natives they were trying to civilise. For example, a British expatriate asserted: 'The [British] officials in general are honourable, honest gentlemen; in good discipline, not cruel and not bribeable.'[20] Dame Margery Perham eulogised that Lugard 'carried the highest standards of his country and civilization into lands far beyond their influence, and once there he did not abandon them. He was always just and humane; he judged each man on his merits and was as quick to like and to trust an African as a white man.'[21]

How true are these accounts of genial British conduct? While many British residents and district officers doubtless ingratiated themselves with locals and went to great effort to solve the problems of the communities they administered, that was not always the case. Although the generation of colonial officers who worked in Nigeria during the final few decades of colonial rule were generally more temperate, some of the first generation were very different. Like Goldie before him, Lugard immersed himself in hard work to try to forget his unhappy personal life, and was 'a hard driving and often ungracious master'.[22] Goldie also 'had the name of being a hard man to serve'.[23] Colonial accounts usually focus on the action and policies of the apex colonial officers such as Lugard and Hugh Clifford, yet it was their subordinates who carried out most of the day-to-day business of governing.

A remarkable aspect of modern Nigeria is how many of its monuments are named after colonial oppressors. For example, the main road through the town of Owerri is called Douglas Road and the Imo State Government guest house in south-east Nigeria is named Douglas House. The naming would suggest that Douglas was a remarkable man. Who was he?

Harold Morday Douglas was one of the most notorious colonial officers in Nigeria. He worked for the British colonial service for over twenty years and in 1902 was appointed as the first district commissioner of Owerri (in modern-day Imo State in south-east Nigeria). Prior to this, he was a political officer attached to the British army during its invasion of Arochukwu.

The memory of Douglas endured and the people of south-east Nigeria recalled him long after his departure. When someone spoke to an elder about Douglas more than seventy years after he first arrived in the region, the elder replied: 'it is hard for you, my son, to grasp the degree of our suffering and the fear that was generated in our minds at the time.' A historian has described Douglas as 'the worst D.O. to ever serve in the region'.[24] Another account stated: 'The overwhelming consensus of the local people at Owerri regarding Douglas was that he was extraordinarily autocratic, particularly difficult to deal with, and extremely overbearing. His violent temper, autocratic personality, and insensitivity towards the local Africans, it is said, made him distinctly unpopular throughout the whole of the Owerri district.'[25]

What did Douglas do to make himself so unpopular? Two of his distinguishing traits were his ferocious temper and his liberal use of forced labour. Douglas belonged to a generation of colonial officers who casually or reflexively resorted to force and violence, even when not necessary, and even when dialogue was the easier path.

'The people complained bitterly of your harsh treatment of them'

Douglas was enthusiastic in using severe force against communities that refused to supply labour to him. In March 1904 the people of Eziama rejected Douglas's order to build roads. In response Douglas embarked upon a path of destruction. Firstly, he ordered every compound in Eziama to be burned and destroyed, then he arrested and imprisoned their leaders, and held them hostage for two months until the people agreed to build the roads in exchange for securing their leaders' freedom.[26] Douglas also flogged and assaulted natives, including their chiefs. He manhandled Chief Nwagbaraocha Anumunu for arriving late at a meeting. The chief was so appalled that he resigned from his position as a warrant chief. In 1905 a Nigerian priest witnessed Douglas beating and kicking a young man in the Owerri market square in an unprovoked attack. When the priest tried to mediate, Douglas physically threatened him. The priest reported the matter to Bishop Herbert Tugwell, who wrote to Douglas on 18 December 1905 to say:

> From what I have heard from the people as I pass through your district, and from what I heard subsequently from those who accompany me, your system of administration appears to be well nigh unbearable. The people complained bitterly of your harsh treatment of them, while those who accompanied me do not cease to speak in the strongest terms of your unbearable manner towards them. They say they have never received such treatment at the hands of a British officer.[27]

'I did what you told me, Sir'

Tugwell appealed to Douglas to 'adopt a kindlier and more generous attitude towards a subject people'.[28] Douglas was not receptive to the advice and continued his reign of terror. He continued to subject his personal staff to his outbursts of temper and violence, and to publicly flog native chiefs who crossed him. Douglas confessed that in 1914 he knocked an African interpreter unconscious for answering him back. After the interpreter was discharged from hospital, he claimed that the comment that so outraged Douglas was: 'I did what you told me, Sir'.[29] Douglas proudly claimed to have subdued at least 135 five villages and towns,[30] during which time 'his soldiers terrorised the nearby communities'.[31]

Douglas's outrages led to the death of another Briton. The tragic story of Dr James Stewart has passed into folklore in Igboland. Dr Stewart was a Northern Irish medical officer serving in south-east Nigeria. While riding on a bike on 16 November 1905, he became separated from his escorts, got lost, and ended up in the village of Onicha-Amairi close to Mbaise (in the heartland of the area that suffered at Douglas's hands). Douglas's actions had generated great anti-British hostility in the area and turned it into a dangerous territory that could not be safely visited by Britons without an armed escort. The villagers misidentified Stewart as Douglas and were under the joyful impression that they had captured their tormentor. They murdered Stewart, then arrested and tied his 'iron horse' (his bicycle) to a tree. Since his corpse was never recovered, British authorities assumed that the locals ate him. Another popular account claimed that they instead cut off his limbs and distributed them to different communities. This triggered a massive British military reprisal against the Mbaise, Mbano and Etiti areas of south-east Nigeria, during which hundreds more Nigerians were killed and more villages were destroyed.

Oswald Crewe-Read was Douglas's counterpart on the west side of the River Niger. He was the district commissioner at Agbor (in modern-day Delta State). Crewe-Read's district was in enemy territory, inside the Asaba hinterland, which was the centre of the Ekumeku uprising against British rule. A British army officer who met Crewe-Read was very impressed by the work he had accomplished:

> He was the only white man in the district, but during the few months he had been there he had worked wonders. He had cleared away a large tract of bush, laid out the new station, and houses, offices, and police-barracks were well on the way to completion. In addition, he had filled up a swamp, staked and dammed the banks of the river, across which he had built a rough trestle bridge, and made an excellent thirty-foot road from the river to Agbor town.[32]

Although Crewe-Read got the credit, it was actually native forced labour that did the work. In the middle of the longest-running anti-colonial insurgency in the history of British rule in Nigeria, Crewe-Read thought it would be a good idea to seize and flog native chiefs from the area. He was already unpopular for conscripting natives for unpaid forced labour and on 8 June 1906 increased his unpopularity after he summoned all the chiefs of the village of Owa for a meeting. When the chiefs did not arrive by his deadline of 5 pm, Crewe-Read sent police officers out at night to arrest one of them, Ekuti, whom he blamed for the chiefs' tardiness. Ekuti's supporters would not allow him to be arrested and drove the police away. Crewe-Read persisted and decided to march out at 3 am in another attempt to apprehend Ekuti by force. He did not get the chance to complete his objective. Ekuti's supporters shot Crewe-Read at a place called Owa-Nta and he died from a bullet wound to the chest. The undersecretary of state for the colonies, Winston Churchill, and other officials at the Colonial Office stopped just short of blaming Crewe-Read for his own death. Churchill called for a posthumous 'severe and measured reprimand' of Crewe-Read for his practice of flogging chiefs, and was prevented from doing so only because the British secretary of state for the colonies, Lord Elgin, did not want to censure a dead man. Nonetheless, an inquiry concluded that the floggings Crewe-Read meted out were illegal and improper. Lord Elgin wrote: 'I have learned with great regret that the late Mr Crewe-Read caused native chiefs to be flogged and that much unnecessary and even useless work was demanded, provoking very great discontent amongst a population whose character I gather is not peaceable.'[33]

A Colonial Office official commented (with Churchill's approval) on Crewe-Read's murder in a manner almost suggesting that it was justified:

> Anyone who has imagination enough to turn himself round and look at this incident from the appropriate historical point of view (that of the Maccabees or of the Lays of Ancient Rome or of the Saxon defence of England) will recognise that this man [the killer] acted in a manner which could not but appear not only legitimate, but heroic and noble to his countrymen ... Of course we hang him for it—but we do not get any further by doing that in the face of what every native that knows the facts will think about them.[34]

Crewe-Read's actions caused more deaths and injuries as more than a hundred of the soldiers sent to avenge his death were killed or wounded.

Why did colonial authorities tolerate the outrageous behaviour of men like Douglas and Crewe-Read? The violent methods they used were a means to a greater British objective. In early colonial Nigeria, communication and transport were challenging because the existing narrow roads made it difficult for British officials to travel around. The solution was to build wider roads and railways. Douglas was successful at this task, building more than 200 miles of road in his district. However, the method that Douglas used, forced labour, was controversial and unpopular. Even though it was a primary instrument for the development of colonial Nigeria, forced labour has not been given the attention it merits.

WHAT BRITAIN DID TO NIGERIA

Forced Labour

A popular colonial narrative has it that colonialism brought infrastructural development to Nigeria in the form of improved roads, railways and bridges. Yet the method by which such innovations were accomplished is rarely discussed. Forced labour was the primary tool used to develop early colonial Nigeria. In those days, the colonial government preoccupied itself with the task of 'opening up the country'. The mobility of British military and political officers and communications between them were impeded by the lack of roads and the absence of telegraphs. Consequently, the government used forced labour to build railways, roads, telegraphs and houses for British personnel, and to carry their luggage when they travelled.

In using forced labour, district commissioners could claim the defence of obedience to their superiors' orders. The governor of Southern Nigeria, Walter Egerton, encouraged his staff to avoid 'undue leniency' since he believed it was 'apt to be misconstrued by the natives and regarded as weakness'.[35] He encouraged them to conscript as much forced labour as they desired. This was not a popular method. Being conscripted for a colonial labour project meant travelling far away from home to work on projects without pay. Moreover, the labourers were responsible for providing their own food, which often spoiled since they might work away from home for five or six consecutive days. Working as a carrier was onerous, and some carriers died from thirst or hunger or from carrying heavy loads. When they accompanied British army officers, carriers were also often the first casualties since they were unarmed and untrained.

People were often compelled to work against their own personal interests. For example, forced labourers were sometimes ordered to clear their own farmland (without compensation) to make way for a road or railway. Although these roads were used by the natives, that was not their primary purpose. The objective was to make British colonial administration more convenient, to make it easier to extract and transport produce, and to enable soldiers to march quickly and transport their weapons to areas where they were needed. In one example, people from Asaba and Okpanam were forced to work as carriers for the British army during their war against the Ekumeku insurgents in the early 1900s. Not only was the labour unsettling for carriers forced to travel far from home, but it also exposed them to physical danger by placing them in the middle of war zones.

Moreover, the colonial government did not seem to realise that conscripting forced labour made them appear hypocritical. The colonial government executed natives for keeping slaves, yet did not see the hypocrisy of forcing people to work for the government against their will and without pay. The British seemed unperturbed that, in the native perception, forcing people to work without pay and against their will had the same name as the practice that Britain professed to be committed to eradicating. To the natives, it appeared as if Britain had abolished indigenous slavery so it could replace it with its own system of slave labour.

British officers knew that forced labour was unpopular. A British army officer said: 'The problem of getting labour—which must be forced—and food supplies, is manifestly difficult ... Moreover, no native likes working far away for an unknown white man under new conditions, on a job he does not understand.'[36] Yet Britain defended forced labour as an unavoidable instrument of colonial rule. In 1906 Winston Churchill defended the practice in Parliament by stating: 'In West African Colonies and Protectorates in which there is legal power to demand labour on roads and waterways, the Governor or High Commissioner alone can make an order that such work shall be done.'[37] Forced labour was so routinised that in 1910 a colonial medical officer,

Dr Kent, forcibly seized people from two church congregations at Iseri and Umuku (in modern-day Delta State) during divine service in order to work for him as carriers. The incident provoked so much uproar that the congregation rejected the £5 compensation that the government offered to them.[38]

There are at least three possible reasons to explain why colonial officers employed such unnecessary violence. In some instances, young and inexperienced officers in the colonial service were allowed to exercise too much unsupervised power. Wielding so much power led some to inflate their sense of self-importance, build virtual personality cults, and develop bombastic nicknames for themselves.

Another school of thought maintains that, being isolated thousands of miles away from home in an unfamiliar environment, some colonial officers succumbed to depression, loneliness, mental illness and extreme temper. According to a British expatriate, 'they suffer from climatic irritability'. Can the casual violence that some colonial officers inflicted really be ascribed to a lack of climatic adaptation? Some colonial officers did indeed succumb to mental illness after serving in Nigeria. A prominent example is Sir Ralph Moor, who was the architect of Britain's conquest of Benin and south-east Nigeria. Much of the violence described in this chapter occurred under his watch. He returned to England from Nigeria a broken man. Owing to ill health, he retired in 1903 at the age of 43. Thereafter he suffered from insomnia and, in September 1909, committed suicide by drinking potassium cyanide while suffering from a bout of temporary insanity. We do not know whether these were pre-existing conditions or if they were caused by exposure to unaccustomed tropical conditions and illnesses. Nonetheless, the expatriate advocate of 'climatic irritability' had such deep belief in his explanation that he claimed: 'The mentality and morality of Europeans are also unfavourably affected by the climate. There is

a weakening of the control of the brain which results in outbursts of tropical fury, fits of passion caused by trivial incidents,
which sometimes result in assaults and violent crimes.'[39]

'There is something in the possession of superior strength most dangerous'

While loneliness and culture shock may have contributed to the
behaviour of colonial officers, more credible explanations for the
actions of men such as Douglas and Crewe-Read are to be found
in their attitudes of racial superiority and their perception of
Africans as an inferior, primitive, servile race. A colonial officer
was candid enough to admit:

> There is something in the possession of superior strength most dan-
> gerous, in a moral view, to its possessor. Brought in contact with
> semi-civilised man, the European, with his endowments and effective
> force so immeasurably superior, holds him as little higher than the
> brute, and as born equally for his service ... there are undoubtedly
> still a few who have yet to learn that a black man may be a gentleman
> and a white man otherwise.[40]

Major Arthur Glyn Leonard is another example of a man with
such a racist outlook. Leonard worked in colonial south-east
Nigeria. Before coming to Nigeria, he had worked as a police
officer for the British South Africa Company and he brought to
Nigeria racist attitudes that were prevalent among Europeans in
southern Africa. He referred to the locals in the south-eastern
Nigerian town of Aba as 'black monkey brands',[41] and when he
met a man from the town of Arochukwu, he informed him 'we
white men are "gods" who make you Aro boys'.[42] Although he
had contempt for the locals, Leonard's discerning eye noticed
'the bearing of their women, who, I must say, are ever so much
handsomer and finer than of any of the tribes in the Niger Delta'
and that 'among the women I noticed some very fine looking

specimens'.[43] The high commissioner of Southern Nigeria, Ralph Moor, forced Leonard to resign, not because he frequently beat his African staff or that he killed a man that worked as a carrier for him, but because he committed the far more serious crime of having sexual relationships with two Nigerian women whom he kept as travelling companions.

Whatever its real or perceived justification, British aggression and violence against Nigerians was a choice, not a necessity. The racial attitudes of the time portrayed flogging as the only way to discipline errant Africans. In 1905 Lt Blakiston-Houston of the NNR was acquitted of manslaughter after he flogged a young boy, who died shortly afterwards. Yet there were non-violent ways of achieving British objectives. One more light-hearted way that some colonial officers employed was to use Nigerians' innate belief in the supernatural against them. After realising that 'the faith of the people in the power of others to work magic against them is unbounded',[44] some British officers presented themselves as possessing supernatural powers. For example, a district officer with a glass eye would remove his eye and leave it at his desk when he was not around and managed to convince his Nigerian staff that he was able to observe them even when not at his office. Frank Hives was a district commissioner in south-east Nigeria who exploited his skills as a sleight of hand magician and ventriloquist to convince locals that he possessed supernatural powers.

'The crime of extortion or personation is very prevalent'

An indirect outcome of the terror that colonial officers like Douglas and Crewe-Read sowed was that it allowed unscrupulous Nigerians to add the crime of identity fraud to their unlawful box of tricks. Some Nigerians realised that they could exploit the terrifying power and reputation of the white man and his symbols of power to extort from their fellow Nigerians. For example, a favoured trick for Nigerian fraudsters (especially in the south) was to dress in a fez cap or soldier's uniform, then walk into a village full of illiterates and claim to be an emissary of the British. The fraudster would present the villagers with a piece of paper that he would allege contained British demands for money, food or other gifts (which the illiterate villagers could not dispute or verify). If they refused to pay or provide the items he demanded, he would secure their compliance by threatening to inform the British, who would come to destroy the village as a punishment. Such identity fraud was sufficiently commonplace for Lugard to mention it in one of his annual reports:

> throughout the protectorate, especially in the southern provinces, the crime of extortion or personation is very prevalent. A man wearing a fez and a pair of trousers comes to a village and announces that he has been sent by the white men. He may remain there for months, levying blackmail from the ignorant natives. He will often not content himself with demanding horses, cattle, fowls, and grain (sometimes in large quantities), but by threats that he will bring against the people some serious charge which (he informs them) will result in their extermination by the forces of the Protectorate, he may terrorise them into yielding to him their wives and daughters. The uncomplaining acquiescence of the people, and their extraordinary credulity encourages this form of crime.[45]

Such crimes of impersonation may be considered as the ancestors of Nigeria's modern '419' fraud scams. While Britain cannot be held responsible for such criminality, the fact that fraudsters deployed British motifs to intimidate their victims demonstrates the extent to which encounters with British authorities became synonymous with fear and destruction.

21

THE MISTAKE OF 1914

Perhaps no question makes Nigerians disagree as much as why Britain created their country. Nigerians looking for deeper meaning for their country's existence may be disappointed to find that there was none. Nigeria's existence is little more than the outcome of balancing the colonial accounting books.

In 1900 Britain created two countries with similar-sounding names. These were the protectorates of Northern Nigeria and Southern Nigeria. For 14 years these two countries were separately governed by different high commissioners. Lugard was Britain's first high commissioner for Northern Nigeria and Sir Ralph Moor was his counterpart in Southern Nigeria. The two colonies had different colonial personnel, legal systems, land tenure laws, educational policies and systems of governance. Their eventual amalgamation on 1 January 1914 was not sudden. It was the culmination of a process that, as we have seen, began 16 years earlier with the recommendation of the Niger Committee. Although Lugard is credited as being the architect of Nigeria's amalgamation, the process started long before he became Northern Nigeria's high commissioner or the governor-general of the combined Nigeria in 1914.

WHAT BRITAIN DID TO NIGERIA

'These jolly laughing trading black men'

Some British accounts of the differences between the people in the two Nigerias mentioned (with the usual poor amateur anthropological insight of that era) that 'the inhabitants of Northern Nigeria are very different from the coast Negroes [of Southern Nigeria]' and flippantly described northerners as 'black-faced Mohammedan Arabs with an admixture of negro strain' and southerners as 'these jolly laughing trading black men'.[1] Although this is a very simplistic summary, others offered a more realistic assessment. Sir George Goldie, who advocated the amalgamation of Southern Nigeria and Northern Nigeria, admitted that the two countries were 'as widely separated in laws, government, customs, and general ideas about life, both in this world and the next, as England is from China'.[2] Since Britain was aware of the sharp differences between the two Nigerias, why did it decide to amalgamate them anyway?

Just as British entry into Nigeria was motivated by economic reasons, so was its amalgamation into one country. The duplication of finances and personnel in running two separate colonies in the same area was an impediment to administrative efficiency. The need for British colonies to be self-financing made amalgamation a priority. Since Northern Nigeria had no coastline and was landlocked, it did not receive customs duties, as Southern Nigeria did. This disadvantage was exacerbated because Northern Nigeria imported goods from Southern Nigeria duty-free, and its costs for transporting its goods to Southern Nigeria for export were also high. Since Southern Nigeria received customs duties and Northern Nigeria did not, a small percentage of customs revenue from the former was sent to the latter.[3] Yet this was not enough to offset Britain's cost of administering Northern Nigeria.[4] Northern Nigeria had been running on a budget deficit for ten years, during which time its revenue was not enough to meet even half its cost of administration.[5] As a result the British Treasury paid grants-in-aid to Northern Nigeria (totalling over £4 million) in the 14 years of its existence.[6] These were non-refundable payments rather than loans, and were in addition to the £865,000 that the Treasury paid to the Royal Niger Company as compensation for the revocation of its charter. Such dependency on the Treasury could not continue. Lugard tried to raise revenue by imposing taxation on Northern Nigeria but it was not enough. As early as 1904 he argued:

> Northern Nigeria is as yet largely dependent on a grant in aid ... I feel myself that economy can only be effected by the realization of Mr. Chamberlain's original scheme of amalgamating Northern and Southern Nigeria and Lagos into one single administration. It is only in this way that Northern Nigeria, which is the hinterland of the other two, can be properly developed, and economies introduced into the triple machinery which at present exists. The country, which is all one and indivisible, can thus be developed on identical lines, with a common trend of policy in all essential matters.[7]

'The material prosperity had been extraordinary'

Lugard's advocacy of amalgamation ten years before it actually happened is not surprising. As Northern Nigeria's high commissioner, he faced the problems of the colony's dependency on grants from the Treasury and the need to find alternative revenue sources. Amalgamating the two Nigerias into one country would not only solve these problems for him, but carried with it a potential promotion, in that he would become the governor of the newly amalgamated country. For Lugard, the solution to his problems lay in Southern Nigeria. He observed:

> Southern Nigeria, on the other hand, presented a picture which was in almost all points the exact converse of that in the north. Here the material prosperity had been extraordinary. The revenue had almost

doubled itself in a period of five years. The surplus balance has exceeded a million and a half. The trade of the interior had been greatly developed by the construction of a splendid system of roads, and by the opening to navigation of waterways hitherto choked with vegetation ... And so while Northern Nigeria was devoting itself to building up a system of Native Administration and laboriously rais-ing a revenue by direct taxation, Southern Nigeria had found itself engrossed in material development.[8]

Before southern Nigerians pounce with glee (as they often do) at this evidence of northern economic dependency on the south, one must pause and reflect that amalgamation was a British idea and decision, not a northern one. Northern Nigeria had no more say in amalgamation than Southern Nigeria did (and probably, if given a choice, would have objected to it). One of the north's leaders did, after all, later refer to amalgamation as 'the mistake of 1914'.[9]

'Effect an alliance with a Southern lady of means'

The economic disparity between the two Nigerias made their amalgamation inevitable. In a light-hearted after-dinner speech to the Colonial Service Club in 1913, the secretary of state for the colonies, Lord Lewis Harcourt, used a metaphor to refer to the impending amalgamation:

We have released Northern Nigeria from the leading strings of the (British) Treasury. The promising and well-conducted youth is on an allowance 'on his own' and is about to effect an alliance with a Southern lady of means. I have issued the special licence and Sir Frederick will perform the ceremony ... May the union be fruitful and the couple constant![10]

'An enthusiastic practising paedophile'

In 1913, Lugard named the south-eastern Nigerian city of Port Harcourt after Lord Harcourt. Details of a man's personal life should not ordinarily occupy much space in a history book about two nations. However, the continued prominence of Harcourt's name in contemporary Nigeria justifies an exception. Harcourt ostensibly led an ordinary family life. His wife was the wealthy American heiress Mary Burns, who was a member of the Morgan banking family dynasty and the niece of the banker John Pierpont Morgan (founder of JP Morgan Bank). However, Harcourt (or 'Loulou', as he was known) 'was an enthusiastic practising paedophile',[11] who abused both young boys and girls. Owing to his status, Harcourt's paedophilia was largely unknown to the public, and knowledge of it was restricted to the elite circles in which he moved. Harcourt abused the son and daughter of his friend Viscount Esher (Reginald Brett). Esher's teenage daughter Dorothy was so traumatised after Harcourt tried to sexually assault her that she avoided romantic relationships with men for most of her adult life. Harcourt's predilection for preying on children was so well known that boys at Eton School (where he was a fellow) were warned not to be alone with him. Harcourt also tried to sexually assault a young boy named Edward James during a party at Harcourt's country estate. The boy reported the assault to his mother, who mentioned it to others. Harcourt was found dead early the next year after taking an overdose of sedatives.

The most extraordinary aspect of Nigeria's amalgamation was how little thought the British colonial administrators gave to its long-term consequences. The architects of both the 1914 amalgamation and the Niger Committee's report of 1898 had no guiding vision or objective. Not only did the colonial government fail to contemplate the north–south differences, but they paid little attention to how much British rule had amplified the pre-existing differences between the two regions. The introduction of Christian missionaries in the south had caused a revolutionary change to the region's religious life and created a

Western-educated cadre that was anxious for independence, while the north had little interest in rushing into a union with a southern region that was so radically different in religious and social ethos. British rule had also changed the north by introducing a Christian convert population into the region on the outskirts of the Muslim emirates. The British did not consider stabilising the country by dividing it into territorial units consistent with ethno-linguistic zones. In 1898 the Niger Committee had recommended dividing Southern Nigeria into eastern and western regions. Yet, for unspecified reasons, it did not recommend a similar subdivision of Northern Nigeria. The colonial government belatedly carried out the Niger Committee's recommendation when it split Southern Nigeria into the Western and Eastern Regions in 1939, yet it left Northern Nigeria intact and undivided. As a result, Northern Nigeria ended up being more than twice as large as the two southern regions combined. Creating a country where one region was geographically larger, and had more people, than all the other regions combined became a constant point of contention.

The 1914 amalgamation and the fault lines between north and south remain among the most contentious issues in modern Nigeria. More than 106 years after amalgamation, the wisdom of this step is still being debated in Nigeria, and the country continues to grapple with how to deal with the divisions between north and south and the mutual paranoia they often have about each other. The most spectacular eruptions of instability in Nigeria have emerged on a north–south basis: the military coups of 1966, the civil war of 1967–70, the annulment of the presidential election of 12 June 1993 and the ensuing political crisis it generated, and the crisis over Sharia law in the early 2000s. Each of these controversies has polarised the country on north–south lines. The civil war, which commenced after the south-east seceded, represented one of many attempts to repeal the 1914 amalgamation (the north also threatened secession in 1953 and 1966). It is perhaps unsurprising that conflict would arise in this manner. It was difficult to build patriotism and emotional loyalty to a country created by a foreign invader and inhabited by people whose prior loyalties had never extended beyond their family, village or kingdom.

The lack of British foresight regarding the enormous upheaval that amalgamation would cause is astonishing. For over twenty-five years prior to the merger, British administrators had year after year mentioned the massive cultural, political and religious differences between the north and south. Yet they insisted on amalgamation simply to fix an accounting problem. Even if amalgamation was a necessity for colonial administrative convenience, one wonders why it was not reversed or reconfigured when it became apparent that the unified Nigeria would one day become an independent self-governing country.

With no overriding ideological principle behind Nigeria's creation, it has been left to Nigeria's post-colonial governments to find ways to rationalise the 1914 amalgamation. Nigeria's territorial evolution has followed two opposing trends during its colonial and post-colonial eras. The colonial era was characterised by territorial amalgamation, and followed by the country's fragmentation into smaller and smaller territorial units during the post-colonial era. Starting from 1967, post-independence Nigerian governments started unravelling Britain's territorial consolidation by fracturing both the north and south into smaller states, which currently number 36. It is to Nigeria's credit that it has developed its own home-grown innovations to reduce tension between the north and south, such as an affirmative action quota system and the alternation of the presidency between northern and southern holders.

Perhaps it is pious to expect a colonial government to have contemplated the long-term consequences of its decisions on the people of the colony. As demonstrated again and again in prior chapters, the colonial government's priority was not to create a new nation with a common ethos. The priority of Colonial Office officials was to minimise the financial burden to the British taxpayer, reduce bureaucratic duplication and maximise revenue. In that regard it succeeded from Britain's perspective. Nigeria was just a page in a colonial accounting ledger.

22

CONCLUSION

The Colonial Balance Sheet

What balance sheet can be drawn up for British rule of Nigeria? Unsurprisingly, British colonial administrators believed that they brought peace, order and good government to Nigeria. Lugard's secretary asserted:

> We have, admittedly by force, given the people good government in place of tyranny, we have abolished human sacrifice and slavery, and we have secured for the country a material prosperity which could never have been realised under the chaotic conditions that previously existed ... The bloody tyranny of the king of Benin, the malign influence of the Aros, the oppression of the slave-raiding Fulani Emirs, were replaced by an ordered administration which stood between the long-suffering peasantry and the hereditary tyrants. For the first time in the history of this unhappy land there was peace and security for all.[1]

Another British perspective was that colonial governance was too brief to make a meaningful long-term impact on Nigeria. John Smith, who worked for the colonial government in Northern Nigeria shortly before independence, said: 'We were very few in number. Britain was here for 60 years [in Northern Nigeria]. In the lifetime of a whole nation it is a raindrop in a thunderstorm, and in a sense it was a bit like going around the country with a feather duster.'[2]

How true are these assessments of Nigeria's colonial life? Nigeria would probably not have escaped colonial rule even if Britain had not stepped in. If Britain had not conquered Nigeria, someone else would have. Without Goldie's intervention, Nigeria would almost certainly have become a French colony instead.

Businesses, churches and the colonial administration were the three main sources of British influence on Nigeria. Of the three it was perhaps the missionaries who changed Nigeria the most, even though the colonial government did not charge them with that role. The Royal Niger Company's tenure was a reign of fraud and terror. It never pretended to be anything other than a business whose primary objective was profit and paying dividends to its shareholders. It did not build schools or hospitals, or help to improve the lives of natives living in its charter territories. Its primary interaction with the natives involved killing them or making their lives a misery if it did allow them to live. Goldie's destruction of his and the company's documents concealed the RNC's corporate terrorism for over a hundred years and also buried part of Nigeria's early history with him.

The missionaries left the most indelible marks on Nigeria by giving it a new religion and national language, and by propagating a humanitarian agenda to abolish practices such as twin abandonment and human sacrifice, which had caused unnecessary and tragic loss of life. In some areas British intervention also ended conflicts, such as those between Yoruba groups in southwest Nigeria. It also put an end to the Sokoto Caliphate's practice of raiding what it regarded as 'pagan' communities on its fringes for slaves. These slave raids forced nearby communities to flee into the highland areas and hills where they lived for decades. The great irony is that an objection to enslaving Muslims was one of the causes of the jihad that founded the Sokoto Caliphate. Yet the Caliphate ended up enslaving more people than its pre-decessor Hausa states. At one point the Caliphate had two million slaves, more than any other African state.[3] Lugard claimed that the Caliphate's slave raiding was so prolific that some towns were almost emptied and that 'where a Fulani army passed it left a depopulated desert'.[4] Without British colonialism, these slave raiding sorties and conflicts would probably have continued for several decades.

Yet colonialism was not a uniform process. It touched and transformed some parts of Nigeria more than others, and was also a mass of contradictions. Britain visited the Niger Delta and south-east with more blood and suffering than the rest of Nigeria. In contrast, some other areas like Borno were fortunate to be added to the British Empire without a shot being fired. Yorubaland was also not exposed to the same level of sustained British military violence as the Niger Delta and south-east. Yet, ironically, the same areas of the country that were the primary victims of British attacks were also the most enthusiastic adopt-ers of Britain's language, religion and educational system. The most Christianised and English-speaking areas are today to be found in the Niger Delta and south-east. Yet they were also the areas most in a hurry to get rid of the British coloniser and secure Nigeria's independence. Meanwhile, the Muslim areas of the north, which largely rejected Britain's language, religion and educational system, tried to delay Britain's departure. The parts of Nigeria that enthusiastically adopted Britain's educational sys-tem, language, and religion paid a price for it. The introduction of Christianity and Western education stunted the progress of and, in most cases, replaced indigenous systems of education, writing and knowledge.

WHAT BRITAIN DID TO NIGERIA

Patterns of Resistance

One of the most puzzling aspects of Nigerian resistance to British rule is that it was most fierce where one would not have expected it, yet most fleeting in the areas where one would have expected it to endure. Resistance was most frequent in the Niger Delta, the south-east and the so-called 'pagan' areas of the north from ethnic groups such as the Tiv in the Middle Belt and the Kibaku and Marghi in the north-east. Oddly, British troops who had defeated the large armies of the Sokoto Caliphate and thousands of its mounted cavalry in the north in only two days, struggled for decades to subdue farmers from societies with no standing army, who were armed with little more than machetes, bows and arrows, and elderly hunting rifles. Why did barefoot fighters with rudimentary weapons give the British more trouble than thousands of mounted warriors who were backed by archers?

'Communities of troglodytes and cannibals'

Resistance to British occupation was more sustained and violent in the south and in decentralised societies for several reasons. The first category of explanation is connected to actions taken by Britain. Many British people who encountered decentralised communities perceived and treated them as primitive, blood-thirsty savages with no reasoning—little more than wild animals. The typical British impression of the natives can be seen in this observation of the Igbos in the Niger Delta: 'The physique of this tribe, like most others in the Delta, is poor ... the lady wears her wool in half-a dozen conical tufts ... which adds not a little to her natural hideousness. There is little to admire about these people—in fact there is nothing.'[5] British accounts described people living in the non-Muslim areas of the north as 'pagan tribes in various degrees of savagery',[6] or as varying between 'a collection of tribes with a paramount chief to small communities of troglodytes and cannibals'.[7] These impressions were not without consequence. British officials tended to treat those they regarded as savages in a harsh way that invited opposition.

The second category of explanation is connected to the tactics deployed by the African defenders. The south and 'pagan' areas of the north had physical features that favoured guerrilla warfare and neutralised some advantages that the British enjoyed. In the north, British forces could not use their horses against the hill-dwelling Marghi and Kibaku of the north-east. British mobility in the south was also limited, as it had to be conducted almost entirely on foot, and was slowed down as all ammunition, supplies and weapons had to be physically carried. When the British brought their horses down south, the climate and mosquitoes killed them.

Powerful indigenous kingdoms, such as Ijebu and Sokoto, were so emboldened by their large armies that they made the mistake of confronting British forces in open battle. The British fighting formation of choice was the 'square', and when cavalrymen naively charged it, they were shredded by British machine gun fire. In contrast to the northerners, the southern defenders, who did not have walled cities, wisely made efficient use of their environment. The southern topography was full of thick bush and forests that provided excellent ambush spots and hiding places. 'Roads' were little more than narrow bush paths only about three feet wide. Their narrowness limited the ability of British troops to march quickly and made them vulnerable to ambush since they often had to move slowly in single file. Small groups of fighters using guerrilla tactics were more effective than confrontation on the open battlefield against British forces. As a result, the memoirs of British veterans of campaigns in Nigeria are replete with complaints about the persistently annoying resistance of 'highly trained savages'[8] from the south.

The disparity in weaponry between Nigerian and British forces seems an obvious reason for Britain's victories, but it tells only part of the story. Given the tremendous technological advantage that Britain enjoyed, it is remarkable that any Nigerians resisted at all. Some Nigerian 'armies' carried only rudimentary implements such as machetes and spears, yet time and time again they confronted British forces armed with machine guns and artillery that could decimate them from long range. The disparity in weaponry was a deliberate measure under the Brussels Act of 1890, pursuant to which European countries forbade the export of arms to Africa. Even before this embargo, Europeans deliberately sold defective, inferior or obsolete guns to Africans. One British officer admitted that the guns that British arms dealers supplied to Nigerians 'consist of nothing more deadly than old-fashioned flint-locks and percussion guns—more dangerous, in all probability, to the firer than to anyone else'.[9] Even the gunpowder they supplied to Nigerians was 'of the most harmless description ... with propulsive powers hardly sufficient to discharge a bullet from a musket'.[10] Before confronting African armies, Europeans had thus already 'rigged' the outcome of battles by ensuring that they enjoyed superiority of weaponry. When Britain and France invaded Togo in 1914, the local forces used rifles from a war fought almost forty-five years earlier.

What is more, many Nigerian societies did not have professional standing armies or full-time soldiers. In most communities men were engaged in other occupations but could be conscripted to fight during times of war. In contrast, Britain used professional soldiers drilled to fight in formation, and trained to make the most efficient use of their weapons. Not only did Britain have better weapons, but their soldiers were more experienced at operating them. On the rare occasions when Africans obtained modern weaponry, they did not know how to use them effectively. For example, the Satiru Mahdists captured a Maxim gun and several rifles during their first battle against British forces but did not use them to defend themselves when the British returned to attack several weeks later.

CONCLUSION

Inter-ethnic divisions and rivalries also made it difficult for Nigerians to resist British invasion. Nigerian patriotism was non-existent when Britain arrived and the native armies rarely formed alliances with each other. Nigeria's ethnic groups were as much foreigners and strangers to one another as the British were. British soldiers were just another enemy on their lengthy list of adversaries. This lack of inter-ethnic military cooperation also influenced the disposition of Nigerian soldiers whom the British army recruited. They were akin to mercenaries. While a soldier might, for example, object to attacking his own village, he was less likely to have such reservations if ordered to attack a neighbouring community—even if its inhabitants spoke the same language. A Briton wrote in 1900: 'Patriotism, however, in our English sense of the word, is a virtue unknown in West Africa.'[11] Given these inter-ethnic divisions, Nigerians allowed Britain to take its time and conquer their lands one after the other when it was ready. Almost sixty years elapsed from the time Britain annexed Lagos in 1861 to its conquest of some communities in Igboland in the early 1920s.

Credit must also be given to the British for their extraordinary determination and tactical flexibility. They faced different armies with different tactics, they fought against swordsmen, cavalrymen, snipers, cave-dwelling archers and secret warrior cults; they fought in different climates and terrains, on land, on rivers, on hills, in dense forests and bushes, and in open fields, and they encountered ambushes and booby traps. Yet no matter what challenge their opponents presented and what tactics they used, the British always adapted to the new circumstances, even if they lost individual battles. They studied their defeats and setbacks and learned from them. When Tivs shot poisoned arrows at them, they picked them up and sent them for toxicology tests to determine the source of the poison. When Igbos hid in the bush and ambushed them from their flanks, British soldiers revised their tactics and marched while firing barrages of gunfire into the bushes on either side of the road to clear snipers, and used scouts to march in the bush parallel to the main column on the road. When they succumbed to malaria and fever, they developed quinine and slept under mosquito nets. When the Satiru Mahdists broke their square in their first confrontation, they learned the hard way and returned several weeks later to exact retribution by forming the square before arriving in the village. British intelligence was also excellent. They almost always knew more about their enemies than their enemies knew about them. Before marching on a city or village they would usually recruit locals (at gunpoint if necessary) who knew the area, to accompany them and act as their guides and escorts.

Reverse Influences

While colonialism scarred Nigeria and affected it greatly, the price of colonialism to Britain was slight. Fewer than fifty British soldiers were killed during its wars of Nigerian conquest. Since Britain used indigenous soldiers to fight these battles, after each battle both sides of the battlefield would be littered with native corpses. Britain also suffered less physical damage since the battles were fought in foreign lands.

Yet colonial impact in the long run has not been all one way. Another outcome of colonialism was that it introduced Nigerian immigrants and culture to Britain. A hundred years ago, British missionaries evangelised and converted Nigerians to Christianity. Nowadays, Nigerians are among the most enthusiastic Christian evangelisers. The largest church congregation in Western Europe is located in London at the Kingsway International Christian Centre, which was founded by a Nigerian pastor, and whose weekly services are attended by approximately 12,000 people. The children of Nigerian immigrants in British schools and universities have demonstrated educational achievements that are remarkable for people from a country where most of the population was illiterate only fifty years ago. Nigeria now has more English speakers and Christians than England, Scotland, Wales and Northern Ireland combined. Nigerian influence extends to many social institutions that represent Britain. Britain's sports teams are filled with the children and grandchildren of Nigerian immigrants, such as Dele Alli and Ross Barkley. Britain's best-known boxer, Anthony Joshua, is the son of Nigerian immigrants. In the political sphere, the British MP Chuka Umunna is the son of a Nigerian father. These reverse influences are still very much in progress. One day, there may be good cause to write a book about the influence of Nigeria on Britain.

APPENDIX

COPY OF TREATY BETWEEN THE SULTAN
OF SOKOTO AND THE NATIONAL NIGER COMPANY[1]

Article I

For the mutual advantage of ourselves and people, and those
Europeans trading under the name of the 'National African
Company (Limited)', I, Umaru, King of the Mussulmans of the
Soudan; with the consent and advice of my Council, grant and
transfer to the above people, or other with whom they may
arrange, my entire rights to the country on both sides of the
River Benue and rivers flowing into it throughout my dominions
for such distance from its and their banks as they may desire.

Article II

We further grant to the above-mentioned Company the sole
right, among foreigners, to trade in our territories, and the sole
right, also among foreigners, to possess or work places from
which are extracted articles such as lead and antimony.

Article III

We further declare that no communication will be held with
foreigners coming from the rivers except through the above-
mentioned Company.

Article IV

These grants we make for ourselves, our heirs, and successors for ever, and declare them to be irrevocable.

Article V

The Europeans above named, the National African Company (Limited), agree to make Umaru, Sultan of Sokoto, a yearly present of goods to the value of 3,000 bags of cowries, in return for the above grants.

Signed and sealed at Wurno, the 1st June, 1885.

(*Signature of the Sultan in Arabic*)
(*Seal of the Sokoto Caliphate*)

For the National African Company (Limited)

Joseph Thomson, F.R.G.S.

Witnesses: W.J. Seago, D.Z. Viera, T. Joseph

NOTES

INTRODUCTION

1. BBC podcast, 'The Empire's Last Officers', 2010, https://www.bbc. co.uk/programmes/p02sd1q1.
2. J.D. Falconer, *On Horseback through Nigeria, or, Life and Travel in the Central Sudan* (T. Fisher Unwin, London, 1911), p. 299.
3. E.A. Ayandele, 'The Task before Nigerian Historians Today', *Journal of the Historical Society of Nigeria*, vol. 9, no. 4, June 1979, p. 4.

1. TRADING PEOPLE

1. Lt-Colonel A.F. Mockler-Ferryman, *British West Africa: Its Rise and Progress* (Swan Sonnenschein and Co., London, 1898), p. 359.
2. Mockler-Ferryman, *British West Africa*, p. 360.
3. Toyin Falola and Matthew M. Heaton, *A History of Nigeria* (Cambridge University Press, Cambridge, 2008), p. 53.
4. Elizabeth Isichei, *A History of the Igbo People* (Macmillan Press, London and Basingstoke, 1976), p. 49.
5. Mockler-Ferryman, *British West Africa*, pp. 360.
6. Hugh Crow, *Memoirs of Captain Hugh Crow of Liverpool* (Longman, Rees, Orme, Brown, and Greene, London, and G. and J. Robinson, Liverpool, 1830), p. 169.
7. Alan C. Burns, *History of Nigeria* (George Allen & Unwin, London, 1929), p. 80.

8. Lt-Colonel A.F. Mockler-Ferryman, *British Nigeria: A Geographical and Historical Description of the British Possessions adjacent to the Niger River, West Africa* (Cassell and Co., London, 1902), p. 239.

2. CURIOSITY AND EXPLORATION

1. Jesse Page, *The Black Bishop: Samuel Adjai Crowther*. Hodder & Stoughton, London, 1892, p. 1.
2. Mungo Park, *Travels in the Interior of Africa*, vol. 1 (Cassell & Co., London, Paris, New York, Melbourne, 1887), p. 186.
3. Perhaps Ishaku or Isako.
4. Mungo Park, *The Life and Travels of Mungo Park* (Harper & Brothers, New York, 1854), p. 211.
5. Fred Shelford, 'Sir George Dashwood Taubman Goldie', *Journal of the Royal African Society*, vol. 25, no. 98 (January 1926), p. 133.
6. Major Dixon Denham, Captain Hugh Clapperton and Dr Walter Oudney, *Narrative of Travels and Discoveries in Northern and Central Africa, in the Years 1822, 1823, and 1824*, vol. II (John Murray, London, 1826), p. 427.
7. Denham et al, *Narrative of Travels and Discoveries in Northern and Central Africa*, p. 266.
8. Denham et al, *Narrative of Travels and Discoveries in Northern and Central Africa*, p. 336.
9. Denham et al, *Narrative of Travels and Discoveries in Northern and Central Africa*, p. 332.
10. Denham et al, *Narrative of Travels and Discoveries in Northern and Central Africa*, p. 335.
11. Denham et al, *Narrative of Travels and Discoveries in Northern and Central Africa*, p. 353.
12. Denham et al, *Narrative of Travels and Discoveries in Northern and Central Africa*, p. 435.
13. Denham et al, *Narrative of Travels and Discoveries in Northern and Central Africa*, p. 336.
14. Lady Glover, *Life of John Hawley Glover* (Smith, Elder & Co., London, 1897), p. 65.

3. THE KINGS IN THE NORTH AND SOUTH

1. Lieutenant Seymour Vandeleur, *Campaigning on the Upper Nile and Niger* (Methuen & Co., London, 1898), p. 235.
2. His name is also sometimes transliterated as Fodiyo or Fodiye. He is also sometimes referred to as Othman dan Fodio, Shehu or Sheikh. In this book I will use the more common Usman dan Fodio.
3. Samuel Johnson, *The History of the Yorubas: From the Earliest Times to the Beginning of the British Protectorate* (CMS Bookshops, Lagos, 1921), p. 17.
4. *Guardian*, 18 March 2016.
5. *Guardian*, 18 March 2016.
6. Michael Crowder, *The Story of Nigeria* (Faber & Faber, London, 1973), p. 55.
7. H. Ling Roth, *Great Benin, Its Customs, Art and Horrors* (Routledge & Kegan Paul Ltd, London, 1903), p. vi.
8. Lt-General Pitt Rivers, *Antique Works of Art from Benin* (London, 1900), pp. iii–iv.

4. PALM OIL RUFFIANS

1. Mockler-Ferryman, *British Nigeria*, p. 1.
2. Scott R. Pearson, 'The Economic Imperialism of the Royal Niger Company', *Food Research Institute Studies in Economics, Trade, and Development*, vol. 10, 1971, p. 70.
3. K. Onwuka Dike, *Trade and Politics in the Niger Delta 1830–1885: An Introduction to the Economic and Political History of Nigeria* (Oxford University Press, London, 1956), preface.
4. John Edgar Flint, *Sir George Goldie and the Making of Nigeria* (Oxford University Press, Accra, Ibadan, London, 1960), pp. 10–11.
5. Flint, *Sir George Goldie*, p. 10.
6. Burns, *History of Nigeria*, p. 115.
7. Burns, *History of Nigeria*, p. 117.

5. JAJA OF OPOBO

1. Dike, *Trade and Politics in the Niger Delta*, p. 184.

2. Dike, *Trade and Politics in the Niger Delta*, p. 184.

3. British and Foreign State Papers, 1886–1887, vol. 78 (William Ridgway, London, 1894), p. 1210.

4. Sir William M.N. Geary, *Nigeria under British Rule* (Frank Cass & Co., London, 1927), p. 281.

5. British and Foreign State Papers, 1886–1887, vol. 78, p. 1210.

6. Letter from Jaja to the prime minister, 24 January 1887. British and Foreign State Papers, 1886–1887, vol. 78, pp. 1217–18.

7. Letter from Jaja to the prime minister, 13 January 1887. Papers Relative to King Jaja of Opobo, 1888.

8. Geoffrey L. Baker, *Trade Winds on the Niger: The Saga of the Royal Niger Company, 1930–1971* (Radcliffe Press, London, New York, 1996), p. 104.

9. Roseline Okpete Kanu, 'The Life and Times of King Ja Ja of Opobo, 1812–1895', MA diss., Dalhousie University, 1970, p. 43.

10. Hansard, 31 May 1888, vol. 326.

11. Harry H. Johnston, *The Story of My Life* (Bobbs-Merrill Company, Indianapolis, 1923), p. 180.

12. Johnston to prime minister, 12 August 1887, Papers Relative to King Jaja of Opobo, 1888.

13. Geary, *Nigeria under British Rule*, p. 281.

14. Kanu, 'The Life and Times of King Ja Ja of Opobo, 1812–1895', p. 43.

15. Papers Relative to King Jaja of Opobo, 1888.

16. British and Foreign State Papers, 1886–1887, vol. 78, p. 1219.

17. Johnston, *The Story of My Life*, p. 181 and Geary, *Nigeria under British Rule*, p. 282.

18. Geary, *Nigeria under British Rule*, p. 282.

19. Cookey Gam, Shoo Peterside, Albert Jaja and Sunday Jaja.

20. Kanu, 'The Life and Times of King Ja Ja of Opobo, 1812–1895', p. 182.

21. British and Foreign State Papers, 1886–1887, vol. 78, p. 1219.

22. Burns, *History of Nigeria*, p. 161.

23. Papers Relative to King Jaja of Opobo, 1888.

24. Jaja reunited with the delegation he sent to Britain (who were on their way back home to Opobo) at Accra.

25. Hansard, 31 May 1888, vol. 326.

26. Many accounts claim that he died on 7 July 1891, but he wrote a letter to his people on 14 July 1891, telling them to prepare for his return home.

27. Geary, *Nigeria under British Rule*, p. 285.

28. Geary, *Nigeria under British Rule*, p. 290.

6. GOLDIE

1. Major Leonard Darwin, 'Sir George Goldie on Government in Africa', *Journal of the Royal African Society*, vol. 34, no. 135, April 1935, p. 143.

2. The Nunnery was originally the site of a monastery of nuns. It is now the location of University College Isle of Man's International Business School.

3. Dorothy Wellesley, *Sir George Goldie, Founder of Nigeria: A Memoir* (Macmillan & Co., London, 1934), p. 94.

4. Wellesley, *Sir George Goldie*, p. 94.

5. Wellesley, *Sir George Goldie*, p. 94.

6. Wellesley, *Sir George Goldie*, p. 93.

7. Geary, *Nigeria under British Rule*, p. 9.

8. *West Africa*, 18 August 1975, p. 960.

9. M.E. Chamberlain, 'Lord Aberdare and the Royal Niger Company', *Welsh History Review*, vol. 3, 1966, pp. 51–3.

10. Samuel Ajayi Crowther was a shareholder of the West African Company (on behalf of the Church Missionary Society). In the 1870s his son Josiah was in charge of the company's trade on the River Niger.

11. Mockler-Ferryman, *British Nigeria*, p. 75, said there were 250 treaties. Vandeleur (*Campaigning on the Upper Nile and Niger*, p. 156) said there were 'no less than 400' treaties.

12. Wellesley, *Sir George Goldie*, p. 98.

14. Vandeleur, *Campaigning on the Upper Nile and Niger*, p. xx.

15. Baker, *Trade Winds on the Niger*, p. 24.

16. Goldie's older half-brother, John Senhouse Goldie-Taubman, was the secretary of this company.

17. Prospectus of the National African Company, reproduced in *Truth*, vol. XII, 20 July 1882, p. 140.

18. A.H.M. Kirk-Greene, 'Expansion on the Benue 1830–1900', *Journal of the Historical Society of Nigeria*, vol. 1, no. 3, December 1958, p. 224.

19. Chamberlain, 'Lord Aberdare and the Royal Niger Company', p. 51.

20. Geary, *Nigeria under British Rule*, p. 214.

21. Renamed Niger Coast Protectorate on 13 May 1893.

22. Born Henry Austin Bruce. He derived much of his wealth from the coalfields of the Aberdare Valley, close to Aberdare, Glamorgan, Wales. He also later became the president of the Royal Historical Society and Royal Geographical Society.

23. The Constabulary moved their headquarters to Lokoja in 1889 and also had a detachment at Ibi near the River Benue.

7. THE ROYAL NIGER COMPANY

1. Geoffrey L. Baker, 'Research Notes on the Royal Niger Company: Its Predecessors and Successors', *Journal of the Historical Society of Nigeria*, vol. 2, no. 1, December 1960, p. 162.

2. Wellesley, *Sir George Goldie*, p. viii.

3. Wellesley, *Sir George Goldie*, p. 114.

4. Robert W. Hannah, 'The Origins of Indirect Rule in Northern Nigeria, 1890–1904', PhD thesis, Michigan State University, 1969, p. 142.

5. Isichei, *A History of the Igbo People*, p. 120.

6. Wellesley, *Sir George Goldie*, p. 32.

7. Wellesley, *Sir George Goldie*, p. 29.

8. Burns, *History of Nigeria*, p. 296.

9. Flint, *Sir George Goldie*, p. 199.

10. John Edgar Flint, 'British Policy and Chartered Company Administration in Nigeria, 1879–1900', PhD thesis, University of London, 1957, p. 394.

11. Some sources say he was a German citizen, while others say he was Swiss.

12. Charles Henry Robinson, *Hausaland, or Fifteen Hundred Miles through the Central Soudan* (Sampson Low, Marston and Company, London, 1900), p. 262.

13. E.A. Ayandele, 'The Relations between the Church Missionary Society

and the Royal Niger Company, 1886–1900', *Journal of the Historical Society of Nigeria*, vol. 4, no. 3, December 1968, p. 410.

14. Flint (*Sir George Goldie*, p. 149) and the undersecretary of state, Sir James Fergusson, claimed that six were killed. However, MP Thomas Bayley claimed that 17 were killed (Hansard, 15 September 1893, vol. 17, c.1290).

15. Hansard, 14 December 1888, vol. 332.

16. Robert Gascoyne Cecil.

17. Flint, 'British Policy and Chartered Company Administration in Nigeria, 1879–1900', p. 246.

18. W.R. Brownlow, *Memoir of Sir James Marshall* (Burns & Oates Ltd, London and New York, 1890), p. 142.

19. Flint, 'British Policy and Chartered Company Administration in Nigeria, 1879–1900', p. 246.

20. Henry Thurstan Holland.

21. Flint, *Sir George Goldie*, p. 147.

22. Flint, *Sir George Goldie*, p. 149.

23. Flint, *Sir George Goldie*, p. 149.

24. Flint, *Sir George Goldie*, p. 188.

25. Flint, 'British Policy and Chartered Company Administration in Nigeria, 1879–1900', pp. 464–6.

26. Flint, 'British Policy and Chartered Company Administration in Nigeria, 1879–1900', pp. 463–4.

27. Hansard, 7 September 1893, vol. 17, cols. 485–555.

28. Hansard, 7 April 1887, vol. 313, cols. 676–7.

29. Hansard, 13 April 1896, vol. 39, cols. 742–3.

30. Burns, *History of Nigeria*, p. 54.

31. Harold Bindloss, *In the Niger Country* (William Blackwood & Sons, Edinburgh and London, 1898), p. 91.

32. Henry Galway, 'The Rising of the Brassmen', *Journal of the Royal African Society*, vol 34, no. 135, April 1935, p. 149.

33. Flint, *Sir George Goldie*, p. 28.

34. Samuel Onwo Onyeidu, 'The Anglican Mission to Asaba, Nigeria, 1875–1930', PhD thesis, University of Aberdeen, April 1985, p. 185.

35. Flint, *Sir George Goldie*, p. 98.

36. Galway, 'The Rising of the Brassmen', pp. 149–50.

37. Burns, *History of Nigeria*, p. 170.

38. The RNC had only two substantive agent-generals in its history: David McIntosh, who retired early due to ill health and later died in 1888, and Joseph Flint, who became agent-general on 15 November 1888 and remained so until 1 January 1900.

39. Galway, 'The Rising of the Brassmen', p. 156.

40. It is unclear whether this was the island's actual name or whether it acquired this moniker owing to the human remains found there.

41. Hannah, 'The Origins of Indirect Rule in Northern Nigeria, 1890–1904', p. 98.

42. Hannah, 'The Origins of Indirect Rule in Northern Nigeria, 1890–1904', p. 99.

43. Hannah, 'The Origins of Indirect Rule in Northern Nigeria, 1890–1904', p. 103.

8. GLOVER'S HAUSAS

1. Glover, *Life of John Hawley Glover*, pp. 81–2.

2. Glover later became the administrator of Lagos and was fondly known by the Yoruba locals as 'Oba Golober' (a mispronunciation of 'king Glover').

3. The expedition leader, Dr Baikie, lived without supplies and communications for 18 months.

4. Glover, *Life of John Hawley Glover*, pp. 77–9.

5. Stanhope Freeman, governor of the British West African possessions resident in Sierra Leone, to the Duke of Newcastle, 9 October 1862.

6. Captain W.D. Downes, *With the Nigerians in German East Africa* (Methuen & Co., London, 1919), p. 3.

7. Vandeleur, *Campaigning on the Upper Nile and Niger*, p. 170.

8. Robinson, *Hausaland*, pp. 27–8.

9. Vice-Admiral H.L. Fleet, *My Life, and a Few Yarns* (George Allen & Unwin, London, 1922), p. 180.

10. Lennox, *With the West African Frontier Force*, p. 49.

11. Formerly an inspector of the Royal Irish Constabulary.

12. The WAFF comprised six units overall: Northern Nigeria Regiment, Southern Nigeria Regiment, Lagos Battalion, Gold Coast Regiment, Sierra Leone Battalion, and Gambia Company.

13. Lennox, *With the West African Frontier Force*, p. 51.

14. Tim Stapleton, 'Barracks Islam and Command Christianity: Religion in Britain's West African Colonial Army (c.1900–1960)', *War and Society*, vol. 39, no. 1, 2020, p. 8.

15. Colonial Reports, 1900, p. 25.

16. Stapleton, 'Barracks Islam and Command Christianity', p. 24.

17. M.J. Dent, 'The Military and Politics: A Study of the Relation between the Army and the Political Process in Nigeria', in Robert Melson and Howard Wolpe (eds.), *Nigeria: Modernization and the Politics of Communalism* (Michigan State University Press, East Lancing, 1971), p. 373.

18. Colonial Reports, 1902, p. 46.

19. Colonial Reports, 1902, p. 46.

20. Larymore, *A Resident's Wife in Nigeria*, p. 25.

21. Colonial Reports, 1907, p. 46.

22. Stapleton, 'Barracks Islam and Command Christianity', p. 27.

23. Downes, *With the Nigerians in German East Africa*, pp. 12–13

24. Downes, *With the Nigerians in German East Africa*, p. 7.

25. Alhaji Sir Ahmadu Bello, *My Life* (Cambridge University Press, Cambridge, 1962), p. 23.

9. THE SOUTH-WEST INVASION

1. Lagos Papers, 1852, Beecroft to Palmerston, 3 January 1852, enclosure no. 69.

2. Lagos Papers, 1852, Captain Lyster report to Captain Jones, 29 December 1851, enclosure 3 of 70, and Burns, *History of Nigeria*, p. 133.

3. Lagos Papers, 1852, Beecroft to Palmerston, 3 January 1852, enclosure no. 69, pp. 188–9.

4. Johnson, *The History of the Yorubas*, p. 620.

10. THE INVASION OF BENIN

1. Alan Maxwell Boisragon, *The Benin Massacre* (Methuen & Co., London, 1897), p. 73.
2. Boisragon, *The Benin Massacre*, p. 70.
3. Boisragon, *The Benin Massacre*, p. 74.
4. Boisragon, *The Benin Massacre*, p. 83.
5. Boisragon, *The Benin Massacre*, p. 84.
6. Boisragon, *The Benin Massacre*, p. 101.
7. Felix N. Roth, 'A Diary of a Surgeon with the Benin Punitive Expedition', *Journal of the Manchester Geographical Society*, vol. 14, 1898, pp. 209–10.
8. Lt-Colonel W.C.G. Heneker, *Bush Warfare* (Hugh Rees, London, 1907), p. 168.
9. Hamilton to the Chief of the Staff, Benin Expeditionary Force, Benin City, 21 February 1897, enclosure no. 3 in 65, Benin Papers, 1897.
10. Roth, 'A Diary of a Surgeon with the Benin Punitive Expedition', p. 218.
11. Geoffrey Rawson, *Life of Admiral Sir Harry Rawson* (Edward Arnold, London, 1914), p. 113.
12. It seems that this patrol was actually searching for Oba Overami, who was still a fugitive at this time.
13. Heneker, *Bush Warfare*, p. 29.
14. Ologbosere was Ogbemudia's paternal great-grandfather. His maternal grandfather Obakhavbaye also fought against the British during the invasion but fled and evaded capture.
15. Mary Lou Ratté, 'Imperial Looting and the Case of Benin', MA diss., University of Massachusetts, Amherst, 1972, pp. 87–8.
16. Galway to Foreign Office, Benin Papers, no. 54, 21 January 1897.
17. Rawson, *Life of Admiral Sir Harry Rawson*, p. 140.
18. Ratté, 'Imperial Looting and the Case of Benin', p. 82.

11. FOUNDERS OF NIGERIA

1. *Saturday Review*, 29 May 1897.
2. G.N. Uzoigwe, 'The Niger Committee of 1898: Lord Selborne's Report',

Journal of the Historical Society of Nigeria, vol. 4, no. 3, December 1968, p. 471.

3. Uzoigwe, 'The Niger Committee of 1898', p. 471.

4. Margery Perham, *Lugard: The Years of Authority 1898–1945* (Collins, London, 1960), p. 18.

5. Perham, *Lugard: The Years of Authority*, p. 65.

6. Margery Perham, *Lugard: The Years of Adventure, 1858–1898* (Collins, London, 1956), p. 61.

7. Perham, *Lugard: The Years of Adventure*, p. 62.

8. Perham, *Lugard: The Years of Authority*, p. 53.

9. *The Times*, 8 January 1897.

10. *The Times*, 8 January 1897.

11. *Saturday Review*, 29 May 1897.

12. The speech was on Tuesday, 6 July 1897. The next year Goldie seems to have changed his mind and used the term 'Niger Sudan' to describe the northern province. See foreword in Vandeleur (*Campaigning on the Upper Nile and Niger*, p. xix).

13. Henry M. Stanley, *Africa: Its Partition and Its Future* (Dodd, Mead, and Company, New York, 1898), p. 168.

14. River Benue.

15. Stanley, *Africa*, p. 170.

16. Hannah, 'The Origins of Indirect Rule in Northern Nigeria, 1890–1904', pp. 98–9.

17. Hannah, 'The Origins of Indirect Rule in Northern Nigeria, 1890–1904', p. 165.

18. This royalty was repealed in 1949.

19. Wellesley, *Sir George Goldie*, p. 73.

20. *West Africa*, 18 August 1975.

12. THE NORTHERN INVASION

1. For example, Frederick D. Lugard, 'Northern Nigeria', *The Geographical Journal*, vol. 23, no. 1, January 1904 and Hugh Anthony Stephens Johnston, *The Fulani Empire of Sokoto* (Oxford University Press, London, Ibadan, Nairobi, 1967).

2. Lugard, 'Northern Nigeria', p. 8.

3. Johnston, *The Fulani Empire of Sokoto*, p. 275.

4. Colonial Reports, 1903, p. 105.

5. Colonial Reports, 1903, p. 100.

6. Colonial Reports, 1903, p. 101.

7. D.J.M. Muffett, *Concerning Brave Captains: Being a History of the British Occupation of Sokoto and Kano and the Last Stand of the Fulani Forces* (André Deutsch, London, 1964), p. 46.

8. Colonial Reports, 1903, p. 101.

9. Johnston, *The Fulani Empire of Sokoto*, p. 283.

10. Johnston, *The Fulani Empire of Sokoto*, p. 243.

11. Notes on Nassarawa Province, Nigeria, 1920, p. 7.

12. Colonial Reports, 1903, p. 12.

13. Larymore, *A Resident's Wife in Nigeria*, p. 54.

14. Lugard, 'Northern Nigeria', p. 8.

15. Geary, *Nigeria under British Rule*, p. 217.

16. Colonial Reports, 1903, p. 102.

17. Brigadier-General F.P. Crozier, *Five Years Hard* (Jonathan Cape, London, 1932), p. 149.

18. Crozier, *Five Years Hard*, p. 148.

19. Crozier, *Five Years Hard*, p. 149.

20. Crozier, *Five Years Hard*, p. 149.

21. Crozier, *Five Years Hard*, pp. 149–50.

22. The king of Gobir captured Aliyu and handed him into British custody.

23. Lugard, 'Northern Nigeria', p. 8.

24. Crozier, *Five Years Hard*, p. 158.

25. Lugard, 'Northern Nigeria', p. 26.

26. Lugard, 'Northern Nigeria', p. 4.

27. Lugard ('Northern Nigeria', p. 27) gave a figure of 700 native casualties while Crozier (*Five Years Hard*), who fought against Sokoto, claimed that over 1,000 were killed.

28. Crozier, *Five Years Hard*, p. 167.

29. 100 years in the Muslim calendar.

13. THE SOUTH-EAST INVASION

1. Basden, *Among the Ibos of Nigeria*, p. 208.
2. W.P. Livingstone, *Mary Slessor of Calabar: Pioneer Missionary* (Hodder & Stoughton, London, 1916), p. 191.
3. Major Arthur Glyn Leonard, 'Notes of a Journey to Bende', *Journal of the Manchester Geographical Society*, vol. 14, 1898, p. 203.
4. Leonard, 'Notes of a Journey to Bende', p. 193.
5. Leonard, 'Notes of a Journey to Bende', p. 203.
6. Leonard, 'Notes of a Journey to Bende', p. 203.
7. Robert D. Jackson, 'The Twenty Years War: Invasion and Resistance in Southeastern Nigeria, 1900–1919', PhD thesis, Harvard University, 1975, pp. 128–9.
8. Leonard, 'Notes of a Journey to Bende', p. 191.
9. Galway, 'The Rising of the Brassmen', p. 162.
10. Galway, 'The Rising of the Brassmen', p. 162.
11. Jackson, 'The Twenty Years War', p. 140.
12. Heneker, *Bush Warfare*, p. 9. This officer was a Canadian serving with the British army.
13. Jackson, 'The Twenty Years War', p. 139.
14. Jackson, 'The Twenty Years War', p. 140.
15. Jackson, 'The Twenty Years War', p. 141.
16. E.A. Afigbo, *The Warrant Chiefs: Indirect Rule in Southeastern Nigeria, 1891–1929* (Longman Group, London, 1972), p. 68.
17. Galway, 'The Rising of the Brassmen', p. 162.
18. Samuel N. Nwabara, 'Encounter with the Long Juju: A Prelude to the British Military Expeditions in Iboland', *Transactions of the Historical Society of Ghana*, vol. 9, 1968, pp. 86–7.
19. Colonial Reports, 1902, Southern Nigeria, p. 5.
20. Jackson, 'The Twenty Years War', pp. 260–1.
21. Jackson, 'The Twenty Years War', p. 262.
22. Jackson, 'The Twenty Years War', pp. 9–10.
23. Jackson, 'The Twenty Years War', p. 346.
24. Felix K. Ekechi, 'Portrait of a Colonizer: H.M. Douglas in Colonial Nigeria, 1897–1920', *African Studies Review*, vol. 26, no. 1, March 1983, p. 26.

25. Lennox, *With the West African Frontier Force*, pp. 13–14.

26. This officer was a veteran of wars against the Ashanti in Ghana.

27. Lennox, *With the West African Frontier Force*, p. 14.

28. Lennox, *With the West African Frontier Force*, p. 10.

29. Lennox, *With the West African Frontier Force*, p. 11.

30. Lennox, *With the West African Frontier Force*, p. 10.

31. Lennox, *With the West African Frontier Force*, p. 29.

32. Lennox, *With the West African Frontier Force*, p. 29.

33. Lennox, *With the West African Frontier Force*, p. 31.

14. THE NORTHERN RESISTANCE

1. Telegram from Sergeant Gosling, 15 February 1906, Colonial Reports, 1907, p. 7.

2. Colonial Reports, 1907, p. 19.

3. Colonial Reports, telegram no. 8, received 11.46 am, 20 February 1906.

4. Colonial Reports, telegram no. 9, received 1.40 pm, 25 February 1906.

5. Colonial Reports, letter from Major Burdon to Lugard, 21 February 1906, p. 19.

6. Colonial Reports, letter from Major Burdon to Lugard, 21 February 1906, p. 21.

7. Letter from Lugard to Lord Elgin, 7 March 1906, Colonial Reports, 1907.

8. Goodwin to Lugard, 11 March 1906, Colonial Reports, 1907.

9. Letter from Lugard to Lord Elgin, 14 March 1906, Colonial Reports, 1907, p. 27.

10. Dusgate, *The Conquest of Northern Nigeria*, p. 247.

11. Goodwin to Lugard, 11 March 1906, Colonial Reports, 1907.

12. Goodwin to Lugard, 11 March 1906, Colonial Reports, 1907.

13. Letter from Lugard to Lord Elgin, 14 March 1906, Colonial Reports, 1907, p. 28.

14. Letter from Lugard to Lord Elgin, 14 March 1906, Colonial Reports, 1907, p. 27.

15. One camel, 46 donkeys, and 15 horses—which they handed over to the resident, Major Burdon.

16. Letter from Lugard to Lord Elgin, 14 March 1906, Colonial Reports, 1907, p. 28.

17. Mallam Isa (son of the 1904 self-professed mahdi) was killed during the first battle on 14 February.

18. Letter from Lugard to Lord Elgin, 14 March 1906, Colonial Reports, 1907, p. 28.

19. J.S. Hogendorn and Paul Lovejoy, 'Revolutionary Mahdism and Resistance to Early Colonial Rule in Northern Nigeria and Niger', University of the Witwatersrand, African Studies Seminar Paper, no. 80, 1979, p. 32.

20. Hogendorn and Lovejoy, 'Revolutionary Mahdism', p. 31.

21. Hogendorn and Lovejoy, 'Revolutionary Mahdism', p. 31.

22. Colonial Reports, Northern Nigeria, 1908, p. 37.

23. Colonial Reports, Northern Nigeria, 1908, p. 38.

24. Colonial Reports, Northern Nigeria, 1908, p. 37.

25. Colonial Reports, Northern Nigeria, 1908, p. 38.

26. Downes, *With the Nigerians in German East Africa*, p. 11.

27. Falconer, *On Horseback through Nigeria*, pp. 175–6.

15. EKUMEKU: THE SILENT ONES

1. Frank Hives (told by and written down by Gascoigne Lumley), *Ju Ju and Justice in Nigeria* (John Lane the Bodley Head, London, 1930), p. 30.

2. Hives, *Ju Ju and Justice in Nigeria*, pp. 32–4.

3. Hives, *Ju Ju and Justice in Nigeria*, p. 63.

4. Isichei, *A History of the Igbo People*, p. 123.

5. Isichei, *A History of the Igbo People*, p. 124.

6. Colonial Reports, 1902, p. 11.

7. Isichei, *A History of the Igbo People*, p. 131.

8. Lethbridge, *West Africa the Elusive*, p. 223.

9. Basden, *Among the Ibos of Nigeria*, p. 205.

10. *Church Missionary Intelligencer*, 1906, p. 696.

11. Igbafe, 'Western Ibo Society and Its Resistance to British Rule', p. 442.

12. Onyeidu, 'The Anglican Mission to Asaba', p. 181.

13. Basden, *Among the Ibos of Nigeria*, p. 206.

14. Basden, *Among the Ibos of Nigeria*, p. 205.

15. Ohadike, 'The Ekumeku Movement', p. 101.

16. Basden, *Among the Ibos of Nigeria*, p. 206.

17. Brownlow, *Memoir of Sir James Marshall*, p. 139.

18. Alan Lethbridge, *West Africa the Elusive* (John Bale, Sons & Danielson Ltd., London, 1921), p. 223.

19. Captain W.E. Rudkin, 'In British West Africa: The Operations in the Agbor District, Southern Nigeria, June to August 1906, Consequent upon the Murder of Mr. O.S. Crewe-Read, District Commissioner', *United Service Magazine*, vol. 35 (April to September 1907), p. 434.

20. Don C. Ohadike, 'The Ekumeku Movement: Western Igbo Resistance to the British Conquest of Nigeria, 1883–1914', PhD thesis, Ohio University, Athens, 1991, p. 105.

21. Philip A. Igbafe, 'Western Ibo Society and Its Resistance to British Rule: The Ekumeku Movement 1898–1911', *Journal of African History*, vol. 12, no. 3, 1971, p. 446.

22. 215 native soldiers, 6 British officers and 4 British non-commissioned officers.

23. Captain Ian Hogg, *Asaba: Report on Aaba Hinterland Operations. From the Officer Commanding Asaba Hinterland Expedition Force, to the Officer Commanding Southern Nigeria Regiment*. 14 March 1904, CO 520/24, p. 12.

24. Hogg, *Asaba*, p. 7.

25. Rudkin, 'In British West Africa', p. 434.

26. Rudkin, 'In British West Africa', p. 436.

27. Rudkin, 'In British West Africa', p. 440.

28. *London Gazette*, 13 March 1908.

29. Rudkin, 'In British West Africa', p. 449.

30. Rudkin claimed 113 were wounded; however, another officer on the mission claimed the number of wounded was much higher ('In British West Africa', p. 193).

31. Rudkin, 'In British West Africa', p. 448.

32. G.T. Basden, *Among the Ibos of Nigeria: An Account of the Curious and Interesting Habits, Customs, and Beliefs of a Little Known African People*

by One Who Has for Many Years Lived amongst Them on Close and Intimate Terms (J.B. Lippincott Co., Philadelphia, 1921), pp. 206–8.

33. Daniel Olisa Iweze, 'The Role of Indigenous Collaborators during the Anglo-Ekumeku War of 1898–1911', *Ufahamu: A Journal of African Studies*, vol. 39, no. 1, 2016, p. 99.

34. Isichei, *A History of the Igbo People*, p. 132.

16. THE WOMEN'S WARS

1. Sessional Paper no. 28 of 1930, *Report of the Commission of Inquiry Appointed to Inquire into the Disturbances in the Calabar and Owerri Provinces, December 1929* (Lagos, Government Printer, 1930), p. 20.

2. Sessional Paper no. 28 of 1930, p. 68.

3. Sessional Paper no. 28 of 1930, p. 70.

4. Sessional Paper no. 28 of 1930, p. 66.

5. Sessional Paper no. 28 of 1930, p. 66.

6. Sessional Paper no. 28 of 1930, p. 67.

7. Sessional Paper no. 28 of 1930, p. 70.

8. Sessional Paper no. 28 of 1930, p. 69.

9. Sessional Paper no. 28 of 1930, p. 69.

10. Sessional Paper no. 28 of 1930, p. 77.

11. Sessional Paper no. 28 of 1930, p. 76.

12. Sessional Paper no. 28 of 1930, p. 79.

13. Marc Matera, Misty Bastian and Susan Kingsley Kent, *The Women's War of 1929: Gender and Violence in Colonial Nigeria* (Palgrave Macmillan, London, 2013), p. 184.

14. Sessional Paper no. 28 of 1930, p. 78.

15. Matera et al, *The Women's War of 1929*, pp. 170–1.

16. Okezie founded and became the leader of the Ngwa Women's Association and dedicated her life to supporting women's rights in Nigeria. She died in 1999.

17. Toyin Falola, *Colonialism and Violence in Nigeria* (Indiana University Press, Bloomington and Indianapolis, 2009), p. 91.

18. Two of their other sons also became prominent. Dr Beko Ransome-Kuti became a human rights activist who campaigned against military rule in Nigeria, and his brother Professor Olikoye Ransome-Kuti

became the minister of health in a military government that his brothers Beko and Fela campaigned against.

19. Judith A. Byfield, 'Women, and the Colonial State: Egba Women's Tax Revolt', *Meridians*, vol. 3, no. 2, 2003, p. 270.

17. THE CRESCENT AND THE CROSS

1. Pew Centre, Religious Composition by Country, http://assets.pewresearch.org/wp-content/uploads/sites/11/2012/12/globalReligion-tables. pdf.

2. Constance Larymore, *A Resident's Wife in Nigeria* (George Routledge & Sons, London, 1908), p. 122.

3. Captain Lord Esme Gordon Lennox, *With the West African Frontier Force in Southern Nigeria* (H.J. Ryman, London, 1905), p. 46.

4. Mockler-Ferryman, *British West Africa*, p. 487.

5. Mockler-Ferryman, *British West Africa*, p. 487.

6. Diana Rosenberg, 'Ibo Resistance to British Colonial Power', *Ufuhamu: A Journal of African Studies*, 1991, p. 4.

7. Michael Crowder, *West Africa under Colonial Rule* (Hutchinson & Co. Publishers, London, 1968), p. 356.

8. Burns, *History of Nigeria*, p. 257.

9. Crowder, *West Africa under Colonial Rule*, p. 356.

10. Lennox, *With the West African Frontier Force*, p. 60.

11. Ben Fulford, 'An Igbo Esperanto: A History of the Union Igbo Bible 1900–1950', *Journal of Religion in Africa*, vol. 32, no. 4, November 2002, p. 472.

12. Fulford, 'An Igbo Esperanto', p. 475.

13. Dmitri Bersselaar, 'Creating Union Igbo: Missionaries and the Igbo Language', *Africa: Journal of the International African Institute*, vol. 67, no. 2, 1997, p. 284.

14. James Coleman, *Nigeria: Background to Nationalism* (University of California Press, Berkeley, 1971), p. 102.

18. PEOPLE OF THE BOOK

1. Colonial Reports, 1914, p. 18.

2. Coleman, *Nigeria*, p. 113.

3. Coleman, *Nigeria*, p. 133.

4. *West Africa*, 18 August 1975, p. 960.

5. *West Africa*, 18 August 1975, p. 961.

6. Frederick D. Lugard, *The Dual Mandate in British Tropical Africa* (William Blackwood & Sons, Edinburgh and London, 1922), pp. 79–80.

7. Burns, *History of Nigeria*, p. 265.

8. Geary, *Nigeria under British Rule*, p. 14.

9. Thomas Jesse Jones, *Education in Africa* (Phelps-Stokes Fund, New York, 1922), p. 175.

10. Margery Perham, 'Some Problems of Indirect Rule in Africa', *Journal of the Royal African Society*, vol. 34, no. 135, 1937, p. 288.

11. There were 853 schools in the southern region with 64,759 registered students. Meanwhile, the north had only 58 schools with 1,682 registered students. Colonial Reports, 1914, p. 18.

12. Jones, *Education in Africa*, p. 175.

13. Walter Schwarz, *Nigeria* (London: Pall Mall, 1968), p. 96, citing Jones-Quartey.

14. Coleman, *Nigeria*, pp. 120–1.

15. National Bureau of Statistics. National Literacy Survey, 2010, https://www.nigerianstat.gov.ng/pdfuploads/National%20Literacy%20Survey,%202010.pdf, p. 7.

19. INDIRECT RULE

1. Crowder, *West Africa under Colonial Rule*, p. 198.

2. Goldie in Darwin, 'Sir George Goldie on Government in Africa', p. 140.

3. Colonial Reports, 1903, p. 26.

4. Geary, *Nigeria under British Rule*, p. 55.

5. Burns, *History of Nigeria*, p. 305.

6. Brigadier-General Sir James Willcocks, *From Kabul to Kumasi: Twenty Four Years of Soldiering and Sport* (John Murray, London, 1904), p. 176.

7. George Douglas Hazzledine, *The White Man in Nigeria* (Edward Arnold, London, 1904), p. 3.

8. Lugard, *The Dual Mandate in British Tropical Africa*, p. 198.

9. Lugard, 'Northern Nigeria', p. 8.

10. Colonial Reports, 1902, p. 28.

11. Margery Perham, *West African Passage: A Journey through Nigeria, Chad, and the Cameroons, 1931–1932* (Peter Owen Publishers, London and Boston, 1983), p. 66.

12. Captain C.W.J. Orr, *The Making of Northern Nigeria* (Macmillan & Co., London, 1904), p. 277.

13. Hannah, 'The Origins of Indirect Rule in Northern Nigeria, 1890–1904', p. 221.

14. C.N. Ubah, 'Changing Patterns of Leadership among the Igbo, 1900–1960', *Transafrican Journal of History*, vol. 16, 1987, p. 172.

15. Afigbo, *The Warrant Chiefs*, p. 76.

16. Falola, *Colonialism and Violence in Nigeria*, p. 80.

17. Perham, 'Some Problems of Indirect Rule in Africa', p. 17.

18. Jackson, 'The Twenty Years War', p. 119.

19. Afigbo, *The Warrant Chiefs*, pp. 63–4.

20. Afigbo, *The Warrant Chiefs*, pp. 61–2.

21. Ubah, 'Changing Patterns of Leadership among the Igbo, 1900–1960', p. 175.

22. Afigbo, *The Warrant Chiefs*, p. 309. The warrant chief was Obiukwu Nze of Umulolo.

23. Afigbo, *The Warrant Chiefs*, p. 309.

24. Mbabuike Ogujiofo of Ihube, in Afigbo, *The Warrant Chiefs*, p. 316.

25. Falconer, *On Horseback through Nigeria*, p. 300.

26. Axel Harneit-Sievers, 'Igbo Traditional Rulers: Chieftaincy and the State in Southeastern Nigeria', *Africa Spectrum*, vol. 33, no. 1, 1998, p. 59.

27. There are many other examples. The former minister of trade Kingsley Mbadiwe was the nephew of a warrant chief. The grandfather of the famed economist Dr Pius Okigbo was also a warrant chief.

28. Goldie in Vandeleur, *Campaigning on the Upper Nile and Niger*, p. xxii.

29. Perham, 'Some Problems of Indirect Rule in Africa', p. 18.

20. COLONIAL LIFE

1. Hazzledine, *The White Man in Nigeria*, p. 38.
2. Burns, *History of Nigeria*, p. 306.
3. Denham et al., *Narrative of Travels and Discoveries in Northern and Central Africa*, p. 254.
4. Denham et al., *Narrative of Travels and Discoveries in Northern and Central Africa*, p. 338.
5. Denham et al., *Narrative of Travels and Discoveries in Northern and Central Africa*, p. 318.
6. Geary, *Nigeria under British Rule*, p. 15.
7. Geary, *Nigeria under British Rule*, p. 22.
8. Burns, *History of Nigeria*, p. 306.
9. Baker, *Trade Winds on the Niger*, p. 281.
10. Wellesley, *Sir George Goldie*, p. 113.
11. Crozier, *Five Years Hard*, p. 195.
12. Crozier, *Five Years Hard*, p. 144.
13. Crozier, *Five Years Hard*, p. 195.
14. Crozier, *Five Years Hard*, p. 154.
15. Crozier, *Five Years Hard*, p. 161.
16. Crozier did not name the resident (whom he nicknamed 'Ash') but, given the time, it was most likely John Alder Burdon or C.W.J. Orr.
17. Crozier, *Five Years Hard*, p. 161.
18. Richard H. Dusgate, *The Conquest of Northern Nigeria* (Frank Cass, London, 1985), p. 221.
19. Stanhope White, *Dan Bana: The Memoirs of a Nigerian Official* (Cassell, London, 1966), p. 167.
20. Geary, *Nigeria under British Rule*, p. 21.
21. Perham, 'Lord Lugard', p. 235.
22. Johnston, *The Fulani Empire of Sokoto*, p. 232.
23. Wellesley, *Sir George Goldie*, p. 30.
24. Falola, *Colonialism and Violence in Nigeria*, p. 27.
25. Ekechi, 'Portrait of a Colonizer', p. 26.
26. Ekechi, 'Portrait of a Colonizer, pp. 28–9.
27. Ekechi, 'Portrait of a Colonizer, p. 34.

28. Ekechi, 'Portrait of a Colonizer, p. 34.

29. Ekechi, 'Portrait of a Colonizer, p. 35.

30. Falola, *Colonialism and Violence in Nigeria*.

31. Fulford, 'An Igbo Esperanto', p. 486.

32. Rudkin, 'In British West Africa', pp. 437–8.

33. Ronald Hyam, *Elgin and Churchill at the Colonial Office, 1905–08: The Watershed of the Empire–Commonwealth* (Macmillan, London, 1968), p. 541.

34. Jackson, 'The Twenty Years War', p. 249.

35. Jackson, 'The Twenty Years War', p. 258.

36. Crozier, *Five Years Hard*, p. 99.

37. Hansard, November 1906, vol. 164, col. 119.

38. Walter Ofonagaro, 'An Aspect of British Colonial Policy in Southern Nigeria: The Problems of Forced Labour and Slavery, 1895–1928', in Boniface Obichere (ed.), *Studies in Southern Nigerian History* (Frank Cass and Company, London, 1982), pp. 227–8.

39. Geary, *Nigeria under British Rule*, p. 17.

40. Burns, *History of Nigeria*, p. 307.

41. Leonard, 'Notes of a Journey to Bende', p. 191.

42. Leonard, 'Notes of a Journey to Bende', p. 192.

43. Leonard, 'Notes of a Journey to Bende', p. 207.

44. Burns, *History of Nigeria*, p. 256.

45. Colonial Reports, 1902, p. 11.

21. THE MISTAKE OF 1914

1. Geary, *Nigeria under British Rule*, p. 214.

2. Stanley, *Africa*, p. 167.

3. Geary, *Nigeria under British Rule*, p. 232.

4. Colonial Reports, 1916, p. 38.

5. Geary, *Nigeria under British Rule*, p. 232.

6. Geary, *Nigeria under British Rule*, p. 232.

7. Lugard, 'Northern Nigeria', p. 18.

8. Colonial Reports, 1916, p. 38.

9. Bello, *My Life*, p. 133.

10. N.U. Akpan, 'Nigerian Federalism: Accidental Foundations by Lugard', *Journal of the Historical Society of Nigeria*, vol. 9, no. 2, June 1978, p. 6.

11. *Independent*, 29 October 1995.

22. CONCLUSION

1. Burns, *History of Nigeria*, pp. 301–2.
2. BBC, 'The Empire's Last Officers', 2010.
3. PBS, Africa's Great Civilisations', episode five, 2017, https://www.pbssocal.org/programs/africas-great-civilizations/africas-great-civilizations-atlantic-age-hour-five/.
4. Lugard, 'Northern Nigeria', p. 7.
5. Lt-Colonel A.F. Mockler-Ferryman, *Up the Niger. Narrative of Major Claude Macdonald's Mission to the Niger and Benue Rivers, West Africa* (George Philip & Son, London and Liverpool, 1892), p. 13.
6. Orr, *The Making of Northern Nigeria*, p. 110.
7. Geary, *Nigeria under British Rule*, p. 229.
8. Heneker, *Bush Warfare*, p. 4.
9. Mockler-Ferryman, *British Nigeria*, p. 90.
10. Mockler-Ferryman, *British Nigeria*, p. 90.
11. Robinson, *Hausaland*, p. 30.

APPENDIX: COPY OF TREATY BETWEEN THE SULTAN OF SOKOTO AND THE ROYAL NIGER COMPANY

1. Text as reproduced in Burns, *History of Nigeria*, pp. 333–4.

BIBLIOGRAPHY

Afigbo, E.A. *The Warrant Chiefs: Indirect Rule in Southeastern Nigeria, 1891–1929*. Longman Group, London, 1972.

Akpan, N.U. 'Nigerian Federalism: Accidental Foundations by Lugard'. *Journal of the Historical Society of Nigeria*, vol. 9, no. 2, June 1978, pp. 1–20.

Ayandele. E.A. 'The Relations between the Church Missionary Society and the Royal Niger Company, 1886–1900'. *Journal of the Historical Society of Nigeria*, vol. 4, no. 3, December 1968, pp. 397–419.

———. 'The Task before Nigerian Historians Today'. *Journal of the Historical Society of Nigeria*, vol. 9, no. 4, June 1979, pp. 1–13.

Baker, Geoffrey L. 'Research Notes on the Royal Niger Company: Its Predecessors and Successors'. *Journal of the Historical Society of Nigeria*, vol. 2, no. 1, December 1960, pp. 151–161.

———. *Trade Winds on the Niger: The Saga of the Royal Niger Company, 1930–1971*. Radcliffe Press, London, New York, 1996.

Basden, G.T. *Among the Ibos of Nigeria: An Account of the Curious and Interesting Habits, Customs, and Beliefs of a Little Known African People by One Who Has for Many Years Lived amongst Them on Close and Intimate Terms*. J.B. Lippincott Co., Philadelphia, 1921.

BBC Podcast: 'The Empire's Last Officers', 2010, https://www.bbc.co.uk/programmes/p02sd1q1 (accessed 22 July 2020).

Bello, Alhaji Sir Ahmadu. *My Life*. Cambridge University Press, Cambridge, 1962.

BIBLIOGRAPHY

Benin Papers. *Papers Relating to the Massacre of British Officials near Benin, and the Consequent Punitive Expedition.* Presented to Both Houses of Parliament by Command of Her Majesty. Her Majesty's Stationery Office, London, August 1897.

Bersselaar, Dmitri. 'Creating Union Igbo: Missionaries and the Igbo Language'. *Africa: Journal of the International African Institute*, vol. 67, no. 2, 1997, pp. 273–295.

Bindloss, Harold. *In the Niger Country.* William Blackwood & Sons, Edinburgh and London, 1898.

Boisragon, Alan Maxwell. *The Benin Massacre.* Methuen & Co., London, 1897.

British and Foreign State Papers, 1886–1887, vol. 78. William Ridgway, London, 1894.

Brownlow, W.R. *Memoir of Sir James Marshall.* Burns & Oates Ltd, London and New York, 1890.

Burns, Alan C. *History of Nigeria.* George Allen & Unwin, London, 1929.

Byfield, Judith A. 'Women, and the Colonial State: Egba Women's Tax Revolt'. *Meridians*, vol. 3, no. 2, 2003, pp. 250–277.

Chamberlain, M.E. 'Lord Aberdare and the Royal Niger Company'. *Welsh History Review*, vol. 3, 1966, pp. 45–62.

Church Missionary Intelligencer: A Monthly Journal of Missionary Information, vol. 57, 1906.

Coleman, James. *Nigeria: Background to Nationalism.* University of California Press, Berkeley, 1971.

Colonial Reports, Annual, no. 346, *Northern Nigeria. Report for 1st January, 1900 to 31st March 1901.* Her Majesty's Stationery Office, London, 1902.

Colonial Reports, Annual, no. 405, *Southern Nigeria. Report for 1902.* His Majesty's Stationery Office, London, November 1903.

Colonial Reports, Annual, no. 409, *Northern Nigeria. Report for 1902.* His Majesty's Stationery Office, London, 1903.

Colonial Reports, Annual, no. 516, *Northern Nigeria. Report for 1905–6.* His Majesty's Stationery Office, London, 1907.

Colonial Reports, Annual, no. 551, *Northern Nigeria. Report for 1906—April 1907.* His Majesty's Stationery Office, London, 1907.

BIBLIOGRAPHY

Colonial Reports, Annual, no. 878, *Northern Nigeria. Report for 1914*. His Majesty's Stationery Office, London, 1916.

Crow, Hugh. *Memoirs of Captain Hugh Crow of Liverpool*. Longman, Rees, Orme, Brown, and Greene, London, and G. and J. Robinson, Liverpool, 1830.

Crowder, Michael. *The Story of Nigeria*. Faber & Faber, London, 1973.

―――. *West Africa under Colonial Rule*. Hutchinson & Co. Publishers, London, 1968.

Crozier, Brigadier-General F.P. *Five Years Hard*. Jonathan Cape, London, 1932.

Darwin, Major Leonard. 'Sir George Goldie on Government in Africa'. *Journal of the Royal African Society*, vol. 34, no. 135, April 1935, pp. 138–143.

Denham, Major Dixon, Captain Hugh Clapperton and Dr Walter Oudney. *Narrative of Travels and Discoveries in Northern and Central Africa, in the Years 1822, 1823, and 1824*, vol. I. John Murray, London, 1826.

―――. *Narrative of Travels and Discoveries in Northern and Central Africa, in the Years 1822, 1823, and 1824*, vol. II. John Murray, London, 1826.

Dent, M.J. 'The Military and Politics: A Study of the Relation between the Army and the Political Process in Nigeria', in Robert Melson and Howard Wolpe (eds.), *Nigeria: Modernization and the Politics of Communalism*. Michigan State University Press, East Lancing, 1971, pp. 367–399.

Dike, K. Onwuka. *Trade and Politics in the Niger Delta 1830–1885: An Introduction to the Economic and Political History of Nigeria*. Oxford University Press, London, 1956.

Downes, Captain W.D. *With the Nigerians in German East Africa*. Methuen & Co., London, 1919.

Dusgate, Richard H. *The Conquest of Northern Nigeria*. Frank Cass, London, 1985.

Ekechi, Felix K. 'Portrait of a Colonizer: H.M. Douglas in Colonial Nigeria, 1897–1920'. *African Studies Review*, vol. 26, no. 1, March 1983, pp. 25–50.

Falconer, J.D. *On Horseback through Nigeria, or, Life and Travel in the Central Sudan*. T. Fisher Unwin, London, 1911.

BIBLIOGRAPHY

Falola, Toyin. *Colonialism and Violence in Nigeria*. Indiana University Press, Bloomington and Indianapolis, 2009.

Falola, Toyin, and Matthew M. Heaton. *A History of Nigeria*. Cambridge University Press, Cambridge, 2008.

Fleet, Vice-Admiral H.L. *My Life, and a Few Yarns*. George Allen & Unwin, London, 1922.

Flint, John Edgar. 'British Policy and Chartered Company Administration in Nigeria, 1879–1900'. PhD thesis, University of London, 1957.

———. *Sir George Goldie and the Making of Nigeria*. Oxford University Press, Accra, Ibadan, London, 1960.

Fulford, Ben. 'An Igbo Esperanto: A History of the Union Igbo Bible 1900–1950'. *Journal of Religion in Africa*, vol. 32, no. 4, November 2002, pp. 457–501.

Galway, Henry. 'The Rising of the Brassmen'. *Journal of the Royal African Society*, vol. 34, no. 135, April 1935, pp. 144–162.

Geary. Sir William M.N. *Nigeria under British Rule*. Frank Cass & Co., London, 1927.

Glover, Lady. *Life of John Hawley Glover*. Smith, Elder & Co., London, 1897.

Hannah, Robert W. 'The Origins of Indirect Rule in Northern Nigeria, 1890–1904'. PhD thesis, Michigan State University, 1969.

Harneit-Sievers, Axel. 'Igbo Traditional Rulers: Chieftaincy and the State in Southeastern Nigeria'. *Africa Spectrum*, vol. 33, no. 1, 1998, pp. 57–79.

Hazzledine, George Douglas. *The White Man in Nigeria*. Edward Arnold, London, 1904.

Heneker, Lt-Colonel W.C.G. *Bush Warfare*. Hugh Rees, London, 1907.

Hives, Frank (told by Gascoigne Lumley). *Ju Ju and Justice in Nigeria*. John Lane, the Bodley Head, London, 1930.

Hogendorn, J.S. and Paul Lovejoy. 'Revolutionary Mahdism and Resistance to Early Colonial Rule in Northern Nigeria and Niger'. University of the Witwatersrand, African Studies Seminar Paper, no. 80, 1979.

Hogg, Captain Ian. *Asaba: Report on Aaba Hinterland Operations. From the Officer Commanding Asaba Hinterland Expedition Force, to the Officer Commanding Southern Nigeria Regiment*. 14 March 1904, CO 520/24.

BIBLIOGRAPHY

Hyam, Ronald. *Elgin and Churchill at the Colonial Office, 1905–08: The Watershed of the Empire–Commonwealth.* Macmillan, London, 1968.

Igbafe, Philip A. 'Western Ibo Society and Its Resistance to British Rule: The Ekumeku Movement 1898–1911'. *Journal of African History*, vol. 12, no. 3, 1971, pp. 441–459.

Isichei, Elizabeth. *A History of the Igbo People.* Macmillan Press, London and Basingstoke, 1976.

Iweze, Daniel Olisa. 'The Role of Indigenous Collaborators during the Anglo-Ekumeku War of 1898–1911'. *Ufahamu: A Journal of African Studies*, vol. 39, no. 1, 2016, pp. 87–107.

Jackson, Robert D. 'The Twenty Years War: Invasion and Resistance in Southeastern Nigeria, 1900–1919'. PhD thesis, Harvard University, 1975.

Johnson, Samuel. *The History of the Yorubas: From the Earliest Times to the Beginning of the British Protectorate.* CMS Bookshops, Lagos, 1921.

Johnston, Harry H. *The Story of My Life.* Bobbs-Merrill Company, Indianapolis, 1923.

Johnston, Hugh Anthony Stephens. *The Fulani Empire of Sokoto.* Oxford University Press, London, Ibadan, Nairobi, 1967.

Jones, Thomas Jesse. *Education in Africa.* Phelps-Stokes Fund, New York, 1922.

Jones-Quartey, K.A.B. *A Life of Azikiwe.* Penguin Books, Baltimore, 1965.

Kanu, Roseline Okpete. 'The Life and Times of King Ja Ja of Opobo, 1812–1895'. MA diss., Dalhousie University, 1970.

Kirk-Greene, A.H.M. 'Expansion on the Benue 1830–1900'. *Journal of the Historical Society of Nigeria*, vol. 1, no. 3, December 1958, pp. 215–237.

Lagos Papers. *Papers Relative to the Reduction of Lagos by Her Majesty's Forces on the West Coast of Africa.* Presented to Both Houses of Parliament by Command of Her Majesty, 1852.

Larymore, Constance. *A Resident's Wife in Nigeria.* George Routledge & Sons, London, 1908.

Leonard, Major Arthur Glyn. 'Notes of a Journey to Bende'. *Journal of the Manchester Geographical Society*, vol. 14, 1898, pp. 190–207.

Lennox, Captain Lord Esme Gordon. *With the West African Frontier Force in Southern Nigeria.* H.J. Ryman, London, 1905.

BIBLIOGRAPHY

Lethbridge, Alan. *West Africa the Elusive.* John Bale, Sons & Danielson Ltd, London, 1921.

Livingstone, W.P. *Mary Slessor of Calabar: Pioneer Missionary.* Hodder & Stoughton, London, 1916.

Lugard, Frederick D. 'Northern Nigeria'. *The Geographical Journal*, vol. 23, no. 1, January 1904, pp. 1–27.

———. *The Dual Mandate in British Tropical Africa.* William Blackwood & Sons, Edinburgh and London, 1922.

Matera, Marc, Misty Bastian and Susan Kingsley Kent. *The Women's War of 1929: Gender and Violence in Colonial Nigeria.* Palgrave Macmillan, London, 2013.

Mockler-Ferryman, Lt-Colonel A.F. *British Nigeria: A Geographical and Historical Description of the British Possessions adjacent to the Niger River, West Africa.* Cassell and Co., London, 1902.

———. *British West Africa: Its Rise and Progress.* Swan Sonnenschein and Co., London, 1898.

———. *Up the Niger. Narrative of Major Claude Macdonald's Mission to the Niger and Benue Rivers, West Africa.* George Philip & Son, London and Liverpool, 1892.

Morrison, J.H. *The Missionary Heroes of Africa.* George H. Doran Co., New York, 1922.

Muffett, D.J.M. *Concerning Brave Captains: Being a History of the British Occupation of Sokoto and Kano and the Last Stand of the Fulani Forces.* André Deutsch, London, 1964.

National Bureau of Statistics. National Literacy Survey, 2010, https://www.nigerianstat.gov.ng/pdfuploads/National%20Literacy%20Survey,%202010.pdf (accessed 19 July 2020).

Nwabara, Samuel N. 'Encounter with the Long Juju: A Prelude to the British Military Expeditions in Iboland'. *Transactions of the Historical Society of Ghana*, vol. 9, 1968, pp. 79–89.

Nworah, Kingsley Kenneth Dike. 'Humanitarian Pressure-Groups and British Attitudes to West Africa, 1895–1915'. PhD thesis, University of London, April 1966.

Ofonagaro, Walter Ibekwe. 'An Aspect of British Colonial Policy in Southern Nigeria: The Problems of Forced Labour and Slavery, 1895–

1928', in Boniface Obichere (ed.), *Studies in Southern Nigerian History*. Frank Cass and Company, London, 1982, pp. 219–243.

Ohadike, Don C. 'The Ekumeku Movement: Western Igbo Resistance to the British Conquest of Nigeria, 1883–1914'. PhD thesis, Ohio University, Athens, 1991.

Onyeidu, Samuel Onwo. 'The Anglican Mission to Asaba, Nigeria, 1875–1930'. PhD thesis, University of Aberdeen, April 1985.

Orr, Captain C.W.J. *The Making of Northern Nigeria*. Macmillan & Co., London, 1904.

Papers Relative to King Jaja of Opobo, Opening of West African Markets to British Trade. Presented to Both Houses of Parliament by Command of Her Majesty, April 1888.

Park, Mungo. *The Life and Travels of Mungo Park*. Harper & Brothers, New York, 1854.

―――. *Travels in the Interior of Africa*, vol. 1. Cassell & Co., London, Paris, New York, Melbourne, 1887.

PBS, Africa's Great Civilisations', episode 5, 2017, https://www.pbssocal. org/programs/africas-great-civilizations/africas-great-civilizations-atlantic-age-hour-five/ (accessed 22 July 2020).

Pearson, Scott R. 'The Economic Imperialism of the Royal Niger Company'. *Food Research Institute Studies in Economics, Trade, and Development*, vol. 10, 1971, pp. 69–88.

Perham, Margery. 'Some Problems of Indirect Rule in Africa'. *Journal of the Royal African Society*, vol. 34, no. 135, 1937, pp. 1–23.

―――. 'Lord Lugard: A Preliminary Evaluation'. *Journal of the International African Institute*, vol. 20, no. 3, July 1950, pp. 228–239.

―――. *Lugard: The Years of Adventure, 1858–1898*. Collins, London, 1956.

―――. *Lugard: The Years of Authority 1898–1945*. Collins, London, 1960.

―――. *The Diaries of Lord Lugard, vol. 4*. Faber & Faber, London, 1959.

―――. *West African Passage: A Journey through Nigeria, Chad, and the Cameroons, 1931–1932*. Peter Owen Publishers, London and Boston, 1983.

Pew Centre. Religious Composition by Country, http://assets.pewresearch.

BIBLIOGRAPHY

org/wp-content/uploads/sites/11/2012/12/globalReligion-tables.pdf (accessed 24 August 2018).

Pitt Rivers, Lt-General A.H.L.F. *Antique Works of Art from Benin.* London, 1900.

Ratté, Mary Lou. 'Imperial Looting and the Case of Benin'. MA diss., University of Massachusetts, Amherst, 1972.

Rawson, Geoffrey. *Life of Admiral Sir Harry Rawson.* Edward Arnold, London, 1914.

Robinson, Charles Henry. *Hausaland, or Fifteen Hundred Miles through the Central Soudan.* Sampson Low, Marston and Company, London, 1900.
———. *Nigeria: Our Latest Protectorate.* Horace Marshall and Son, London, 1900.

Rosenberg, Diana. 'Ibo Resistance to British Colonial Power'. *Ufahamu: A Journal of African Studies,* vol. 19, no. 1, 1991, pp. 3–21.

Roth, Felix N. 'A Diary of a Surgeon with the Benin Punitive Expedition'. *Journal of the Manchester Geographical Society,* vol. 14, 1898, pp. 208–221.

Roth, H. Ling. *Great Benin, Its Customs, Art and Horrors.* Routledge & Kegan Paul Ltd, London, 1903.

Rudkin, Captain W.E. 'In British West Africa. The Operations in the Agbor District, Southern Nigeria, June to August, 1906, Consequent upon the Murder of Mr. O.S. Crewe-Read, District Commissioner'. *United Service Magazine,* vol. 35, April to September 1907.

Schwarz, Walter. *Nigeria.* Pall Mall, London, 1968.

Sessional Paper no. 28 of 1930. *Report of the Commission of Inquiry Appointed to Inquire into the Disturbances in the Calabar and Owerri Provinces, December 1929.* Lagos, Government Printer, 1930.

Shelford, Fred. 'Sir George Dashwood Taubman Goldie'. *Journal of the Royal African Society,* vol. 25, no. 98, January 1926, pp. 132–137.

Stanley, Henry M. *Africa: Its Partition and Its Future.* Dodd, Mead, and Company, New York, 1898.

Stapleton, Tim. 'Barracks Islam and Command Christianity: Religion in Britain's West African Colonial Army (c.1900–1960)'. *War and Society,* vol. 39, no. 1, 2019, pp. 1–22.

Ubah, C.N. 'Changing Patterns of Leadership among the Igbo, 1900–1960'. *Transafrican Journal of History,* vol. 16, 1987, pp. 167–184.

BIBLIOGRAPHY

Uzoigwe, G.N. 'The Niger Committee of 1898: Lord Selborne's Report'. *Journal of the Historical Society of Nigeria*, vol. 4, no. 3, 1968, pp. 467–476.

Vandeleur, Lieutenant Seymour. *Campaigning on the Upper Nile and Niger*. Methuen & Co., London, 1898.

Wellesley, Dorothy. *Sir George Goldie, Founder of Nigeria: A Memoir*. Macmillan & Co., London, 1934.

White, Stanhope. *Dan Bana: The Memoirs of a Nigerian Official*. Cassell, London, 1966.

Willcocks, Brigadier-General Sir James. *From Kabul to Kumasi: Twenty Four Years of Soldiering and Sport*. John Murray, London, 1904.

INDEX

INDEX

INDEX

INDEX

INDEX

INDEX

INDEX

INDEX

INDEX

INDEX

INDEX

INDEX

INDEX

Visscher, Hans, 274

Wallace, William, 85–7, 155, 163, 205–6, 209
warrant chiefs, 287–306
  Aro conflict and, 191
  proxy conflicts and, 214
  Ekumeku and, 219, 226, 228
  Women's War and, 229–42
weapons, 180–81, 185, 211, 224, 227, 229, 332
West African Frontier Force, 99, 108–16, 155, 158
  Aro War (1901–2), 181–8
  Chibok conflict (1906–7), 207–9
  creation (1897), 99, 158
  Satiru revolt (1906), 195–207
  Sokoto War (1901–3), 166, 168, 171–5
West India Regiment, 105, 124, 125
Western education, 13, 34, 52, 111, 119, 240, 242
'white man's grave', 17
Women's War (1929–30), 229–42
World War I (1914–18), 114–15, 243, 332
World War II (1939–45), 114–15

Wyndham, Thomas, 9

Yoruba people, 18, 23, 32–3, 41, 329
  British annexation (1893), 126
  Egba, 32, 106, 126, 243, 244–7, 258, 259, 261
  Ekiti, 32, 258, 261
  Ijebu, 32, 33, 258, 261
  Ijesha, 32, 258, 261
  Islam and, 253
  language, 135, 258, 259, 260, 261
  Niger Committee on, 146
  Oyo Empire (c. 1300–1896), 27, 31, 32–4, 40, 42, 126, 258–9
  religion, 251
  in Royal Niger Constabulary, 79
  slave trade, 107
  taxation in, 230, 242
Yunfa, King of Gobir, 30–31

Zaghawa people, 28
Zappa, Carlo, 219–20
Zaria, 29, 161, 163, 164, 166, 274
Zungeru, 195, 202, 272
Zweifel, Josue, 85–7